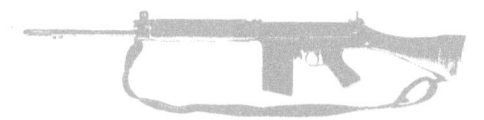

SCRUBBER
MCDADE

(THE CLEANER)

DAVID W. ROBERTS

SILVERBIRD PUBLISHING

Published in Australia by Silverbird Publishing
& David W. Roberts

First published in Australia 2025
This edition published 2025
Copyright © David W. Roberts 2025
Cover design, typesetting: WorkingType (www.workingtype.com.au)

The right of David W. Roberts to be identified as the
Author of the Work has been asserted in accordance with the
Copyright, Designs and Patents Act 1988.

This book is a work of fiction. Any similarities to that of
people living or dead are purely coincidental.

All rights reserved. No part of this publication may be reproduced, stored in a retrieval system, or transmitted, in any form or by any means without the prior written permission of the publisher, nor be otherwise circulated in any form of binding or cover other than that in which it is published and without a similar condition being imposed on the subsequent purchaser.

ISBN: 978-0-6459162-3-2

ABOUT THE AUTHOR

David Roberts migrated as a qualified teacher from the United Kingdom. After seventeen years working as a teacher, deputy principal and principal in country New South Wales, he became a university academic. University appointments and consultancies enabled David to travel widely and broaden his horizons. Now retired, he lives with his wife in Adelaide.

This is his seventh novel.

BOOKS BY DAVID ROBERTS

One Thing Leads to Another

Easytimes

Graham's Story

Eve

Murder on the Heysen Trail

White Rose

PART ONE

1. BEGINNINGS

Norman McDade began to take more notice of the world when he turned three. There was mum, warm, soft and cuddly, the bringer of food and drinks and Lynda, the big noisy sister, who sometimes played with him, but more frequently teased him. He shared the floor with Taffy, a three-legged sheepdog that left hairs everywhere but didn't mind being sat on. Then there was Smokey, an ancient relic of a tabby cat with one green eye that worked and another that didn't. Smokey never wanted to play with Norman and simply ran away whenever he came near. Last of all, there was dad. Dad was huge, with an over-sized tummy. Mum sometimes called it a "beer gut". Dad, whose name was Fred, liked to pick Norman up and throw him around. Thankfully, he always caught Norman in his strong arms, which, more often than not, were smothered in grease and dirt.

The McDade family lived in a modest house behind the only garage in town, "McDade & Sons". The home was red brick veneer with a sun-bleached corrugated iron roof and an ancient chimney stack sticking out the top. Along the front was a faded wooden verandah with holes in the floor. Apart from the obvious repairs needed, Mum kept complaining the house needed "a good lick of paint." Dad always agreed with her, said he would do something about it, but never did.

Behind the house was the vegetable patch with a spade sticking out of it. Sadly, the patch didn't produce any vegetables nowadays, only weeds, that sometimes grew taller than a grown person. Beyond the vegetable patch was dad's private shed. Dad loved his shed and spent many happy hours out there. Only mum was allowed to visit him, if she brought dad a decent cup of tea and a biscuit or two or three. Mum didn't mind Fred having a shed because she understood the weaker sex needed somewhere to escape to from time to time. Dad was always rabbiting on about the latest project he was working on up in his shed. Unfortunately, nobody could remember any of his projects actually coming to fruition, but mum kept saying she, "lived in hope."

All around the house was a dark brown paling fence, except in the front garden, where there was a rusting wire fence. Some of the wooden palings were rotting and had holes at the bottom. Where possible these holes had been blocked up with rocks, assorted bits of timber or even Masonite. It looked like a fence with giant band-aids. The blockages were necessary because three-legged Taffy had recently invented a new sport; crawling under the paling fence to chase old Mrs Korku's free ranging hens. Not surprisingly, Mrs Korku was less than impressed when this happened and had been heard screaming and swearing as she chased Taffy about her garden with a broom. This only added to the fun as far as Taffy was concerned, until one day a particularly well directed swipe of the broom found its mark and it was Taffy's turn to yelp.

A narrow cement path dotted with weeds led from the squeaky front gate to the entrance of the house. Sometimes mum would get enthusiastic and plant a row of pansies along the edge of the path. The flowers would do okay for a while until the snails and slugs feasted on them, or dad accidentally trampled them when pushing the rusty lawn-mower around the scrappy patch of grass and weeds he liked to extol as "the lawn." An ancient green letter-box stood at a rakish angle next to the front gate, its opening too small to take most of the mail. The postie simply dropped oversized letters and circulars on the ground where they lay about for days or even weeks.

Little Norman soon learnt dad was in charge outside the house; mum was the boss indoors. Inside, mum ruled supreme. Everything had its correct place and woe betide anyone who didn't put things back where they belonged. Mum's name was Mary. If somebody forgot to put something away in its proper place dad would gently chastise them, 'Queen Mary'll be after ya!' or 'Queen Mary'll get ya' or 'watch out, her Majesty Queen Mary will have ya guts for garters'. Norman was always puzzled by what this last threat meant, but it sounded far too frightening to risk.

There were three bedrooms at the McDade's residence. Mum and dad occupied the largest with a framed picture of Jesus hanging on the wall above their bed. Lynda had the second bedroom with dozens of cut-out pictures of cats, dogs and horses stuck around the walls with sticky tape. Ever since Lynda started school, she had wanted to be an animal doctor. Dad said Lynda should use the correct wording which was "Veterinary Surgeon," but that was too difficult for a five-year-old to say. Norman slept in the third and smallest bedroom. There was just one large poster on his wall of Blinky Bill looking mighty mischievous in a pair of bright red trousers and carrying a large scary catapult.

The family spent much of the time in the kitchen. Mum was an enthusiastic cook and always seemed to be busily concocting something special to eat. They didn't have much money, but somehow Mary always managed to have a fulsome meal on the table. Nobody went hungry and the children soon learnt not to complain if they didn't like the food mum served up. 'You be thankful you've a full stomach, 'cause there's heaps of kids that don't!' Mum would declare authoritatively, whenever she saw Lynda or Norman turning up their noses.

It was warm and homey in the kitchen and everyone savoured the yummy cooking odours. Mum was for ever making biscuits, baking cakes or scones, washing and peeling vegetables, or stoking up the wood fire under the hot-plate. Mary McDade had even taken out first place in the sponge cake competition at the annual Rinsdorf Show and was narrowly beaten into second place for her dozen lamingtons.

Breakfast was always porridge with full cream milk and a large blob of CSR's brown sugar, there were "seconds" if still hungry. Dad and Lynda took sandwiches and an apple for their lunches neatly wrapped up in grease-proof paper. The McDades enjoyed their big meal of the day together at night, usually meat and two veg.

Grandpa McDade had a small holding on the edge of town where he ran a few sheep. Dad would visit Grandpa every second Sunday and, whilst there, slaughter an old jumbuck. Under Grandpa's watchful eye, dad would butcher the unfortunate animal on a concrete slab, then bring it back to the house in manageable pieces for the family to eat during the week. We always knew when it was a Monday morning because a fresh sheep's head would be staring forlornly at us from out of a large saucepan when we went out the back door to the outside toilet. Mum proudly boasted the McDades wasted nothing because together the family ate through the entire sheep's anatomy including brains, liver, kidneys and offal by the end of each fortnight.

As soon as Norman was able to slide about on his bum, or crawl he showed a keen interest in nature. Inside the house it was lean pickings, there was only the occasional unsuspecting ant to chase across the floor or an unfortunate spider that had lost its way. Flies sometimes zoomed over his head, but Norman could never catch them. One exciting day, Norman came face to face with a surprised gecko. They stared at each other for a moment or two before the puzzled creature decided to beat a hasty retreat and disappeared down a crack in the floor.

Norman's fascination with all things natural exploded whenever he was taken outside. Grubbing about under the washing line on Mondays when mum hung out the washing, never failed to intrigue. Here, in the dirt, he encountered all sorts of interesting creepy crawlies: beetles, slugs, snails, a host of different kinds of ants, millipedes, slaters, the odd ladybird and once a large pink worm that didn't taste as good as he expected. After rain there were puddles to be checked out where Norman sometimes found mosquito wrigglers, water boatmen or silly moths that had fallen in and couldn't get out. Norman knew there was an exciting world out there in their garden, if only he could toddle out there more often.

* * *

On the whole, the McDades lived contentedly in their modest house behind McDade & Sons. Dad and Grandpa McDade looked after the business at the garage while mum looked after the McDades. Since the garage was the only one in town and for many miles around, the locals expected it to be open pretty much all the time. Dad seemed to be working there all day, every day. If he wasn't at the garage he was to be found in his shed behind the vegetable patch. Sometimes, dad would be late home for seven o'clock tea and this would annoy mum no end because she had to reheat his meal especially for him and then clear it away afterwards.

Mum was a trained nurses' aide. She had a certificate to prove it that hung in the hall in case she wanted to show it to anyone. Mary was proud of her certificate and had worked full time as a nurses' aide until just before Lynda was born. The Rinsdorf town folk liked to boast they had their very own hospital, but really it was not much more than a nursing home for a few of the elderly locals who needed full-time care. Occasionally, mum was still asked to do a shift if the hospital was short staffed or at Christmas time. She loved working there.

Rinsdorf had a school too. There were two teachers. When Norman turned five his mother took him there at the start of the school year to enrol him. His sister, Lynda, was by then starting her third year at the school. Norman's teacher's name was Mrs Adams and she looked after the kindergarten as well as the first, second and third grade pupils. The headmaster, Mr Cruickshank, taught the big kids.

Now that you know something about the McDade's family background, it's time to hand over to young Norman to tell the rest of his story.

* * *

I didn't like school because I was no good at the work I was supposed to do. Five other kids began kindergarten at the same time as me and they loved school because they could do the things Mrs Adams wanted them to do. Mrs Adams always did everything too quickly for me and I couldn't keep up. I tried hard to do what she wanted, but it was too difficult. When Mrs Adams looked at my work she would sniff loudly and not say anything, but when she looked at the other children's work she would smile and tell them how well they were doing. Mrs Adams would get out her stamp pad and put an animal stamp on the other children's work. She rarely said anything nice to me, so I didn't like the old bat. I really wanted some of those animal stamps, but all I got were sniffs.

I didn't like to grumble about school. I thought it was a bit like at home when mum told Lynda and me never to complain about our food because we were lucky to *have* food. I reasoned it would be the same with school. I shouldn't winge about school because we had one and I knew there were many children around the world who didn't even have a school to complain about.

Lynda and I would walk home together after school. When we arrived home mum would have a drink and something tasty for us to eat. Lynda would be all excited and bubbly about what she had done at school that day whilst I sat at the kitchen table quietly. After Lynda finished telling her news, mum would make a point of asking me about my day at school. Now, our parents had taught us to always tell the truth so I tried hard to answer mum honestly every time.

'What about you, Norman, what did you do today?'

'The same as always mum, counting and letters.'

'Was it fun?'

'No.'

'Why, dear?'

'Because I couldn't get anything right and the other kids could.'

'Well, I expect it will get easier soon. Keep trying, dear.'

'Yes, I will, mum.'

Sometimes, when we had these little conversations, tears came to my eyes. When this happened, I picked up whatever I was eating and fled to my bedroom. A few minutes later mum would come to my room to comfort me and I would have a big cry in her warm comforting arms. Next morning, I would be brave again, eat up my porridge and get ready for another horrible day at school as if nothing was ever wrong.

One evening, dad came home late and I overheard my parents talking about me. Mum had forgotten to close my bedroom door and they thought I was in bed fast asleep.

'I met Mrs Adams when I was down at the store today, Fred.'

'Oh yeah…? Norman's school teacher, isn't she? How's the old girl?'

'Quite chatty, actually.'

'It's about time she brought her bloody car in for its next service. Haven't seen her at the garage for months.'

'Mrs Adams wanted to speak to me about Norman.'

'Has he been playing up?'

'Not exactly. Mrs Adams says she thinks he's a slow learner.'

'What's wrong with that? Some kids pick up stuff really fast, others are slower. That's life.'

'Well, Mrs Adams thinks he may need special teaching because he's so slow. She says there are special classes for kids like Norman.'

'What's she trying to say? Does she think he's some kind of a gormless idiot or something?'

'No dear. Mrs Adams reckons Norman will always struggle to learn to read and write unless he has extra help from a specially trained teacher. She has twenty-five kids in her classroom across four grades and she simply doesn't have the time to give Norman the help he needs.'

'Well, that's stiff shit. He's only been going to school for a few weeks. Give it time and he'll come good.'

'Mrs Adams is an experienced teacher Fred and says she can pick the kids quickly who can't manage in a normal school. And Norman is one of them. She wants him to go to the special school in the city.'

'She must be kidding. It's fifty bloody miles to the city. He's only flipping five years old.'

'I'm only telling you what she told me, dear. Perhaps we need to think seriously about it in the future. The high school kids go into town on the school bus every day so he could go with them.'

'Over my bloody dead body!'

Dad's last comment puzzled me. I never quite understood why the bus had to drive over dad's dead body. Like many other things in life, it didn't make sense.

2. STARTING TO GROW UP

My big sister Lynda loved books and most nights mum would sit us both down on the couch and read a book from the school library. We were allowed to take one book home for a week at a time. Lynda would sit there bright eyed and eager to hear the story, but I usually found it plain boring. Sometimes I fell asleep leaning up against mum, often I climbed off the couch and played with Taffy who loved me to chase him about the house. After a few minutes of chasing Taffy one, or both of my parents, would get cranky and shout at me. When they yelled, I crawled into my special hiding place in the little room we called the pantry. This was where mum kept her spuds, onions and pumpkins in wooden boxes on the floor. Sometimes I'd take out a couple of handfuls of dirty spuds and they'd become the boys in Mrs Adams' classroom. The onions were the girls because they were cleaner. Mrs Adams was always a big ugly pumpkin standing out in front of the class.

I didn't have any friends at school. I wanted to play with the boys, but they were always playing cricket or football and were too fast and skilful for me. Sometimes the boys let me field when they were playing cricket, but for some reason my turn to bowl or bat never came round. The only time I ever got to touch a soccer ball was when someone kicked it at me when I wasn't looking. At playtimes I would sometimes line up to be picked in one of the soccer teams, but the captains never chose me until the very last and then they weren't keen to have me.

The only person who would play with me was a girl in first grade who was a bit slow like me. She had her own little private spot in the playground underneath a shady peppercorn tree. Her name was Janice. If I couldn't play with the boys, I would run down to Janice's peppercorn tree. She always smiled and let me join in whatever game she was playing. Often it was dollies, sometimes it was hospitals and only occasionally, schools. At the end of the school day mum would often ask me who I had been playing with. When I told her truthfully, that it was Janice, she would look surprised and say things like, 'Norman, you should be playing with the boys' or 'Janice is a girl, dear.'

At weekends mum would often suggest I walk up to the garage to see what dad was doing. I badly wanted to be like dad fixing cars and trucks for people. So, I would pick up my toy hammer and head up there determined to help. It was always noisy and smelly in the garage. Dad and grandpa frequently had their bottoms sticking up out of a car's engine or were lying underneath a truck doing things to it. There was always a lot of banging and hissing sounds. The radio blared all day and dad and grandpa had to shout at each other about their work. There was some swearing too. In the office there were large coloured pictures of smiling ladies with no clothes on except for high heeled shoes, but I never saw photographs of naked men.

The garage was a dirty place, I don't think anyone ever went in there to clean. I didn't mind the dust and dirt though, because it attracted heaps of different kinds of spiders that knew they could safely build their sticky webs and be sure they would be left undisturbed for years. Wherever there were spiders' webs, there were all sorts of exciting insects that became trapped. Some mornings I found several kinds of moths stuck to the fibres; at other times there might be house flies, midges and even mosquitoes flapping about trying to escape. Best of all was when a hungry spider detected a catch and came racing across to eat it on the spot or drag it away for a later feast.

More often than not dad and grandpa wouldn't notice me come into the garage so, after I thoroughly checked out my favourite spider webs, I would find my hammer and start bashing things pretending I was fixing someone's car for them. I liked the idea of doing something to help somebody else. At some point either dad or grandpa would finally spot me fixing the cars and order me home. They always said it was too dangerous for small children to play around in the garage while they were working. So, I would pick up my hammer and feeling sad and unwanted, mooch off home.

One evening grandpa came round to have tea with us. Grandma, he told us, was in hospital and so he had nobody to cook him his evening meal. After dinner dad and grandpa sat down and enjoyed a couple of beers and were soon in a chatty mood. Mum read to Lynda and me and then sent us off to bed. I was a bit naughty though. I left my bedroom door open and lay there wide awake and listening. And I overheard an intriguing conversation…

'How are the kids doing at school, Mary?' asked grandpa.

'Lynda's doing fine, but poor little Norman's getting nowhere, fast.'

I tried to understand mum's strange comment that "I was getting nowhere, fast." It didn't make sense. How could I go nowhere? Then, dad joined in the conversation.

'The silly bugger's got no brains. No more brains than one of those bloody sheep I slaughter at your place every other Sunday, dad.'

'Yes, I suspected as much,' replied grandpa.

'I'd like to send him into town to go to a special school that can help him,' remarked mum.

'Waste of bloody time,' growled dad.

'You do realise son, you're the third generation of McDades to run this family business? My old man opened up the workshop back in 1879. It was horses and carts, mail coaches, drays and only horsey things back in those days.'

'I sure do, dad. The family business is safe with me for another twenty-five years until I'm sixty-five and then I'll get to put my feet up for the rest of my life.'

'What worries me son, is what happens to the business when you retire. Is Norman ever going to have the brains to run the show and keep this family business going?'

'I bloody doubt it! You don't have to be a brain-box to run a business like ours, but at least you need to be able to read and write and do the accounts. A good dollop of common sense doesn't go astray either. To be quite candid dad I can't see our Norman is ever going to make the grade.'

'That's an awful thing to say, Fred.' Mum sounded really angry, 'Norman's only five years old. If you would just allow him to go into that special school in town, he might really blossom.'

Dad snorted. He never liked it when mum had a go at him.

'Well, perhaps you can produce another boy for us Mary? One with the brains to run the garage?'

'Don't be ridiculous, Fred. You know as well as I do, the doctor said I shouldn't have any more children. Having Norman nearly killed me, I was lucky to survive.'

I didn't hear any more after that because the three grown-ups picked up their plates and dishes and moved off into the kitchen. I'd heard more than enough though to keep me thinking for a while. I might be hopeless at my schoolwork, but I certainly understood what they had been saying about the future of the family business. Apparently, I was supposed to take over the family business when dad retired, the same way dad took on the responsibilities when grandpa turned sixty-five. However, dad thinks I'm useless and won't ever be smart enough to run the business.

The last thing mum said really intrigued me too. I had never really thought about where children come from. How did they arrive on this earth? In my five-year-old brain I believed mothers simply went to the hospital when they wanted a baby and the hospital would give them one. Sometimes, if the hospital was extra kind, it might give the mothers two babies to take home. Janice told me once that a few very special mothers were allowed to bring more than two babies home at the same time, but I don't think that can be true.

The most mysterious thing mum said was, "having Norman nearly killed me." What could she possibly have meant by that? I would never do anything to kill my mum. Very strange…!

The other statement I didn't understand was what dad said to mum, "perhaps you can produce another boy for us?" Can mothers "make" children, like they make cakes or salads? I've never seen mum doing anything remotely like that in the kitchen. When mum produces a salad she gets tomatoes, beetroots, lettuce leaves, cheese and anything else she wants and puts them all together in a salad bowl. Perhaps mum also has a kitchen cupboard full of bones, blood, hair and skin so she can produce a baby? When she made me she must have made a big mistake because she only put in half the quantity of brains I needed. Mum ought to read her recipe book more carefully.

Next time I'm in the kitchen, and nobody is around, I'll see if I can find an extra cupboard or a drawer containing baby parts.

3. DON'T PANIC: STAY CALM!

When I was seven, I had a super-scary adventure. Dad, grandpa and a mate of his called Charlie, sometimes went out in the bush to cut wood. Charlie drove an old Ford truck, but he needed someone to help him because he was getting too old to bring in the wood on his own. Charlie was oven older than grandpa! The three men would spend the whole day out working and come back late with the ancient Ford groaning with enough logs to keep the fireplaces at Charlie's, grandpa's and our place burning for the next few months.

I desperately wanted to go out with them. Every time I asked if I could go dad would say, 'No mate you're too young' or 'sorry mate this is men's work.' This didn't seem fair because I often brought in the kindling wood for mum so she could get the fire going in the mornings. Then one day, dad must have been feeling especially kind because he finally agreed to take me. Mum woke me early, kitted me out in my knock-about clothes and gum boots, gave me extra porridge for breakfast and handed me a picnic lunch to take, 'Here's you tucker, son. Don't do what your dad does and eat it all at once and then tell me he didn't have enough.'

It was a squash in the truck with the three large men on seats and me curled up on the floor at their feet being deafened by the roar of the engine. But I didn't mind, because I was going to be one of the men today. The first part of the journey wasn't too bad as we drove along proper bitumen roads. Soon though, we turned off onto a dirt road and then the dust started puffing into the truck all around me. We bounced our way on and on for miles. The dust gradually covered me and soon I had a sore bum from being thrown about so much. Finally, we opened and closed a gate and left the dirt road behind us and began trundling across a rough paddock to reach a strand of mature grey box trees.

It was a sunny day and pleasantly warm. The last few days had been rainy though and dad reckoned he'd measured over three inches in the gauge. When the old truck finally pulled up, I couldn't get out quickly enough after being cramped up on the floor for so long. We had arrived in a large paddock with plenty of fallen timber lying about and low blue coloured hills surrounding us. The grass was as high as the top of my gum boots with the native kangaroo grasses over my head in places. I loved the musty smell of the bush after rain.

I was anxious to begin exploring, there was so much out here that was new to me. Dad must have sensed this because he called me over and gave me a stern warning.

'Now Norman, you listen to me. Out here in the bush you need your wits about you. Beautiful as it is there are plenty of dangers. Snakes are about this time of year and redbacks live in some of the old timber. Walk, but don't run. That way the snakes have enough time to get out of your way. Wear these gloves if you're picking up any wood. They'll stop you getting splinters or being bitten by spiders. Do you understand mate?'

'Yes dad. Can I help you collect the wood?'

'Of course you can, but remember its bloody heavy stuff so only pick up small bits one at a time.'

I watched as the men unloaded their gear and prepared to begin work. Between them they had two chain saws that needed filling with two stroke petrol, a couple of axes I could barely lift and a kind of wedge thing to help them split apart the largest logs. It wasn't long before the chain-saws were in action drowning out the sounds of the bush.

The gloves dad gave me were far too large and kept falling off. For a short time I picked up small bits of wood and carried them over to the back of Charlie's truck where I did my best to throw them up. It wasn't long, however, before I grew tired of collecting timber. The men were busy. Behind the truck I spotted a line of trees winding away into the distance, a sure sign of a creek and somewhere interesting to go exploring for creatures. With all the rain that had fallen over the last few days, I reasoned there should be water there and where there's water there are animals. For a moment or two I delayed, wondering whether I should tell dad where I was going, but he was a long way off and wouldn't hear me anyway.

As I moved off behind the truck heading for the creek, I thought about the animals I might find. Yabbies, I knew, liked the muddy banks of a creek and frogs were bound to be there. A few times mum and dad had taken Lynda and me for picnics down to the creek near our home. I remembered seeing heaps of insects: dragon-flies, bees, wasps and butterflies. Dad told me insects loved the water and then the birds came because they liked to catch the insects. So, there should be swarms of insects and birds along this creek too. Perhaps there would be fish in the water or some frog spawn? Full of anticipation, I hurried on as fast as my galumphing gum boots would allow.

My older sister, Lynda, loves animals too and wants to look after them when she's grown-up. She tries to bring sick animals home to look after them, but mum always says she doesn't want any creepy crawlies in the house. My sister even has a secret spot in the garden, in the middle of the overgrown vegetable patch, where she has set up her "surgery" to treat the sick animals. Sometimes, she takes me there if she has a special patient. She reckons she's looked after a few dozen caterpillars, a couple of worms, a butterfly that crashed and hurt its wing and a gecko that had lost its tail. Once she found a bird with a sore leg, but it escaped. Lynda would be really chuffed if I found an injured insect or animal to bring home for treatment at her surgery.

As I neared the creek, the sound of chain-saws faded and I could hear the calls of the birds. A kookaburra cackled from somewhere high in the branches of an ancient red-gum and small birds with blue fronts or waggly tails darted about in the undergrowth. I stopped at the top of the river bank thrilled to see water flowing in the creek below me. This was a magic spot. Looking down at the still muddied swirling water, I glimpsed a rabbit flash its white tail before dashing off to seek refuge under some bushes.

To get to the water I had to scramble down the slippery bank hanging on to branches and tree roots. My gum boots were no help as they slipped and slithered about on the muddy ground. There were a few small rocks and low shrubs to grab hold of as I went down, if necessary. There was a dead tree branch hanging out over the bank which I decided would be the best place to start. I grabbed the branch with both hands and swung myself out over the bank. Just below me, a convenient rock jutted out which would be helpful as my next point of contact. My weight was enough to bend the branch down, yet I was still a few inches short of the rock platform. I needed the branch to bend over a few more inches so I rocked it up and down. It began to do what I wanted until, snap! The branch broke.

It happened so suddenly I had no hope of grabbing anything. I tumbled down the bank, desperately reaching out to catch hold of something, a root, a plant, a rock, anything to help break my fall. The roughness of the bank slowed my slide somewhat, but not enough. In an instant I hit the muddy water. This terrified me because I couldn't swim. Luck was with me though, because where I landed wasn't deep and my feet quickly found the sludgy bottom. I had enough time to stand up and discover the water here was only waist-deep. Panicked, I tried to scramble back onto the bank only to find the water was flowing too fast and I couldn't make it. Yelling for help and thrashing about hopelessly, the water propelled me along and dumped me, spluttering for air, on a gravel bank on the opposite side of the creek. I was soaked, freezing cold and shaking with fear, but alive and relatively safe where I had ended up. I struggled to my feet and started calling for help, but the noise of the fast-flowing creek drowned out my cries.

I have no idea how long I remained stranded on the wrong side of the creek. After a time, I stopped shouting for help; nobody could hear me anyway and I was getting a sore throat. I reasoned that after a time dad would wonder where I was and come looking. In an effort to get warm and dry, I found a fallen tree trunk bathed in sunshine. I climbed up onto it and stretched out, lizard-like, waiting for someone to appear. I remembered dad saying once, 'If you ever get into trouble, the worst thing you can do is panic. Always stay calm.' Now that I was in trouble, I was determined to try and follow my dad's advice.

It was peaceful lying there on the log. Soon the sun began to warm me so I turned over on my back and pulled my T-shirt over my eyes to lessen the glare of the sun. A number of grazes and scratches from my ordeal began to hurt. The worst was a long scratch down my shin. It had stopped bleeding, but I could see there was mud and muck in the wound. Blow flies seemed particularly interested in the wound and hovered around incessantly. Mum was a whiz at cleaning up injuries with cotton wool, warm water and salt and would have it fixed up in no time. For now, my job was to stay calm and not panic. I was sure I would be rescued soon.

As I lay there, I wondered if dad would be horribly angry with me for wandering off and not telling him where I was going. He'd been reluctant to bring me and had only agreed after I'd pestered him. Now, he might forbid me ever coming out again to help with a wood drive. My total contribution to the day's work effort was to collect half a dozen small logs. And now, having to get rescued because I'd stupidly fallen in the creek, wasn't likely to make dad feel any happier.

Time dragged on and I started feeling hungry. I spent my time carefully observing the birds that came closer and closer as they became accustomed to my presence. I knew the names of a few breeds. There were cute willy wagtails dancing about and magpies strutting around as if they owned the place. High up in the branches of the giant red gums I glimpsed parrots, galahs and sulphur crested cockatoos. Around the creek there were scrub wrens and cheeky blue wrens flitting about.

Before I left the truck, I'd heard the men agreeing to knock off for "smoko" sometime during the morning, which was probably when they would first notice I was missing. Mum said she'd put in a biscuit for me to have during "smoko," but I'd left my picnic box in the front of the truck. Dad might forget he'd brought me, but one of the men would surely find my picnic box and realise I was missing. No need to panic, I assured myself… just stay calm.

Not far from my sunny log was an ant heap. I watched fascinated, as thousands of small brown ants busily went about their duties bringing back little pieces of bark or sticks to the nest and then leaving again, empty clawed, to forage for more. The constant movement of tiny feet had created an ant highway that looped its way into the grassy scrub beyond. Often the ants bumped into each other. This didn't seem to matter; they simply rubbed antennae, side-stepped and politely kept going. Clever little creatures. I thought about Lynda and how she would be intrigued by so much ant activity. Perhaps, somewhere along the ant highway I could find an injured ant to take home for Lynda to look after in her surgery in the vegetable patch? The problem was how to carry an injured ant home without a box or something suitable to carry it in. I was still pondering this challenge when I heard shouting.

It was the three men about a hundred yards away searching for me on the opposite bank, but moving in the wrong direction. I must have been washed downstream farther than I realised and the men were walking upstream. I jumped off my friendly log shouting and waving vigorously, but to no avail. They were not even looking in my direction and couldn't hear me anyway. So, in my still squelchy wellington boots and half dry clothes, I set off running up river to make contact. A couple of times I fell over branches and clumps of grass in my haste to catch up, but kept telling myself to remain calm and not look as though I was panicking.

It only took a few minutes before they spotted me. Dad started yelling.

'Christ's sake son, what the bloody hell have you been doing? How the hell did you get across the creek?'

'Hi dad,' I called out, still trying to look calm and in control, 'I fell in and the current carried me downstream.'

'Are you hurt, Norman?'

'Just a few scratches dad and a couple of bruises.'

'You're lucky, son. You could have bloody drowned!'

Dad turned to Charlie and said something I couldn't hear. The old man nodded and headed off towards his truck.

'Norman, we're going to have to throw a rope across to you. You're lucky we brought a few ropes to tie the wood down on the back of the truck. Don't try and catch the rope. Wait till it falls on the ground and then grab it. Understood?'

'Yes, dad.'

'Why the bloody hell didn't you tell me where you were going?'

'You were busy. I wasn't planning to fall in. I just went exploring. I'm sorry.'

A few minutes later Charlie returned with a coiled rope. He tied one end around a strong sapling before flinging the rest across to me.

'Now, hang on tight while we slowly pull you in. Whatever you do don't let go. Are you ready?'

My heart was thumping like mad. I was nervous about how this was going to work. Outwardly, I made sure I still looked calm and followed the instructions dad was giving In the end, it was easier than expected. They dragged me across the creek and then hauled me up the bank, where I emerged wet and muddy, but on the right side of the creek at last. Dad gave me a hug and we went back to the truck for a much delayed "smoko." There, dad dabbed some sort of antiseptic on the worst of my cuts. It stung like mad, but I didn't cry. I sat in the sun to dry out and ate my biscuit.

Later that afternoon we arrived back in town and dropped piles of logs off at Charlie's, grandpa's and the remainder at our place. Dad ordered me in for first shower and told me to ask mum to patch me up afterwards.

That evening, when I was ready for bed, dad said something that made me feel proud.

'Norman, you were a bloody twit to get yourself into such a mess down at that creek today. The good thing though, was that you remained calm and didn't panic. That's a big lesson in life, son. Whatever happens, don't panic, stay calm.'

I slept well that night. I felt I was one step closer to being a man.

4. HONESTY PAYS...

I don't know why I couldn't do my schoolwork. The letters in the alphabet were hard for me to remember and I became confused when they looked alike. I could never distinguish "d" from "b" or "n" from "u" for example. Numbers were a problem too; the numbers 5 and 2 always muddled me, as did numbers 6 and 9. I tried really hard to get them right, but I wasn't getting any better. I even found it difficult knowing which way to read across the page. Was it left to right or the other way? And which was left and which was right? Mrs Adams gradually became kinder and sometimes even smiled, but I'm sure she had given up trying to help. I think she felt sorry for me.

One day, a psychologist came from town specially to see me. I liked him and the two of us spent a fun couple of hours playing games together. He told me he was trying to diagnose my learning problems to see if there was some way I could be helped. He never told me what he thought I needed. He said he would write a report to give to my school principal and Mrs Adams. A couple of weeks later mum and dad were invited to come to the school to speak to the principal, but I wasn't allowed to attend. Dad was too busy at the garage so mum went along on her own.

That evening, I knew mum would want to tell dad what the principal had told her so I hatched a little plan. I told them I was tired and wanted to go to bed early, much to my parents' surprise. They even wondered if I was feeling sick or something. As soon as mum finished saying goodnight and closed my bedroom door I crept out of bed and quietly opened the door again and sat on the floor listening. I didn't have to wait long.

'I'm sorry you couldn't spare the time to come and see Mr Cruickshank today, Fred.'

'I'm bloody flat out, like a lizard drinking love. A whole bunch of bleeding safety checks have to be done at the moment. Usually dad does them, but he's had a couple of days off recently so I'm way behind.'

'Well, it was actually most interesting.'

'Let me get a beer then you can tell me about it.'

'Do you remember the shrink who came to see Norman a couple of weeks back?'

'Yup… a child psychologist.'

'That's right. Norman spent the whole morning with him doing tests. Anyway, Mr Cruickshank has received the psychologist's report and that's what he wanted to talk to us about.'

'So, what does he reckon?'

'Norman has something called dyslexia. I had to get Mr Cruickshank to write it down on a piece of paper for me.'

'And what the hell is that when the cows come home?'

'Dyslexia is a problem some kids have when they mix up their letters and numbers. They get all confused.'

'Well, we bloody knew that didn't we?'

'Yes, but now it has a proper medical name. Because they know he has dyslexia, it will be much easier to get him into that special school in town where they can help him learn to read and write.'

'I still don't want Norman traipsing off to a bloody school for numb-skulls. The kid's okay. He speaks okay, he understands things, he's got plenty of common sense. Give him a bit more time and he'll sort it all out for himself.'

'The principal and the psychologist don't agree with you, Fred.' He has another problem too. Nearly everybody is either left-handed or right-handed. It seems that our Norman is neither and this makes it difficult for him with his learning. He gets confused about which direction to look at things. Everyone knows when you write or read you go from left to right across the page, but Norman gets mixed up and often tries to do it right to left.'

'Sounds bloody stupid to me.'

'Mr Cruickshank says it's as though the wiring in Norman's head is all jumbled up. You know what it's like if you have your battery leads wrongly positioned, don't you? You have to get the positives and negatives correct. Well, it's as if Norman's leads are buggered, the positives and negatives are all over the place.'

Dad was quiet for a moment or two. Mum continued...

'Poor little fella was born with these problems; it's not his fault. Mr Cruickshank wants him to go to this special school in town where they can help kids like Norman.'

'Let him finish primary school here. If Norman still hasn't sorted things out when it's time to go to high school, he can go to this special school then.'

'But Fred, that won't help him now. The psychologist says the earlier he starts on one of the special programs they have, the easier it will be for him.'

'Mary, I'm not having Norman going on a bus to a special school for abnormal children along with all those high school kids. I don't want everyone in town thinking we have a weird kid. Besides, he's bound to get bullied big time on the bus by those high school kids. No way, Mary. Norman will just have to do the best he can and we'll help him here at home.'

'You're making a bad decision, Fred. Norman will probably grow up illiterate, unable to read and write. How's that going to help him get a job? He certainly won't be able to take over the family business.'

'Mary, I've made my mind up and that's it. I'm the head of this bloody household and what I say goes. No point in discussing it anymore. Topic closed. Now, I'm going down the pub. Do the bloody washing up on your own.'

I scrambled to my feet, quietly closed my bedroom door and jumped back into bed. Dad would walk past my door on his way out to the pub. This was the first time I'd heard my parents having an argument and it made me sad. It didn't help that the fight was about me and the strange sicknesses I have. I loved my parents so much, it was horrible to hear them falling out like this.

* * *

Next morning dad was in a foul mood at breakfast time. I had seen him like this a few times before and knew to keep well out of his way and my mouth firmly shut. Mum served up Lynda and my porridge in silence and gave us a severe look that meant, "beware." A moment later Lynda accidentally spilt milk on the tablecloth and we held our collective breaths expecting an angry outburst, but it never came. Fortunately, dad hadn't seen the misdemeanour. Soon after that, dad left his porridge virtually untouched, declaring he wasn't hungry. Grabbing a piece of dry toast and his lunch-box, he left the room without another word.

The three of us finished our breakfast in silence listening for the front door to close, signalling that dad had left for work. We didn't have to wait long. He clumped down the corridor in his RM Williams boots and slammed the front door shut behind him. Lynda and I looked at mum pleading for an explanation.

'What's up with dad?' I asked, tentatively.

Mum picked up her cup of tea for a refill. 'Dad was out late last night and didn't get much sleep.'

'He looked really grumpy,' said Lynda, 'I was scared when I spilt that little bit of milk. I thought I was going to be in big trouble.'

'You were lucky dad didn't see it, Lynda. Now, hurry up and finish that piece of toast please.'

'I know where dad went last night,' I blurted out without stopping to think, 'he went to the boozer.'

'It's not called a boozer Norman, it's called a pub thank you. And how do you know where dad went anyway?'

I coloured deeply, furious with myself for stupidly letting slip that I had been listening to their conversation last night. My parents have told me numerous times to be honest and always tell the truth. Now that mum was confronting me, I knew my honesty was being challenged. I looked up at mum with a guilty look on my face.

'Sorry mum. My bedroom door was open last night and I heard you and dad talking.'

Mum put her hands on her hips and glared at me, 'Are you telling me you heard everything we were saying about *you* last night?'

I nodded, miserably.

'That was very naughty of you. When we put you to bed your door should always remain firmly shut, unless you want to go to the toilet. Is that clear? Now tell me what you heard.'

Lynda and mum were both looking daggers at me and I knew I had to confess. Feebly, I said, 'You were talking about which school I should go to.'

'I see. And what did we decide, may I ask?'

'To stay where I am,' I mumbled.

'And what do you think of that idea, Norman?'

I shrugged my shoulders. To say I was happy to stay with Mrs Adams would seem to be taking dad's side, to say I wanted to go to the special school in town was to side with mum. I might be hopeless at school work and have some weird medical problems, but I knew instinctively not to get involved in a mum versus dad disagreement. It would have been nice, however, if I had been asked what I wanted to do! Given a choice in the matter, I would definitely have opted to attend the special school. I already realised, even at my tender age, that if everyone else could read and write and do maths except me,

I'd be disadvantaged. It was like Johnny Pratt at school, who had been born with withered legs and would be in a wheel chair for the rest of his life. He was disadvantaged because he couldn't go places or do things that the rest of us could.

'Well Norman, I asked you a question?'

'Sorry, mum.'

I was truly torn. I didn't want to take sides, but I knew if I said nothing I wasn't being totally honest. Mum still had her hands on her hips, a sure sign she wasn't happy. I could feel her anger brewing like a volcano. There was no way out.

'I think I'd like to go to the special school,' I answered softly.

'At least you and I agree, then. Now, go and clean your teeth and get ready for school.'

Lynda and I left the room together. My older sister was full of questions because all this was news to her. 'Norman, are you going to this other school then?'

'No, sis.'

'Why not?'

'Dad says I can't go until I'm in high school.'

'I'm glad because we can go on walking to school together and both be in Mr Cruickshank's class.'

I smiled, then raced her to the bathroom to be the first to clean my teeth.

* * *

My parents claimed "honesty always pays." Sometimes, I found this hard to believe. When mum asked me which school I preferred to attend I picked the special school, but it made no difference. Despite my honesty I stayed at my local primary until I was old enough to go to high school. Four years with Mrs Adams and three years with Mr Cruickshank did little to help me overcome my learning difficulties. At least Mr Cruickshank was considerate. He recognised he wasn't trained to meet my special needs so did his level best to find me useful tasks to do around the school when it was time for reading, spelling, composition and maths. I became the refuse monitor, a fancy term for the kid who collects the school's rubbish each day and properly disposes of it in the big bins.

The position of refuse monitor steadily expanded as Mr Cruickshank came to appreciate how reliable and hard working I was. Additional responsibilities soon started coming my way. The school was entitled to a gardener/maintenance man for three hours a week, which Mr Cruickshank told me was grossly inadequate. Frank Leadbeater was that man, but he had nasty respiratory problems from a lifetime of smoking, so he was delighted to have me to help with some of the heavier, more strenuous tasks. Before long, I was doing a range of outside jobs: mowing the grass. painting the school fence, putting sand out around the play-ground equipment and sweeping up leaves. I wasn't paid to do these jobs, but that didn't worry me, I was just pleased to escape from the classroom to be doing something useful. Mum said doing all these jobs helped my "self-esteem," whatever that meant.

When I was in sixth grade, the final year of primary school, the regular school cleaner went off work with a broken ankle. Mr Cruickshank found a replacement, but then she fell ill and he couldn't find another cleaner at short notice. In desperation, Mr Cruickshank asked me if I would fill in for a few days until he could find another adult cleaner. And so it was, that literally by accident my life as a cleaner began.

Of course, employing a twelve-year-old as a cleaner was illegal, so Mr Cruickshank used what he called "creative accounting" to get around the problem. He paid me out of some discretionary funds he had available. I became a temporary cleaner for five days in a row. Mum and dad agreed to let me do the work after school finished. At the end of the five days, Mr Cruickshank gave me the grand total of twenty-five pounds and commended me for my work and especially for my honesty.

4. Honesty Pays...

When I asked the principal why he was impressed with my honesty, he said I had respected everything in the school and hadn't stolen anything. I was surprised by this comment because I had known ever since I was tiny not to touch things that didn't belong to me and certainly not to steal them! It was part of being "honest."

As it turned out, Mrs Adams had left her purse at school one afternoon and I had simply handed it in to Mr Cruickshank for safe keeping. Mrs Adams was enormously relieved because the purse held nearly two hundred pounds as well as her driver's licence. So, perhaps honesty does pay because now I'm trusted by Mr Cruickshank, Mrs Adams, old Frank as well as my parents. What's more, if there's another cleaning job to be done, they all know I'm reliable and trustworthy.

* * *

As I went up through the grades at my infants/primary school the kids stopped teasing and eventually came to accept me. Everyone knew I couldn't read or write. It became a recognised fact; Norman McDade can't read or write. It was no big deal, no more important than Sylvia has red hair, Michael can speak German, or Jessica's parents are divorced. Increasingly, I came to enjoy going to school especially when Mr Cruickshank made special allowances for me.

I was still not much good at sports. If I could find other things to do during playtimes, I did. Not being sporty, or able to read or write, made finding something to do difficult. Sometimes I would finish off a job for Mr Cruickshank or offer to wash Mrs Adams' car. Often, I would join Janice, the sweet little girl who was kind and welcoming when nobody else was. No longer did we sit under her shady peppercorn tree, unless it was fiercely hot. Janice, it turned out, had learning difficulties too. When the experts started trying to work out why Janice was slow, they discovered it was a simple problem to solve; she couldn't see properly! Surprisingly, nobody had picked this up earlier. Janice's eyes looked normal, but her vision was impaired. The solution, a thick pair of glasses.

I still remember the first day seven-year-old Janice came to school with her newly fitted glasses, she immediately became an object of ridicule. Children can be very cruel to each other and Janice was called horrible names such as "fog-lamps," "glassworks" and "four eyes." She was inconsolable and during playtime retreated back to her peppercorn tree in the playground. I hated hearing the nasty things the children were saying to her so I went down to her tree to try and comfort her. She had been kind to me so it was only fair I should show her I was her friend. Janice wanted to throw her new glasses away, but I told her the teasing wouldn't last long and after a time it would die down. I already knew this from my own experience of being teased.

Without realising it, Janice and I had become close friends. Our shared learning challenges had helped our friendship.

* * *

My frightening experience of being washed downstream while collecting wood had convinced me patience and not panicking were two important attributes for a successful life. Mum and dad had always told me that being honest was just as important. I knew this already when I looked after Mrs Adams' purse, but in grade four the importance of being honest was reinforced.

I was eight years old and trusted to take Taffy, our three-legged sheep dog, for walks on my own. Taffy was missing a back leg, but could walk almost as well as any other dogs. Sadly, running was too much for him and he would either refuse point blank to run or try to run a few yards and then fall in a heap with his tongue hanging out looking up at me with his big apologetic doleful eyes. I loved Taffy to bits and did my best to avoid ever making him run.

Living in a small country town, we had only one public park

located right in the centre of town. Dad said the council looked after the park well because they wanted tourists to stop there and spend their money. The park had the usual amenities: toilets, shady trees, irrigated lawns, playground equipment, barbeques, flower beds and hard concrete tables and seats. One corner of the park was fenced off for a dedicated war memorial where ANZAC ceremonies were held on April 25th each year. I liked it in the park. It was cool in summer and I could let Taffy off the lead to move about freely. Taffy and I would usually visit the park around five o'clock in the evening after I had done any jobs at home that mum had lined up for me.

The park also gave me opportunities to indulge my growing fascination with nature. One of the few subjects I enjoyed at school was natural science and Mr Cruickshank had set up a corner of the classroom as a nature museum. We pupils were encouraged to bring in objects of interest to display there provided they weren't still alive. I think I was the main contributor since I was always discovering intriguing specimens in the park. There were leaves of varying shapes, textures and colours, weird kinds of tree bark, discarded skins of cicadas and scats of several kinds of animals that lived in the park. While Taffy exercised, I hunted for potential new museum pieces.

One evening, after I'd been down the shops for mum, I called Taffy up with my usual call of "walkies" and the dear old thing came bounding towards me as excited as ever. I attached the lead to his collar, ruffled his coat and we set off. It was a lovely evening, still warm with a slight southerly breeze blowing to keep things comfortable. Taffy went through his usual routine of marking virtually every post and shrub we passed along the way, although Mrs Alcott's large dog, next door but one, made it clear his front yard was never to be defiled by a small three-legged canine.

The evening shadows were stretching across the park lawns as we arrived. I let Taffy off the lead and he trotted happily away investigating seemingly endless stimulating scents. Half a dozen kids from school were playing touch football on the largest patch of lawn behind the rose garden and a couple of adults were casually exercising their four-legged friends. Taffy had enough nous to leave other dogs well alone sensing he was at a distinct physical disadvantage. Under the barbecue shelter, a group of tourists were noisily packing up their gear and taking it back to their cars. Three or four hopeful magpies strutted around the barbeque area plucking up the courage to dart in and grab any food scraps. I headed off along the path that meandered towards the glass house containing a collection of exotic ferns.

Half way along the track I heard Taffy whimpering. At first I couldn't see him, then a moment later he emerged limping, from under a thick bush and made his way slowly and painfully towards me. Now, dogs can get around fine on three legs, but trying to remain mobile on two is going a bit too far! There was a park bench nearby so I picked Taffy up and sat there to diagnose his problem. Sure enough, I found a large thorn lodged in the pad of the front left paw. I held Taffy tight, whilst he did his best to lick my face clean and after a couple of attempts extracted the offending item. Taffy gave me a grateful parting lick and jumped to the ground restored to full three-legged mobility. I placed the troublesome thorn carefully in my pocket, it would be a fascinating contribution to the class museum. As I did so, I noticed a woman's purse resting against the leg of the bench I was sitting on, partly obscured by weeds.

I picked the purse up and examined it. It looked as though it was made of crocodile skin, although not having ever seen a crocodile I couldn't be sure. It was in excellent condition so I surmised it had been lying hidden for only a short time, a day or two at most. I'm no expert on ladies' purses, but this one appeared to be excellent quality with a neat golden coloured clasp. I wondered for a moment or two whether I should open the purse, but it didn't feel right to be prying into somebody else's private possessions. Curiosity got the better of me in the end and I unclipped the golden clasp and peered inside.

At first glance the purse appeared empty, but there was another smaller compartment fastened shut by a small zipper. I undid this and discovered what looked like a couple of folded over bank notes. Excited, I pulled the notes out, unfolded them and examined them carefully. After tracing over the numbers with my finger I worked out that my hand was holding a twenty-pound note and a fifty-pound note! I had never seen a fifty-pound note before! Once a week, dad gave me threepence for pocket money and I knew there were 240 pennies in a pound. In my hand was no less than seventy pounds. The maths was too difficult for me, but I knew it would take many years of threepenny bits to come anywhere close to this amount of money.

As you know, mum and dad had always impressed on me the need to be totally honest. Mum had a favourite expression, "do as you would be done by." It made a lot of sense to me. If I had lost this purse, I would certainly want the purse with the seventy pounds returned to me. So, without hesitation, I placed the precious notes back in their compartment, snapped the purse shut and headed off in the direction of the police station. A somewhat mystified Taffy soon caught up surprised I was not heading for home. I attached his lead and we came out of the park and onto the High Street, the main road through town. The police station was only a five-minute walk away.

The sun was close to setting and the air had grown suddenly chilly. There were only a few people still about and the town clock struck once to indicate it was half past five as we walked by. Often, I had driven past the police station with mum or dad, but never had I ventured inside. Taffy and I passed Clarke, the butcher, the Anglican church and two or three houses before we arrived at the four stone steps that led up to the entrance to the police station. There was nothing convenient outside the station where I could tie Taffy up so I was obliged to take my three-legged mate in with me.

It took all my strength to push open the heavy glass door and enter what seemed to be an empty space. There were no tables, no chairs or any other furniture. Fixed to the wall, facing me, were posters covered in writing which I couldn't read. There were also photographs of a few men's faces and I wondered whether these were criminals wanted by the police. At the back of the space was a long wooden counter high enough for me to have to stretch up to see over. On the wall behind the counter was a large coloured photograph of Her Majesty the Queen smiling down at me. Nobody, apart from the Queen, seemed to be about.

I was feeling distinctly nervous. An enormous policeman had come to our school a couple of times to talk to us about safety on the roads, but I had never actually spoken to a policeman before. Armed with revolvers, they didn't seem particularly approachable for a little fella like me. Bravely, I walked up to the empty counter, making sure Taffy was on a short lead and waited. Not a sound, not a sign of life.

After a minute or two, I was still plucking up the courage to yell out when I noticed a small hand bell sitting on the edge of the counter. I reached up and shook it as loudly as I could. There was a muffled sound of movement from somewhere way back behind the counter and I braced myself for what might be a difficult conversation. I didn't have to wait long. Heavy footsteps approached the counter and next minute a ruddy-faced policeman leant over the counter glaring down at me and Taffy, who disgraced himself by starting to bark.

'Shut up, your stupid mongrel,' the policeman ordered, looking crossly at Taffy.

Being chastised only made Taffy further annoyed and he voiced his displeasure even more intensely.

'If you're bringing me a lost dog this is the wrong place. Take him down to the vet or the pound, sonny.'

'This is Taffy sir and he's my dog.'

I fumbled in my pocket and pulled out a small rag doll which was Taffy's favourite toy. In emergencies I could usually depend on this bundle of unrecognisable rags to distract him. The barking stopped immediately and Taffy settled down at my feet gnawing away contentedly at the raggedy object.

'I'm sorry sir. I found this in the park,' I thrust my hand into my other pocket and pulled out the crocodile skin purse which I placed carefully on the counter.

The policeman picked it up, turned it over a couple of times and looked down at me.

'Anything in it, sonny?'

'Yes sir, seventy pounds.'

The policeman whistled, 'Wow, that's a lot of money, sonny.'

I had never been called "sonny" before, but this policeman obviously liked the word. I watched as he unclasped the purse, unzipped the inside compartment and squeezed a large hand in to retrieve the notes.

'Anything else in it, sonny? Did you find the owner's name anywhere?'

This was two questions at the same time and I didn't know which one to answer first. So, I simply said, 'No.'

The policeman searched the purse again, more thoroughly this time. While he was doing this, I had a chance to study him more carefully. Like every policeman I had ever seen, he was large. I reckoned he was about the same age as dad, but fatter and with a very red face. There was a moustache that seemed to twitch as he inspected the purse. Finally, he looked at me again with searching blue eyes.

'Well, sonny, you've done the right thing bringing this to the police station. I'll get the lost property form for you to fill in,' and he disappeared into the back blocks again. When he re-emerged he passed down a sheet of paper and a pencil. 'Fill this in sonny. Make sure you answer all the questions neatly.'

'Sir,' I stammered, 'I'm sorry, but I can't read or write.' I suddenly felt small and useless.

The policeman stared at me, 'Give me the form then,' he said tersely. He looked at me again, more carefully this time, 'are you McDade's young fella?'

'Yes, sir.'

'Well, at least you're an honest lad. I'll ask the questions; you give me the answers.'

In ten minutes, we had completed the form and the large policeman smiled down at me, 'Now sonny, do you know what happens next?'

'Not really, sir.'

'The owner of the purse has three months to come to this station and prove this purse and its contents belongs to them. If, at the end of three months, no one has come forward to claim the purse and its contents, then it's all yours.' He gave me a re-assuring wink.

'Wow, thank you, sir.'

'Sonny, you see these three stripes on the top of my arm?'

'Yes, sir.'

'When you come back in three months' time, don't call me "sir," address me as "sergeant." Got that?'

'Yes, sir…I mean… yes, sergeant.'

Three months' later, I returned to the police station and ran home bubbling with excitement. The owner had successfully claimed her crocodile purse with seventy pounds inside. She was so grateful to have it back she left five pounds with the sergeant for the lad who had brought it in to the police station. Mum and dad were right; honesty really did pay!

5. TIME AT SPECIAL SCHOOL

My father eventually relented and permitted me to attend the special school in town when I graduated from primary school. The long bus trip along the dusty dirt road into town took an hour on a good day and rather longer in the rain and in wintertime if we had a snowfall. These tedious bus journeys necessitated getting out of bed an hour earlier, something I didn't enjoy since I was almost a teenager now and needed extra sleep.

I knew most of the kids on the bus because they had attended the same primary school. There were a few other children who came in from one-teacher schools farther out in the bush. We had a couple of bullies to contend with as well and I soon learnt how to keep a low profile and avoid any contact with them. One was a big kid off a sheep station called Andy. Janice, who was a year ahead of me, said Andy's parents were Scottish and had come to Australia from the wild highlands of Northern Scotland. They had brought their three children up to be tough and uncompromising. Andy enjoyed a fight and knew how to handle himself. Several of the local kids had been beaten up by Andy over the years and nobody was known to have got the better of him in a brawl.

Bullies attract other bullies and together they form gangs. Hank was the only other boy on the bus who was close mates with Andy. Hank was the publican's son, not as physically formidable as Andy, but agile and cunning. Whereas Andy was a thug, Hank was simply a nasty piece of work who delighted in creating trouble. The only other person on the bus who knocked about with Andy and Hank was Naomi, a large buxom girl not overly endowed with brains. It was generally accepted amongst the rest of us on the bus that Naomi was their sexual plaything. This was the only reason Andy and Hank let her mix with them. This gang of three occupied the back row of seats on the school bus every day and nobody else dared to even think of sitting back there.

Our bus driver was old Don Egmont. Nobody knew how old Don was. He had been called "old" Don as far back as anyone could remember. Some reckoned he was somewhere up in his eighties. Don was a bachelor nowadays; his wife having died of cancer some years back. Between them they had raised a brood of five children who married young and had families of their own so that half the kids at the primary school were "Egmonts." Most of Don's teeth were missing and the few that remained were badly stained by nicotine. He still smoked his own skinny rolled up cigs, but never in front of us kids. Don was a man of few words. The most you could expect when getting on his bus was a curt, unsmiling nod. Old Don always looked the same, two or three days of stubble, unruly hair shoved in under an ancient footy cap and thin deeply veined hands. It was rumoured he never actually changed his clothes.

I was the only one on the bus enrolled at the "special" school. Old Don had to add a short detour to his run to drop me off at my school in the mornings and again when he picked me up in the afternoons. This meant in the mornings I was first to get off, in the afternoons, last to board.

At first, I found my new school confronting. All up, there were about forty kids who came from all over the district, some as far as fifty miles away. The school was a sort of combined infants/primary/secondary with little five-year-olds through to big kids who must have been sixteen or seventeen. Classes were tiny, about five or six at a time and not based on age, but on ability or the kind of learning problems we were wrestling with. There were eight teachers and eight teachers' aides which meant we were seldom short of help when we asked for it. The head mistress was a Mrs Radcraft, who welcomed mum, dad and myself on the first day of the new term.

We were a strange bunch of kids. There were a few who seldom wanted to join in any of the activities, preferring to stay apart from the rest of us. They didn't want to play or even talk to anyone. A couple of these kids would spend hours just sitting on the floor rocking back and forth and then suddenly yelling out. One of them, a girl, couldn't talk and only made strange grunting noises. I heard a teacher say one of this group was a "savant". Later I discovered what this meant. He was probably a year older than me and had what was called a "photographic memory." The teachers would show him a highly complicated picture for a minute or so and then take it away and ask him to draw what he had seen in the picture. Amazingly, he could re-create every tiny detail on a large piece of paper with virtually no mistakes. You would have to have a very special brain to be able to do that!

There was another group of kids who had something wrong with their brains and were terribly slow to do anything. They looked funny but seemed happy enough. They could talk a bit, but were not much fun because they were so slow. Then there was a group of deaf kids who did sign language and had a special teacher of their own. I made friends with a couple of them, about my age, and tried to learn their language, but found it really difficult. Lastly, there was a group of children who had similar problems to me, dyslexic. They had come to the special school when they were much younger than I and were now doing quite well. Once they were good enough they graduated to normal schools. I soon realised how disadvantaged I was by having to wait until I was twelve to start coming to this special school.

One teacher was my "home" teacher responsible for my every day welfare. His name was Mr Tonks and I liked him from the start. He was always cracking jokes and doing silly things to make learning fun. He wasn't my class teacher, but he made a point of seeing me every day to see how things were going.

Soon, I found I was settling in and with the specialist help of the teachers started to make some slow progress. My parents told me I'd be at the special school until I turned fifteen when I could legally leave school. I now had three years to try and master the basics of reading, writing and arithmetic. The teachers sometimes referred to these three subjects as "the three Rs" although I never fathomed out why because only "reading" started with an "r".

* * *

I had only been at my special school for a few weeks when I noticed dear old Taffy's health seemed to be deteriorating. The extra hour travelling home on the bus every school day meant I was an hour later taking Taffy for his walk in the park. He was as keen as ever when I called out "walkies" seemingly grateful for the opportunity to get out of the house and have a run. We would get across to the park, as before, and I would let him off his lead. Taffy would charge off but I noticed this initial burst of energy didn't last. Within a couple of minutes, he would sit down panting and look at me with those big doleful, loving eyes. After a few moments rest he would get up again and then be content to walk along slowly by my side. This was a marked change in Taffy's behaviour. Previously, I'd had a job to stop him scampering around like a mad thing and always found him reluctant to leave the park.

As the weeks went by our visits to the park gradually became shorter and shorter until Taffy could barely manage to get across the road. He seemed to be losing weight too although his appetite remained the same. He would still look up at me expectantly whenever I called out "walkies" and come to me willingly. Taffy would struggle the fifty yards or so to where we crossed the road and there he would stop and lie down. At this point I would pick Taffy up and carry him to the park, because I was concerned he might be run over with his painfully slow walking. Once in the park I would carry Taffy over to the trees and bushes which were his favourites. Here, I would put him down gently and he'd play about for five or ten minutes and then ask to be taken home.

Several times I told mum and dad about Taffy's declining health. At first, they dismissed my concerns because they had not noticed anything wrong. He was eating well enough and getting about the house normally; it was only when I took him for "walkies" that his declining health was apparent. After a few weeks, I finally persuaded mum to come to the park with us to see for herself. This convinced her that Taffy was unwell so she arranged an appointment with the vet. I was determined to be with Taffy for his appointment and, with mum's concurrence, wagged school that day because the appointment was at one-thirty.

Usually, Taffy loved trips in the car but on this occasion, he refrained from barking at everything along the way and lay quietly next to me on the back seat. I wondered if he knew where we were going. Many years ago, when hit by a car outside our garage, Taffy had endured a number of horrid visits to the vet as they fought to keep him alive and repair his mangled back leg. Miraculously they saved his life, but lost the battle with the leg which had to be amputated.

The vet's surgery was on top of a low hill, a mile out of town. I had sometimes ridden past on my bike but couldn't remember ever having actually entered the building. Mum told me when I was very small she had taken Lynda and me to the vet a couple of times when they were working on Taffy, who was not much more than a puppy, but I had no recollection of this.

Mum drove into the carpark outside the surgery, looked at her watch and urged me to be quick as we were already a few minutes late for Taffy's appointment. As it happened, we needn't have worried because the friendly receptionist told us the vet was out delivering a troublesome calf and was running late. I placed Taffy on the floor and gave him his raggedy doll to play with. Mum started filling out forms for Taffy and came back rolling her eyes and sighing.

'You'll never guess how much a consultation with the vet costs nowadays,' she said, grimacing.

'A pound?'

'And the rest...'

'Two pounds?'

'Go on...'

'Three pounds?'

'Two-pounds, ten. And if Taffy needs treatment or prescriptions, it'll be more.'

I wondered how many sixpences that would be. Now that I was going to high school, dad had doubled my weekly pocket money to sixpence a week. I knew there were two sixpences in a shilling and twenty shillings in a pound so it shouldn't be too difficult to work it out. I never got there though because Taffy was looking up at me with his big pleading eyes asking for a cuddle. I lifted him up, noting he seemed to have lost even more weight and let him snuggle down into my lap. He didn't appear to have any pain; just listless and lacking vitality.

'Do you know how old Taffy is, Norman?'

'Fourteen, I think.'

'Yup, and he'll turn fifteen before the end of the month. That's really old for this kind of dog.'

'So, mum, do you reckon his problem is just old age?'

'One dog year is like seven years for a human. That makes Taffy almost a hundred and five!'

'What! A hundred and five? Nobody lives that long, do they?'

'Hardly anyone makes it to a hundred so a hundred and five would be almost a record.'

I lifted Taffy up and held him up in front of me. Looking into his face, I said, 'I think it's about time you are declared a pensioner, old fella.' Taffy responded with a wriggle and a couple of quick licks.

'Mrs McDade?'

It was the receptionist calling us. 'Doctor Jones will see Taffy now, second door on your left, please.'

With my continuing difficulties with left and right handedness I had to rely on mum to lead the way.

Doctor Jones turned out to be a large, jolly man with a beard that would challenge Santa Clause. He greeted us with a beaming smile and a hearty handshake. A white coat covered him down to below his knees and a kind of peaked cap sat on his head. He was the sort of man who instils complete confidence. I felt Taffy was in safe hands.

'So, this is Taffy, is it?' and he took hold of one of Taffy's paws as if to shake it too, 'now, young man, would you please bring Taffy over to my examination table.' I did as I was bid and laid Taffy down as comfortably as I could on the clean white sheet.

'And is Taffy your dog young man?'

'No sir, he belongs to the family.'

'Aha…' There was quiet for a few minutes as Doctor Jones carried out his examination. This process was punctuated by some more 'ahas' and a few 'umms' along the way. Taffy was beautifully behaved and allowed the doctor to prod and push wherever he wanted. Finally, Doctor Jones looked up and removed his gloves.

'How about you both take a seat and I'll tell you what's what.'

There were two old metal chairs up against the wall of the surgery and mum and I retreated there. Doctor Jones carefully lifted Taffy up, gave him a bit of a cuddle and passed him back to me. I received another generous round of licks while Doctor Jones folded his arms and lent back against his examination table.

'Okay…Taffy's a real old timer you know. I remember treating the poor fellow many years ago when he tried to knock a car off the road and lost a leg in the process.'

'Oh, it *was* you then, Doctor Jones. I wasn't sure,' said mum.

'Taffy has already well and truly exceeded the average lifespan for this breed of dog so he's done remarkably well.'

'He's almost a hundred and five,' I blurted out.

'Quite right young man. So, Taffy's suffering from old age. It gets us all in the end. He's got lumbago, arthritis, rheumatism, poor vision and probably sundry other problems associated with the ageing process.'

'Is there anything you can give him to spark him up a bit, doctor?' asked mum.

Doctor Jones appeared to think about this for a moment before replying. 'I can prescribe something, yes, but I don't think it will do much for the poor old fellow. Taffy has another problem, which is incurable and it will cause his demise quite soon.'

'What's that?' I asked, anxiously.

'He's got prostate cancer and its well advanced.'

'Prostate cancer?' exclaimed mum, surprised, 'I thought it was only men that got that?'

'Men, and men's best friends are the only two animals, as far as we know, to be so inflicted,' replied the vet.

I had heard of cancer but not prostate cancer. I also knew cancer was a terrible disease and many people died from it and suffered dreadfully.

'If Taffy has cancer, why doesn't he have any pain?' I asked.

'He's lucky, young man. You're right he's still pain free, but that won't last. As the cancer spreads, he'll be in an awful lot of pain and it would be cruel to put him through that.'

Mum looked at me and took hold of my hand. 'So, doctor, should we have Taffy put down?'

'My recommendation is that you take Taffy home today and spoil him to bits. Then, as soon as he shows any signs of pain, bring him back to me and I'll gently put him to sleep. It's a quick injection and then it's all over.'

Mum and I left the surgery with Taffy perfectly happy to walk with us. Mum rummaged around in her purse to find the two pounds and ten shillings to pay the receptionist. I remember Mum putting her arm round my shoulders as we headed slowly back to the car. 'Good and bad, eh?' I nodded and again sat with Taffy as we drove home.

'Mum, I've heard of breast cancer and lung cancer but I've never heard of postate cancer.'

'It's prostate cancer dear, with an "r" in it.'

'So, have we got something called a prostate inside us, then?'

'You have...I don't.'

'How come?'

'Men have one, women don't. You better have a man to man talk with your dad about it. Not much good talking to me, dear.'

For a few beautiful weeks we all doted over Taffy and spoiled him rotten. He lapped it up and we began to dare to think that the vet was wrong. Then, quite suddenly one morning, we noticed things had changed for the worse. Taffy was put down that same day.

I asked dad about prostate cancer. He assured me we would have a good chat sometime but it never happened.

* * *

Shortly after dear Taffy left us, something else happened that was upsetting. I had been careful not to have anything to do with the three bullies on our school bus Andy, Hank and their side-kick, Naomi. I even had little strategies worked out to help me keep a low profile and not draw attention to myself.

One afternoon when school had finished, I was walking across the playground to the bus stop where old Don, our bus driver, together with the high school kids stopped to pick me up. I was late, so I broke into a run to be sure to be at the bus stop in time. Some other kids were playing soccer in the playground when suddenly a soccer ball struck me full in the face. It had been kicked hard enough to floor me and I landed in a dazed heap on the concrete. I shook myself and scrambled up wanting to make light of the incident since I realised it had been an accident. In an instant my friend came over to apologise profusely and see if there was anything he could do.

I assured him I was fine and was about to continue on my way when I felt something warm flowing from my nose. Blood! Heaps of it! I scrambled to find my handkerchief to stem the flow while some of the other kids in the playground came over to tell me what I needed to do to stop the bleeding. There were numerous suggestions, mostly sensible, with a couple of crazy ideas thrown in as well. 'Norman, best way to stop it is to stand on your head.' A girl in my class recommended shoving two pebbles up my nostrils, 'It really works Norman,' she assured me.

I plumbed for the method mum had given me the only other time I'd had a nose bleed; hold your nose firmly and sit down quietly until it stops. The trouble with that remedy was that I had to get to the bus stop in time, so sitting down was out of the question. I ran on awkwardly, holding my nose with one hand and carrying my school port in the other. As I came round the corner of the building I saw, to my horror, the bus was already there waiting. I knew old Don was merciless with kids who were running late and had been known on a number of occasions to leave without a moment's delay.

I'm not sure if old Don made allowances for me that day because I attended a "special" school, or if he had arrived a couple of minutes early. Whatever the reason, I was hugely relieved to clamber up the steps to a raucous chorus of not-so-nice comments from virtually everyone on board. Being one of the most junior on the school bus, I always sat in the front somewhere, if possible next to Janice. For some reason the front seats were occupied today so, still clutching my bloodied nose with blood stains down my shirt and even on my shorts, I was forced to head up towards the back of the bus. The only seats still vacant were in the two rows directly in front of the three bullies. This time there was no way I could avoid the unwelcome attentions of Andy, Hank and Naomi.

'Hey Norman, one of the girls beat ya up, eh?'

'Poor little diddums…was she too tough for ya?'

'You're not supposed to fight the girls you know Norm; you're supposed to fuck 'em.'

This last comment, from Naomi, sent the two bully boys into hysterics. After a moment or two Hank calmed down enough to ask Naomi what did she know about fucking? More laughter ensued. I couldn't catch Naomi's response, but it set the boys off again. Things quietened down for a bit until Andy, with his strong Scottish accent, decided to have some more fun at my expense.

'Hey, listen Norm, you gotta girl friend?'

I didn't answer.

'Nah, I reckon he's a queer,' Hank chimed in.

'He can't even get it up yet,' added Naomi, sending the boys into chortles again.

'How would you know, Naomi?' challenged Andy, 'you been with little Norman, have ya?'

Naomi never liked being ridiculed, fearing she might be in danger of losing her privileged position with Hank and Andy and realised she must do something out of the ordinary to re-ingratiate herself with the bullies. What she did took me completely by surprise.

Without warning, she plonked herself down next to me and started making out that she was kissing and hugging me. Hank and Andy thought this was clever and sniggered loudly. It only lasted a few seconds before Naomi scrambled back to her back seat accompanied by a bellow from old Don, angry that someone was out of their seat and moving about his bus.

'Don't worry Norman, we'll get you at the bus stop,' growled Hank.

There was another half hour to go before we were due to arrive at the bus stop; I was truly fearful I was in for a bashing if I didn't do something. I slunk down in my lonely seat hoping that out of sight might mean out of mind with the three bullies. Two stops before mine one of the year eight kids left the bus, so I unobtrusively left my seat and moved down the bus to sit in the vacated seat, desperately hoping my move had not been noticed by the loathsome trio in the back seat.

Nearly all the children leave the bus at the same stop as I do, so my plan was to quietly intermingle with the other kids as they left and hope like mad the bullies forgot their threat to "get me". We pulled up as usual opposite the small park that reminded me of "walkies" with Taffy and I slipped off the bus as surreptitiously as possible. I joined Janice and told her the bully gang had said they were going to bash me up and explained how I hoped they had forgotten. She looked at me sympathetically and even offered to come home with me when I walked across the park to get to my place. If anything did happen, however, I certainly didn't want her involved so, I dissuaded her. There was no sign of the three bullies as we farewelled and I crossed the road to enter the park. It looked as though I had given them the slip.

I hurried along my familiar path past the glass house, under the stand of conifers and into the stand of rhododendron bushes in the centre of the park. There was no sign of the gang and I began to relax; only another hundred yards or so and I'd be out of the park and in sight of home.

Then, suddenly, from behind one of the azaleas came Naomi flaunting herself like a cheap tart. She shimmied herself about in a way she must have considered was seductive as she slowly approached me. There was a nasty smirk on her face and she wobbled her hips and breasts like some sort of grotesque whale. At first, I thought I was only being confronted by Naomi and I wasn't too worried. I was sure I could run faster than this overweight girl, but then with howls of laughter, Hank and Andy dropped down in front of me having hidden in one of the massive branches of the only Moreton Bay Fig in the park. I stopped dead, terrified. There was no way I could avoid what was coming. I was no athlete. Whereas I might out run Naomi, I had no hope of escaping from the two older boys.

There were no sticks on the ground I could grab to defend myself or stones I could throw. I could hold my own against other kids my age with my fists, but here I was out numbered and hopelessly out muscled. There was no escape, I was just going to have to take what was coming. Like all bullies, my persecutors wanted to savour the moment and enjoy the fear they could see in my eyes. Andy took the lead.

'Now, we reckon you can't even get a stiffy, Norman and Naomi here is desperate to find out. So how about you whip off those shorts of yours and you can prove we're all wrong, eh?'

I couldn't believe what they were ordering me to do. I had expected to be bashed up and left bruised and battered to struggle home as best I could. Naomi was up really close now and I could smell her body odour as she cavorted about in my face.

'Come on little Norman, show us what you've got,' she teased and then with a sudden snatch she grabbed my shorts, but I was too quick and managed to wriggle out of her grasp. My escape was short lived, however, as Andy and Hank took hold of me and roughly pushed me to the ground. I did my best to struggle and kick and one of my kicks landed solidly on Naomi's leg.

'You little bugger you're going to pay for that,' she spat out.

Hank held me down by the shoulders and Andy busied himself unbuckling my belt.

'Don't do it here,' hissed Hank, 'pull him in under the bushes. We can be seen out here. Come on Andy get those bloody shorts off him.'

Between them they dragged me along the ground as I screamed, wriggled, squirmed and kicked. I even tried to bite an arm near my shoulder. There was nothing more I could do, as like some kind of captured wild African beast, I was forced into the cover of the bushes. By now my shorts were down around my ankles and between them they were trying to hold me still long enough to yank my underpants down. Whatever they were planning was about to happen.

'What the hell are you doing? Leave that kid alone!'

It was an angry man's voice coming from somewhere on the pathway. The tone and authority of the challenger was enough to stop the bullies and they immediately switched into defensive mode.

'Just having a bit of fun, mister,' Andy responded.

'It's a game we play,' added Hank.

I'd been dropped like a sack of potatoes. Fumbling for my shorts, I scrambled to my feet and at the same time managed to hitch the shorts up my legs. It was then I realised I'd wet myself.

'Doesn't look much like a game to me,' the stranger continued.

The three bullies looked sheepish and seemed unable, or unwilling, to say anything more. I found my school port lying nearby on the ground and half ran, half walked back to the path where the stranger was standing.

'You okay, young fella?'

'Yes, thanks, sir.'

I hurried off, anxious to get home and check out my injuries. My sister, Lynda, always went to a friend's place for half an hour before coming home so she wouldn't find out what had just happened. Reaching the gate on the edge of the park, I glanced back. There was no sign of the stranger or my three tormentors. In another minute or two I swung open our front gate, charged up the garden path and let myself in. Mum was out the back getting in the washing. I hesitated for a moment, wondering whether I could handle everything on my own without letting my parents know what had happened. One look in the mirror convinced me that wasn't going to work. There were blood stains on my shirt and shorts, grass stains on the back of my clothes and I needed to get out of my urine-soaked underpants. I discovered several minor scratches on my arms and legs and my school shoes were filthy too. Better to explain...

Mum was furious when she saw the state I was in, but calmed down after she heard my explanations about the nose bleed and the three bullies. I changed out of my dirty school clothes and had a long refreshing shower. Mum insisted on bathing my wounds in diluted Dettol and then let me have a couple of extra chocolate biscuits to cheer me up after my ordeal.

That evening there was much discussion over dinner about what action, if any, should be taken. Mum was all for going to the police and registering a formal complaint against the three bullies. Dad was more circumspect. He knew Hank and Naomi turned fifteen soon and both were expected to leave high school, thereby breaking up the group. He said he knew their fathers and serviced their vehicles. Dad promised to have a word with their fathers next time they came in for petrol or had their vehicles checked. Dad's views always prevailed in our household, so nothing more was done.

6. ANOTHER CLEANING JOB

Before I knew it, I was into my second year at the special school. I tried hard at school work but made painfully slow progress. My teacher used what was called the Dolch list of words to help me to read. Apparently, a man called Dolch had rigorously analysed written English language and documented the 220 words which were most commonly used. My teacher believed that if I could memorise these 220 words correctly, then I might be able to get by with basic reading. I admit it helped, but I never reached a point where I could read things easily or fluently. Reading remained an awful struggle which meant spelling and writing were almost impossible. I did make some progress with arithmetic though. My teacher told me when I turned thirteen that my arithmetic was now about the same standard as a child in second grade. As you can imagine that didn't impress me, or my parents, for that matter.

Dad was right about the bullies leaving school and moving on. Hank hung about his dad's pub for a few months then went off and joined the army as some kind of an apprentice. Andy joined his dad working on their property, but soon fell afoul of the law. The last I heard, he was doing six months in some gaol for young offenders. Naomi gave birth to a baby girl at the age of sixteen. Nobody knew who the father was and Naomi wasn't telling. She moved back to live with her parents which was a big help in looking after the child.

6. Another Cleaning Job

Lynda and I pleaded with mum and dad to allow us to have another dog for a pet. Mum weakened but dad stood firm. 'Vets are too bloody expensive,' he declared. Mum told us later that dad's garage business was struggling and money was getting "tighter". We had had a couple of years of serious drought and some of the local farmers had walked off their land or sold their properties. Not so many farm labourers were required nowadays. So, with the size of the local population dropping, McDade's garage had fewer customers and hence our family's income was declining. There was no need for grandpa to work in the garage anymore as there wasn't enough work. Dad was hopeful there would be sufficient work to keep the business going for a few more years, but he had dropped a couple of hints to me that McDade's garage might be coming to the end of its life, unless something major happened to suddenly boost the local population. 'We need a bloody great gold mine to open up near town,' became one of dad's favourite comments to friends and neighbours.

Common sense told me that with Dad's business struggling to survive and my inability to overcome my learning disabilities, I needed to look elsewhere for employment. Somebody who is illiterate has few work options. I had to find employment that didn't require reading or writing skills or even basic arithmetic. Farm labourer or factory worker were possibilities, but neither appealed. Then, quite by chance, another work opportunity opened up for me.

Grandma had been unwell for years. She had suffered a massive stroke that left her without the use of her left side. Her left arm hung loosely and she could only get about with much difficulty in a wheel chair. Even her speech was affected and her words were slurred. Fortunately, grandpa remained fit until shortly after he stopped working at McDade's garage. While he was fit, he had been able to do all the domestic duties at home as well as look after grandma.

Out of the blue, grandpa was diagnosed with stage four prostate cancer. The doctors and surgeons didn't mess about. Within days he had surgery to remove his prostate, followed by debilitating chemotherapy and finally radiotherapy. Poor grandpa fell in a heap and in the space of a few days tumbled from being a fit seventy-year-old to a mere shadow of his former self. Fighting cancer took everything out of him and there was no way he could continue to look after poor grandma and keep the house going as well. Mum went over to help whenever she could, but was working part time at the hospital now as well as looking after her family.

As if we didn't already have enough to contend with, Lynda had a nasty accident and broke her leg and an arm falling out of a tree. Her leg was in plaster and her arm in a sling. The doctors had advised her to take six weeks off school and to rest as much as possible. As a family we were over stretched with grandma, grandpa and now Lynda out of action and mum and dad working. One evening, after the dishes were cleared away, dad told me to sit down at the kitchen table because he and mum wanted to put a proposal to me. This sounded serious stuff and I didn't know what to expect.

'Norman, your grandpa has asked me to speak to you about an idea he has. They're doing it tough with grandma invalided and now grandpa fighting cancer and feeling very unwell. As you know, Mum has been giving them a hand whenever she can, but they need someone to help on a more regular basis. They've been trying to get someone local to help out, but haven't had any luck. Now, grandpa has come up with a brilliant idea that involves *you*.'

I was intrigued to know where this conversation was heading. I've always got along well with my grandparents, ever since I was little. I probably dropped round to see them at least once a week. Sometimes I delivered something from mum, a jar of home-made jam or a few spare eggs from our chooks. Occasionally my grandparents rang up because they had something they wanted to give us. Grandpa's pride and joy was his vegetable patch and if he had any vegetables surplus to needs, he liked us to have them. Over the years there had been apples, spuds, tomatoes, cabbages and frequently pumpkins. Usually, I went over to their place to collect these items. At other times I popped over just to say hello and ended up staying to have a chat with grandma while munching on her homemade biscuits which she still managed to bake with grandpa's help. The poor lady couldn't do much, but she did like to listen to my news.

'I think you might like what grandpa has suggested Norman,' mum added, looking enthusiastic.

'He wants to give you a job, son,' announced dad.

'What sort of a job?' I asked, thinking it might be a one-off such as painting the fence or digging up the vegetable patch.'

'A paid job,' smiled dad, 'how does that sound?'

'Okay,' I said, cautiously, 'what sort of a job?' I repeated.

'It would be cleaning and doing odd jobs,' mum chimed in.

'Grandpa is asking you to do two hours a day, excluding weekends. What's more, he's happy to pay you a proper wage.'

'But I'm only thirteen. Am I allowed to get paid?'

'No problem if it's just in the family and grandpa will pay you in cash. The tax office won't ever need to know.'

For several months I had been saving up my pocket money to buy a new bike. The one I had my eye on was for sale in town for twenty pounds. I already had five pounds from the grateful owner of the crocodile purse plus sixpence a week pocket money which had so far reached the grand total of eighteen shillings and sixpence. Then, there was one pound and two shillings from when I worked at the primary school. Mum told me that I now had the grand total of seven pounds and sixpence. I might not be good at arithmetic, but I knew it was going to take me years to save up enough money to get that bike. I also knew that grandpa was not short of a quid. My grandparents lived in one of the best houses in town surrounded by a large garden and a spacious garage for their car. When grandpa had the dealership of McDade's garage business it was booming and he had done very well, far better than my dad.

Mum took over. 'Grandpa has suggested you come over as soon

as you get off the school bus and do your two hours then. Guess how much he's prepared to pay you, if you do a good job?'

'I don't know. Perhaps sixpence an hour?'

'Norman, have you learnt about the basic wage at school?'

'No, dad.'

'I know you can't get your head around maths so I'll explain it for you. It's important you start to understand this stuff.'

'I'll try.'

'In Australia it's the law that nobody gets paid less than the basic wage. Now the basic wage currently is nineteen pounds for a thirty-eight-hour week. That's ten bob an hour. But you're only a thirteen-year-old kid, so that's far too much to pay you. Grandpa is prepared to pay you half the basic wage which will work out as five shillings an hour or ten bob for every two-hour stint.'

'That's very generous of him Norman,' added mum, nodding enthusiastically.

I was at a loss for words. This was simply amazing. So much money! That fifteen-pound bicycle was now definitely within reach.

'So, what do you think?' asked dad.

'Yes, definitely. When does it start?'

'Tomorrow.'

'Tomorrow, wow! What will I have to do?'

'Basically, it's all the housework; dusting, sweeping, vacuuming. But you're going to have to be really flexible because neither grandma or grandpa are capable of doing much for themselves. It's very likely they'll ask you to do the washing up sometimes or to go shopping, tidy up the garden or even prepare vegetables for their evening meal.'

'I'm not very experienced at doing some of those things.'

'Well, you're going to have to learn in a hurry son,' laughed dad, giving me an affectionate slap on the back.

'What about poor Lynda? If she wasn't laid up, she'd be keen to do this work and earn some money?'

'Well, Lynda's out of action for at least a couple of months until she heals and gets her strength back. They need help now. At the moment it has to be you. If they still need help after a couple of months, then perhaps you could let Lynda replace you or share the duties?'

'Yes, of course, that's a good idea. How about I give Lynda some of the money I get because it's not fair she can't earn anything for another two months.'

'That's very considerate of you, Norman. How about you give her 10 per cent of your earnings?'

'How much is 10 per cent dad?'

'That's easy,' said dad, 'for every ten shillings you earn, you give Lynda one shilling. Does that sound about right?'

'No way. Lynda should get half of what I'm earning because she would be doing the work for them if she could.'

'That's more than generous of you son, I'm impressed,' dad responded, 'now, how about you ring them straightaway and tell them you accept their kind offer of employment?'

Grandpa answered. He sounded excited that I was going to start work around four-thirty the next day.

And so it was that my next job as a cleaner came about. My previous experience at my primary school would be help.

7. JANICE

Janice and I had remained friends throughout primary school and this continued when we both caught the school bus into town to attend our respective schools. Often, we would sit together on the bus. It felt perfectly natural, almost as if we were siblings. I sat next to Janice on the bus the day after the job with my grandparents was arranged. She was so pleased!

'That's great Norman. Maybe, being a cleaner is what you should do when you leave school?'

'I'll see whether I like it first,' I replied, 'I'm certainly not improving much with my reading and writing so I'm going to have to find work that doesn't require any literacy skills.'

Janice was silent for a few moments, thinking over what I had just said.

'I can always help you with your reading or writing Norman, if you want.' She was looking at me through her thick glasses that made her eyes look small and far away.

'Thanks Janice, but mum and dad can help me.'

'I'm thinking more about when you leave school and go out into the big wide world.'

'That's kind of you Janice, but people go off in all directions as soon as they leave high school. I doubt if we'll be living near each other by then.'

7. Janice

'Don't say that, Norman,' and Janice gently put her hand on top of mine. I was surprised by this intimate move and didn't quite know what to do. I left my hand where it was and Janice soon removed hers. My parents are not particularly demonstrative, but I remember thinking at the time how pleasant that brief touching of our hands was.

'What are you going to do when you leave school, Janice?'

'If I work really hard, I'm going to try to get into a teachers' college.'

'Wow! You're going to be a teacher!' I exclaimed.

'Don't sound so surprised Norman. Don't you think I'd make a good teacher?'

'I don't know, I've never thought about it. Have you got the brains?'

'Umm…that I don't know. Apparently, around the top ten percent of school leavers make it to university. I don't think I'm *that* clever, but I might just make it to a teachers' college.'

'So, you'll be staying at high school until the end of fifth form?'

'Of course.'

'I'm going to leave as soon as I turn fifteen. School's not much help for me, I'll be much better leaving early and earning some money.'

'That sounds sensible. Now you've landed this job, you can start your CV.'

'My CV? What the heck is that?'

'CV is short for curriculum vitae. That's Latin. When you leave school, you need to write up a list of all the jobs you've done and the qualifications you have. It helps you find better jobs.'

I laughed. 'I can't write up a CV, I'm flat out writing my own name correctly!'

'Oh Norman, I'm so sorry that was insensitive of me. Anyway, I can help you with your CV.'

Once again, I was reminded how tough it was going to be in the future surviving as an illiterate adult.

* * *

A few minutes before four-thirty our school bus pulled up opposite the park as usual and everyone scrambled off. For me this was the start of a new adventure. It was a ten-minute walk to my grandparents' place, but I was so keen to start earning that money that I ran all the way and arrived hot and sweaty.

My grandparents lived in one of the handsomest houses in town, built when McDade's garage was a booming business struggling to cope with the huge demand for its services. Grandpa had had a big hand in the design of their family home after working closely with an architect. Like most expensive homes erected in the 1910s, it was red brick and boasted a wide verandah which ran the full length of the front of the building. The garden, with its stone statues and splendid ornate birdbath, was already somewhat run down since grandpa fell ill.

It was the interior of their Federation style house I liked most. High ceilings with fancy plaster work, floral wall paper and bay windows to let in the sunlight. In the centre of the impressive dining room ceiling was a lyre bird motif which was repeated in the three large stained-glass windows. When the light was right the lyre birds in the windows positively glowed. Around the house were no less than six fine marble mantlepieces each one unique. Nowadays, my grandparents only bothered to have a wood fire crackling away in the sitting room during the winter months. Only if they were entertaining in the evenings would they also have a wood fire blazing in the dining room. The house was about fifty years old now, erected shortly after my grandparents married. The home sat in the centre of town on a large block with well-established trees and was referred to by the locals as the "grand old lady" of the town.

I skipped up the four marble steps to the main door and rang the bell excitedly. It seemed to take for ever before I heard grandpa unlocking the bolts on the inside and I watched as he slowly opened the heavy timber door. I hadn't seen him for three weeks and his appearance shocked me. I had expected him to look the same as

7. Janice

always not realising the ravages cancer, and its treatment, can inflict on a person's appearance. Grandpa had lost weight, his face was pale and gaunt, there were shadows under the eyes and his hair had fallen out. Grandpa's welcome remained cheerful enough though.

'Norman, good to see you young fella.'

'And you, grandpa.'

'Now, I understand your mum and dad have spoken to you at length about what we're proposing. Is that right?'

'Yes, that's right, grandpa.'

'Good, come on in then. Say hello to grandma if she's not still snoozing.'

He led me down the hallway to the sitting room where they spent most of their time nowadays. As I followed grandpa, I noticed I was almost as tall as him now. I knew I was having a growing spurt, but it seemed grandpa had shrunk. Perhaps cancer does that to you? It wasn't only that he was shorter in stature, but he had lost condition as well. I felt sorry for him. Grandma was, indeed, snoring softly in her favourite armchair so we went through to the spacious kitchen where grandpa asked me to find a stool to sit on. On the kitchen table he had placed a tall glass of orange drink and a plate loaded with several kinds of bought biscuits.

'Get stuck into these,' he said, pushing the plate of biscuits in my direction, 'young blokes like you are ravenous after school, I know.'

I didn't need any more encouragement and started on the two chocolate ones first.

Grandpa fumbled around in his top jacket pocket and pulled out a ten-shilling note which he slapped down on the table.

'There you are, your first ten bob for two hours work.'

'Thanks grandpa,' I replied, through a mouthful of biscuit crumbs, 'what would you like me to do?'

Grandpa slid an open folder towards me, 'it's all in here for you, Norman.'

I looked in horror at the two open pages sitting in front of me full of writing. Then I recognised five words I knew at the side of the first page: Monday, Tuesday, Wednesday, Thursday and Friday. I couldn't make head or tail of the other words on the page and immediately felt panicked.

'Look at the pictures Norman,' my grandfather added, gently.

When I studied the pages again, I noticed grandpa had drawn small pictures for me next to the words. All I had to do was find the day of the week and then follow along the line to see pictures of the jobs listed for that day.

'That's clever grandpa, thanks.'

Today was a Thursday. I ran my finger along Thursday's line and recognised five pictures: washing up, dusting, sweeping, vacuuming and digging.

'Do the jobs in this order, please Norman. On Thursdays it's washing up first, then dusting, then sweeping and so on. Now, have a look at the pictures on the other days. Do they make sense to you?'

I scanned the other days, marvelling at grandpa's neat miniature illustrations. It was laid out simply for me. I recognised laundry, grass cutting, shopping, wood chopping and ironing on other days.

'When you arrive each day, you must check with me where everything is. For example, grass cutting is a big job so one week you'll do the front lawn, next week the side lawn and another week the back lawn. Got the idea?'

I nodded enthusiastically as I skolled the dregs of my orange drink and reached for one of the last two biscuits. Then, I stopped and guiltily passed the almost empty plate over to grandpa. Selfishly, I hadn't thought he might like some biscuits too. He shook his head, though.

'No thanks Norman, I don't seem to be hungry these days.'

I thanked grandpa for the snack and moved to the kitchen sink where I started running hot water to begin the washing up. I often did the washing up at home so this was an easy task for me, although I had to ask for grandpa's help to know where to put things away.

7. Janice

With only the occasional assistance from grandpa, I satisfactorily managed my other designated tasks for Thursday. Grandma woke up while I was doing the dusting and seemed surprised to see me, however, grandpa explained what was happening and she relaxed again. By six thirty, my time to leave, I hadn't quite finished digging over the small vegetable patch grandpa had selected for me so I stayed an extra twenty minutes to get the job done. Grandpa was genuinely impressed.

* * *

Next day, I managed to sit with Janice again on the school bus coming home. She wanted to know how things had worked out at my grandparent's place and told me it was "cute" I was so domesticated.

'You'll make someone a good husband one day,' she laughed, lightly.

I glanced at her, thinking this was a strange thing to say and she blushed.

A few minutes later she spoke again, 'are you doing anything special tomorrow, Norman?'

Usually, on a Saturday morning, I rode my ancient bike about town with two or three mates who lived nearby or spent a couple of hours helping dad with small jobs up at the garage. Saturday afternoons were a drag, unless the weather was inviting and I went off on my own to do a bit of bird-spotting. Interestingly, a few people in town were now purchasing televisions, but dad said we couldn't afford an "idiot box." He reckoned in a year or two they might start coming down in price and he might think about it then. Janice, I realised, was still waiting patiently for my answer.

'No. not much. Why?'

'It's my birthday tomorrow, I'll be fourteen. Mum says I can ask five or six friends round for the afternoon and we'll have a bit of a party. You know, a few balloons, a couple of games, something to eat.

Just a small celebration. Three girls are already coming and a couple of boys. Would you like to come as well?'

Kids' parties are few and far between in our town and I was rarely invited. The occasional ones I'd been to were for boys only and had ended up being scrappy, noisy affairs with the kids often being naughty, silly or uncooperative. The parents couldn't control us. Towards the end, after we had scoffed all the food, we would run around the place wildly doing crazy things. I guess we were pretty disrespectful to the parents who had invited us. But Janice's party would probably be different with some girls attending.

'That's kind of you, Janice. What time?'

'Two o'clock.'

'I've never been to a party where there are girls before. Will I have to wear a dress?'

'Don't be stupid Norman,' and she punched me playfully on the leg.

'Okay, I'll be there. What number are you?'

'Number fifteen. It's just past the beautiful big gum tree on the left as you go up the hill.'

I knew the street Janice lived in, but had never been to her place before.

'Thanks, Janice. I'll probably ride my bike over.'

As soon as our bus pulled in, I gave Janice a wave and trotted off to my grandparents to start my Friday chores. The pictures in the blue folder reminded me Fridays were for shopping and grass cutting. Grandpa advised me to do the shopping first before the general store closed. Grandma had dictated a list of things she wanted to grandpa who, in turn, had written these items down on the back of a large brown envelope. Because I couldn't read, I knew I would have to ask one of the staff in the store to help me. Most embarrassing! Without further delay, I set off for the general store. Scrunched up in my pocket was the ten-shilling note Grandpa had given me for Friday's work together with a

7. Janice

pound to buy the goods that grandma wanted. While I was in the general store, I planned to look around to find a suitable present to take to Janice's party.

8. PARTY TIME...

Once again, I did a bit of voluntary overtime at grandpa's place. We had problems with the grass cutting and I had to thoroughly clean the spark plugs before the ancient mower would fire up. It was almost seven thirty when I finally arrived home and sat down for dinner with mum, dad and Lynda. I apologised for being late. Mum doesn't miss much and had noted I had a small parcel when I arrived home.

'Did you go shopping this afternoon, Norman?'

'Sure mum, I do their shopping on Fridays.' I went on to explain how grandpa gave me the list of items they wanted and how I had to ask one of the shop assistants to find the things for me.

'How do you know the shop assistant is getting you the right stuff?' inquired dad, with a large forkful of sausage poised ready to disappear into his cavernous mouth.

'I just have to trust them,' I replied.

'And what about the money? What if the assistant makes a mistake and gives you the wrong change?' mum asked.

'Again, mum, I have to rely on their honesty and good maths skills.'

They made no further comment and we attacked our sausages and mash, accompanied by carrots and mushy peas. But mum hadn't found out yet what was in my mysterious parcel and wasn't about to let it pass.

She poured herself a glass of water and caught me by surprise.

'And what about that little parcel you came home with, dear? What was that?'

I felt myself reddening as an uncontrollable deep blush enveloped my face. Three sets of eyes peered at me, expectantly. There was nothing for it, I had to give them an answer.

'Oh…that…that was some…soap,' I stammered, trying my best to look nonchalant as if I often went to the general store to purchase soap.

'Soap?' came the stunned chorus.

'Why on earth are you wasting your money buying soap when we have heaps of soap here at home?' demanded mum.

'It's not for here,' I mumbled.

The interest in my responses had suddenly gone up another notch and it was my sister Lynda who first sensed what might be happening.

'Normans got a girlfriend, Normans got a girlfriend,' she chanted, accusingly.

'No, I haven't,' I retorted.

'Yes, you have. Who is it? I bet it's one of the pretty girls at your special school,' she declared, triumphantly.

'No, it's not.'

'Who is it then?'

'Be quiet Lynda, Norman might have bought it for you, or mum,' came dad's more reasoned observation.

'Well dear?' asked mum, gently.

At some stage I was going to have to ask my parents' permission to go to Janice's birthday party tomorrow, so I thought it timely to mention it then.

'I've been asked to go to a birthday party tomorrow afternoon at two o'clock.'

Lynda couldn't contain herself, 'It must be a girls' party,' she sang out, excitedly.

'It's for boys and girls, if you must know,' I snarled.

'So dear, who's having a birthday?' asked mum.

'Janice Fenton.'

'Of course,' squealed Lynda, 'they've been keen on each other ever since kindergarten.'

'It's just a birthday party Lynda. You have to take a present so I bought some soap for her, that's all. You're just getting all silly about it.'

'Oh, come on Norman, you two often sit together on the bus,' continued Lynda, determined to squeeze everything she could out of this sniff of a romance.

'Well dear, if you'd like to bring the soap down to the kitchen, I'll help you wrap it up nicely,' offered mum as a way of ending the conversation.

I waited until Lynda and dad were somewhere else before I quietly made my way back to the kitchen clutching my brown paper parcel. I had relied entirely on the shop assistant to select some appropriate soap for a teenage girl and hadn't even looked at the soap yet. When we took it out of its brown paper bag, I was surprised at what she had chosen. There were three bars of pretty coloured soap, two rectangular in shape with rounded edges, but the one in the middle was pink and shaped like a heart. There was some writing on the heart-shaped soap, which I couldn't decipher.

'What does it say, mum?'

'It says, "With all my love."'

'Oh crikey, I can't give Janice that!'

'Why ever not?'

'It's a heart and it's got sloppy words written on it.'

'Too late now, Norman. The shops aren't open tomorrow so it'll have to do. Anyway, Janice probably won't even notice the writing on the heart.'

I wasn't so sure. Within five minutes mum had the soap wrapped up in "feminine" sort of paper with a pink bow. I shoved it back in its brown paper bag and went off to bed.

8. Party Time...

* * *

Saturday dawned sunny and warm. No clouds in sight and a light south westerly breeze blowing to prevent the day exploding into a fierce hot cauldron. At breakfast, Lynda spared me any further interrogation and the meal passed without incident. Dad was already up at the garage so I joined him for most of the morning. Under dad's supervision, I was now able to do a few things to help the business. Over the last couple of years dad had shown me how to replace a car's engine oil, check battery fluid, correctly measure tyre pressures and wash vehicles before having them ready for customers to collect. Dad was running the business on his own now and I think he was slowly coming to depend on me helping out on Saturdays. Sadly, he could no longer afford to pay an apprentice to work at the garage.

Around mid-day, I reminded dad I had to go to a party in the afternoon. I needed to get back home, shower, change, have lunch and jump on the old bike to get round to Janice's place by two o'clock. To my surprise, this party business had sparked some interest from dad too.

'I reckon I was about fourteen when I first got interested in girls,' dad announced, 'I had a few girlfriends before I met your mum though,' he boasted. 'Are you really interested in this Janice girl or is Lynda just carrying on stupidly about nothing?'

'No, it's nothing dad. We've been at school together for many years, that's all.'

He wiped his hands on the oily rag that always hung out of his back pocket and was silent for a moment. 'When you start wanting to spend time with the lassies, you and I will need to have a "father-to-son" chat. Okay?'

'Sure dad.'

What, I wondered, is a "father-to-son" chat about?

* * *

Janice Fenton's house was barely visible from the road because it was set well back on the block and partly obscured by a row of mature radiata pines running along the front fence. I had ridden past many times before, but never realised it was where Janice lived. When I arrived, I felt distinctly nervous, this was the first time I'd been to a party with girls present. I've never been an outgoing sort of person, in fact, I've always been rather shy most likely because of my disability. I rode my bike up the scrunchy driveway and left it leaning up against the side of the car-port. There were two other boys' bikes there and I recognised one as belonging to Scott Treevers, who I occasionally sat next to on the school bus.

Smoothing my hair down and hoisting up my socks, I made my way slowly to the front door with Janice's present safely stowed in its brown paper bag. I could hear loud excited voices inside as I approached, it sounded as though the party was already in full swing. Mrs Fenton must have been waiting for me because the front door swung open before I even had time to ring the bell.

'Well now, you must be Norman McDade. Come on in Norman, lovely to meet you,' and she held out a large flabby hand that I shook politely. 'This way dear. Did you ride your bike over? They're all in the lounge. Isn't it a lovely day? Here we are then. It's so nice you could come. Janice often mentions you. They're playing some sort of game.'

Mrs Fenton deposited me in the doorway of the lounge before making a hasty retreat back to the kitchen. I still hadn't uttered a single word; such had been the barrage of uninterrupted chatter coming from Janice's mother.

I stood in the doorway feeling stupid, until someone noticed me and there was a chorus of welcoming remarks. They were playing "Twister," a recently invented game that required players to contort themselves into weird positions without falling over in order to stay in the game. I was soon involved and found it great fun. For the first time in my life, I found myself crawling about on the floor in close proximity to attractive teenage girls. It was a heady experience. The girls were wearing perfume and sometimes, as we reached for another part of the Twister mat, they would brush up against me. On one occasion Janice was on the mat with me and the way she had to lean over made the front of her dress sag open and I had a peep at her breasts. Janice's party was my awakening. Although still only thirteen, that afternoon I became aware of girls being something mysterious, something beautiful, intriguing, something to be cherished. I guess I was suddenly growing up.

Janice had planned things well, the party consisted of four girls and four boys. It soon became clear that Scott Treevers, my friend from the bus, considered one of the other girls, Beatrice, to be *his* special girlfriend. Another boy, Colum, was doing everything he could to win Janice over to be his girlfriend. He was making eyes at her, joking secretively and being particularly attentive. I felt left out and rather inadequate. This whole business of flirting was new to me and it certainly didn't come naturally. I realised, for the first time, I was keen on Janice, but didn't know how to show it.

Towards the end of the party, two others seemed to have paired off and Janice was spending most of her time with Colum. Obviously, they were attracted to each other and as I watched them flirting, I experienced my first pangs of jealousy. Colum attended the Catholic high school in town and this school had its own private bus. I found myself wondering about Colum. How had Janice met him? What was he like? At one stage, I overheard Colum telling Janice about a game called rugby union which, he said, was revered at his Catholic high school. Colum proudly declared he played in the rugby union's first fifteen, whatever that meant. Physically, Colum was strong and muscular with broad shoulders. I was small and rather puny in comparison.

Around five o'clock the party came to an end. Janice had blown out her fourteen candles and we sang "happy birthday." Janice had one last duty to perform, opening her birthday presents. The girls had brought perfumes and hand creams, the boys a small chess set, a book and a box of chocolate biscuits. My present was the last to be opened. Janice looked across at me as she tore off the wrapping paper that mum had taken so much trouble with. There was an expectant hush as Janice held up my set of three attractive soaps for everyone to see, followed immediately by the reactions of everyone present. A boy daring to give pretty soaps to a girl was thought to be a bit forward, especially if it included a heart shaped soap displaying a loving message. Once again, I was deeply embarrassed and wished I'd thought of something else.

    I felt unsettled riding home that afternoon, but didn't know why. Then I realised it was because I had developed feelings for Janice and wanted her to be my girlfriend. What hope did I have though, with Colum so obviously attentive? He had it over me in every respect; excellent at sport, tall and strong, good looking, attending a private school and undoubtedly a good reader. What did I have to offer? Not much!

9. MY FOURTEENTH BIRTHDAY

The regular cleaning job at my grandparent's place continued, as planned, for another six weeks. Then it was time to start sharing the cleaning duties with Lynda now that her leg was better. We worked out a simple system of taking it in turns that suited everyone involved. My bank balance steadily increased and together we estimated I'd be able to purchase my new bike in time for Christmas. It soon became apparent my sister and I had very different likes and dislikes with regard to grandpa's jobs. Lynda loved doing the shopping and housework but bluntly refused to do some of the out-door jobs such as cutting the grass, gardening and chopping wood.

Our grandparents' health was not improving. Grandma had another stroke that kept her confined to her armchair for most of the day and grandpa finally had to have his prostate gland surgically removed. When he returned from hospital, he told me he was incontinent and had to wear adult nappies. I remembered poor old Taffy had to be put down because he had cancer of his prostate. When I tried to gently quiz grandpa about his condition he wouldn't tell me much, except that when you lose your prostate you can't have children.

I turned fourteen on November 7th which became a special day for me for several reasons. Mum, dad and my grandparents ganged up to purchase the bike I had been longing for. I was only two pounds ten shillings short of the amount I needed to get it myself from my earnings, however, receiving the bike early was a thrill I didn't expect. Mum asked me whether I wanted a birthday party. I thought about the idea for a while and decided against it.

November 7th was a school day and Janice made a point of sitting next to me on the school bus on the return trip. Somehow, she had discovered it was my birthday.

'Happy birthday Norman,' she said, as she plonked herself down next to me, 'you're not having a party?'

'No. Mum offered me one, but I decided not to bother.'

'That's a shame. Would you have invited me?'

'Yes, of course.'

I looked at Janice, she was prettier than ever. Whatever had been wrong with her eyes when younger was virtually corrected and now she only wore glasses for reading and other close work. Soon she'd be able to dispense with spectacles altogether. Although only a few months older than me, she was maturing into an attractive young woman with a neat figure. No wonder the likes of Colum were attracted to her. Janice lifted up her school satchel and started rummaging around inside. For a moment or two she couldn't find what she was looking for, but then with a sigh of relief, she pulled out a white envelope and handed it to me.

'You're not to open this until you get home. Promise me?'

I nodded.

'And open it in private,' she added, with a shy blush.

I must have looked surprised, because she repeated herself. 'Promise you'll look at it in private Norman or I'll take it back,' and she held out her hand ready to receive it.

'I promise, Janice. Nobody else will see it.'

'Good, it's a secret just between you and me,' she smiled.

I said nothing for a few minutes, simply enjoying Janice's close company.

'How's school?' I asked.

'Great. I'm definitely staying on to do my leaving certificate so I have another two years to go. What about you?'

I shook my head. 'As soon as I turn fifteen, in twelve months' time, I'll be out of school like a bat out of hell.'

Janice laughed, 'how's the job with your grandparents going?'

'Terrific,' I said, and proceeded to update her on the situation there.

When our bus pulled in, she gave my knee a quick squeeze and was up and gone before I could gather up my gear. I made sure Janice's mysterious white envelope was safely stowed away and feeling on top of the world set off for my grandparents' place.

On arrival, grandpa ushered me into the lounge where grandma sat in her usual chair with her feet up and a shawl around her shoulders. Normally, grandpa would let me in, invite me to partake in the refreshments he had left for me in the kitchen and I would start my chores for the afternoon. Today, however, he had something special on his mind. After they both wished me a happy birthday, grandpa asked me to sit down.

'Norman, your fame has spread.'

I looked at him, puzzled.

'Currently, you are sharing the cleaning duties with your sister and you only have cleaning and gardening jobs every second day during the working week. How would you like to earn some extra money?'

'Possibly,' I replied, guardedly, 'what's on offer, grandpa?'

'Do you know Miss Norah Malden?'

'Yes, she's that crazy old woman who lives on her own at the disused railway station.'

'Correct. She's not crazy though, she's what we might describe as "eccentric".'

'What does that mean?'

'Miss Malden is a character, an interesting personality you might say. She's eighty something years old, holds some strange ideas and is wealthy. Anyway, she wants someone well-mannered and energetic, like you, to help in the house and out in her garden and orchard. I know her from church and last Sunday, she asked me if I could suggest anyone. I think the work might be too physically demanding for your sister so I gave her your name. If you're interested, she wants someone for four hours a week to start with, although this might increase at busy times of the year such as fruit picking. What do you think?'

'Do you know what she's prepared to pay, grandpa?'

'Same as me, five bob an hour.'

'Wow, sounds good. When does she want me to start?'

'As soon as possible and preferably at weekends. If you're interested, she wants you to go round to her place at five o'clock tomorrow. She told me she doesn't want any old nincompoop, but someone with a good work ethic.'

'What's that mean?'

'Someone that works hard. I told Miss Malden you're almost fourteen and work as hard as any grown up and are very polite.'

'Thanks grandpa, I'll definitely go and see her tomorrow.'

My jobs completed, I went back to the lounge where my grandparents were still seated. Grandma was snoring quietly with her head on a pillow, but grandpa was awake and reading the paper. I was sorely tempted to ask grandpa to help me with the contents of Janice's white envelope, although I had promised Janice I would open the envelope in private. If she had written me a letter, I wouldn't be able to read it so I needed someone to read the letter to me. It would be too embarrassing to ask mum or dad or Lynda to read the letter. In the end, I kept my promise and walked back home with the white envelope safely tucked into my back pocket, unopened.

I went straight to my bedroom and pulled out the white envelope. Why had Janice been so insistent that nobody else should see what was inside? It was something "private" she had said. If she had written me a letter, I wouldn't be able to read it so what was the point? Perhaps she wanted me to get her to read it to me? Now,

9. My Fourteenth Birthday

more than ever before, I hated myself for not being able to read and write. Finally, I plucked up the courage to tear open the envelope. Inside was one sheet of paper folded over and smelling of some kind of perfume. I unfolded the single sheet to find a simple drawing in pencil of two hands joined together. I knew Janice was good at drawing and I was sure this was her work. Underneath the slightly larger hand I recognised my name, underneath the more delicate hand was written another name I recognised... Janice.

* * *

Our railway line was closed almost twenty years ago, leaving a string of stations and station masters' houses unoccupied and gradually falling into disrepair. They were an open invitation to squatters, vandals and graffiti sprayers. The state railway still owned the buildings, but was at a loss to know what to do with its redundant real estate. There was no point wasting money on the upkeep of the buildings so the buildings were offered up for sale.

It so happened that Miss Norah Malden retired about the same time that these railway buildings were coming on the market for sale to the public. For nigh on forty years, Miss Norah Malden had been in the business of selling ladies clothes. "Norah's" had proudly opened its doors to the more genteel ladies of the district decades ago and had steadily built up an enviable reputation. The success of the business was due largely to the flamboyant lifestyle of its owner, Miss Norah. It was said that locals would enter Norah's shop just to see what exotic outfit she was wearing on any particular day and would come away having spent far more money than their husbands would ever have approved.

Norah had been a saleslady par excellence. She had led a colourful life, was a member of the society set, enjoyed a drink or two and was always rumoured to be having a ravishing "affair" with someone or other. Despite innumerable liaisons, Norah was never known to have married or have children. Indubitably, Norah had a genuine flare for fashion and did her utmost to stay abreast of the latest trends and to stay in touch with whatever was in vogue overseas. Whether or not you bought anything at Norah's, you always came away on a high because Norah had the happy knack of making everyone feel they were the most important person in the world.

At three score years and ten, Norah suddenly decided she had had enough and put her business up for sale. With its prime position and high profit margins over many years, "Norah's" sold almost immediately and Norah was left wondering what to do next. She had increasingly hankered after a quieter life in the country, so when the station masters' houses came on the market, she was quick to purchase. The station master's house she selected appealed because it had an unusually large garden and a well-established orchard at the back. The house itself was still in reasonable shape and within a few months she was happily ensconced and living the life of a country retiree.

Miss Norah Malden had moved into her station master's house shortly after I was born and was soon perceived by the locals to be a "delightful character." She led a quieter life these days, but still dressed outrageously and could often be found enjoying a couple of gin and tonics down at the local. Age had slowed her down somewhat, but she still drove her old Ford about town and enjoyed a yarn with anyone who had a few minutes to spare. Surprisingly, Norah had recently returned to her Catholic faith and it was at the local Catholic church she had befriended my grandfather and hence found out about me.

Shortly before five o'clock I let myself out through the back gate to walk the half mile to Norah's place close by the dis-used railway tracks. The woodwork at the station master's house had recently been re-painted and was looking smart in the bright sunlight. The lawn, I noticed, was in need of a mow and the rosemary hedge required trimming. Not surprising if Norah was in her eighties. At the gate I was welcomed by a long dark brown sausage-like dog, a dachshund. The dog was friendly, wagging its tail frantically and keeping up a steady stream of yapping. As I went through the gate, I gave the dog a pat and was reminded of dear old Taffy. There was an old-fashioned black door knocker on the front door that I used respectfully. I waited for what seemed like ages and was about to knock a second time when the front door finally opened.

I couldn't believe the sight of the apparition standing before me. Miss Norah Malden was tall and angular with prominent cheek bones, a sharp nose and eagle-like eyes that seemed to bore through me. She wore a long dress right down to her feet that was multi-coloured like Joseph's coat of many colours. There were bangles on her wrists matching two giant ear-rings hanging from the lobes of her strangely elongated ears. We looked blankly at each other for a moment or two before she spoke.

'Who are you, darling?'

I don't think anyone had ever addressed me before as "darling," but I had been forewarned by mum to expect anything from this eccentric old lady.

'I'm…I'm… Norman, Norman… McDade.'

'Are you now, darling. And what, may I ask, is Norman McDade doing standing on my doorstep looking like a shag on a rock?'

'You asked me to come here at five o'clock.'

'Did I? Ah… yes, now it's coming back to me. Aren't you a bit young to be fixing my plumbing, darling? I was expecting a much larger, brawny sort of man.'

'You asked me to come and see you about a cleaning and gardening job for four hours a week.'

'Of course, so I did. My memory's not what it used to be, darling. Aren't you a bit weedy to be doing physical work?' she said, eyeing me up and down as if inspecting a prize pony.

'I was fourteen yesterday, Miss Malden, and I work many hours a week for my grandparents doing the cleaning and gardening for them,' I responded, feeling rather put down.

'Yes, yes of course. Come on in then. It's all coming back to me now. You're Fred McDade's young fella from up at the garage?'

'That's right,' I replied with some enthusiasm, pleased that at last we seemed to be connecting.

'Gin and tonic? Oh no you can't have one yet, can you darling. Now do sit down and we'll talk business.'

Norah moved to a sideboard and proceeded to pour herself a generous gin and tonic which gave me a chance to look around the extraordinary room I was sitting in. The walls were so heavily festooned with paintings and photographs I could scarcely see the colour of the walls. Some photographs were famous female models showing off bizarre outlandish costumes. Another wall was cluttered up entirely with faded landscapes in heavy wooden frames. The picture that grabbed my attention most, however, was a huge painting that hung above the mantlepiece of a nude woman reclining on a sofa. The artist had cleverly hidden the private parts with a shawl. The colouring was exquisite and to my surprise, I found myself wondering if Janice looked anything like this.

I was struck also by the quantity of furniture in the room; there hardly seemed sufficient space to move about. I knew nothing about antiques except that they were valuable relics from the past and needed to be carefully cared for. The thought of trying to polish and clean so many pieces of furniture was daunting. Furthermore, what looked like valuable ornaments were displayed on the mantlepiece, along the window sills and atop several of the tables and cupboards. The room was more like a museum, certainly a cleaner's nightmare!

Miss Norah Malden, armed with her gin and tonic, lowered herself down gingerly into the large armchair opposite and looked me over again. After another generous mouthful, she seemed confused.

'What were we going to discuss, darling?'

'Miss Malden, you said you wanted to discuss business.'

'Yes... quite. If I remember correctly, you're going to clean and garden for me for four hours a day.'

'No, no Miss Malden, four hours a week!'

'Ah yes, of course. Now your grandpa, what a nice man he is, suggested I should pay you ten shillings an hour. Is that right?'

'No, Miss Malden, my rates are ten bob for *two* hours, so you only have to pay me five bob an hour.'

Miss Malden laughed at her silly mistake and took another comforting swig of gin and tonic. It was abundantly clear the good lady was starting to lose her marbles. I had heard it said that elderly folk often find it difficult to remember things or become confused, or both. Such people were easy prey for the unscrupulous. But I had also learnt that honesty always pays and so I had no intention of swindling this eccentric old lady.

'Five bob an hour…five bob an hour. So… if you work four hours a week, I only need to give you a pound. Is that correct, darling?'

It was finally settled. Next, we had to decide when I would come to her house and what the work would entail. This took another two gin and tonics, but in the end we got there. I was booked to work four hours straight on Saturday afternoons from two o'clock to six o'clock. Miss Malden, conscious of her unreliable memory, asked me to ring her around mid-day on Saturdays to remind her of my imminent arrival. I was to spend three hours on the cleaning: dusting, polishing, sweeping the whole house and the paths around the building and then an hour "on the garden," as Miss Malden put it. It was left entirely to me to decide what I thought most needed doing in the extensive garden and orchard.

At the end of our discussions, Miss Norah Malden escorted me, rather unsteadily, to her front door with a gin and tonic still firmly in hand. She farewelled me there, along with another half dozen "darlings," and I made my way home slowly wondering what I might have let myself in for. Would this new job prove to be another good thing to come from my fourteenth birthday?

10. SATURDAY AFTERNOONS

Before the next Saturday came round, I quizzed mum on how best to go about polishing antique furniture and the safest way to dust around the many valuable ornaments Miss Malden had on display. I was terrified of accidentally dropping an item on the floor, seeing it smashing into small pieces and then having to find hundreds of pounds to replace or repair it. Mum and dad had never been interested in antiques. The only piece of furniture we owned that was remotely "antique" was a nest of side-tables that dad's grandfather had left him. Dad wouldn't have them standing about in the lounge because he kept falling over the pesky things so they'd been banished to somewhere out in his garden shed. However, mum sought them out and showed me what to do.

Sadly, my parents had little time or interest in gardening, so it was to grandpa that I turned to get some gardening background. Unable to do much gardening himself these days, grandpa was delighted to pass on his knowledge. I think it made him feel he was still capable of doing the hard physical work himself. So, when Saturday came round, I felt I had enough basic knowledge to survive my first adventure at the home of the notorious Miss Norah Malden. I remembered to telephone at mid-day to remind her I was coming and a few minutes before two o'clock I was again standing at her front door poised to use her black door knocker.

10. Saturday Afternoons

This time, my new employer was better organised. She opened the door with a flourish, wearing what looked like a bright red jumpsuit with a huge matching red bow in her hair. No gin and tonic in evidence, but she was clearly expecting me for she had laid out certain items I should use for the dusting, polishing and sweeping. Norah Malden had also given some thought to how things were to proceed during the afternoon.

'Welcome darling, come on in. Here are the cleaning items you'll need. Now, do you have a watch?'

I replied in the affirmative.

'A bit before four o'clock you are to down tools and make us both a nice cup of tea. Bring it into the lounge please. You and I will then have a bit of a natter. I like company, you see. Do you think you can manage that, darling?'

I assured Miss Malden I could manage and went to work. A feather duster made out of what I thought were ostrich feathers, had been provided for the dusting. Taking a deep breath, I moved first into the lounge; the room that most terrified me with its many valuables. With great care, I followed the modus operandi mum had suggested, first dusting and then polishing. This room alone took me half an hour, but I did the job thoroughly and with a sigh of relief moved on to the next room, hopefully leaving everything back in its proper place and intact. Dusting the other rooms was far less demanding. I didn't enter her bathroom or toilet, considering them to be too private. On the dot of four o'clock, I returned to the lounge carrying a tray with what I hoped was the afternoon tea Miss Malden expected. She was there in an armchair, fast asleep.

As quietly as possible, I placed the tray on the table nearby and took the opportunity to more closely observe my employer. She was covered in wrinkles and her hair was almost snowy white which accentuated the redness of the bow that had now slipped down out of position. Miss Malden's hands were wrinkled too and prominent blue veins stood out on the surface of the skin. Norah Malden had been lavish with the application of her bright red lipstick which in a couple of places had missed its mark. A pair of reading glasses sat on the side table together with a book she had been reading. As if by magic, her eyes suddenly sprang open and she saw me looking down at her.

'Good God, who are you? What are you doing in my house?' and she started to struggle up before falling back when the penny dropped and she remembered I was there to do her house work. She recovered her wits quickly, however, adjusted the wandering red bow, and gave me a big smile.

'And how are you, young man? Did you break anything? The one thing you *can* break, darling, is that dreadful looking lion over there in the corner. It's Ming dynasty you know but as ugly as Hades.'

Ming dynasty and Hades meant nothing to me, of course, but I assured Miss Malden nothing had been broken and asked her if she was ready for her tea. Sitting down formally for afternoon tea was foreign to me. At home, if someone was thirsty, they grabbed a glass out of the cupboard and filled it with tap water; job done.

'Where are the biscuits, darling?'

'I didn't know there were any, Miss Malden.'

'There are always biscuits, darling. You'll find them in the bread container. Get them will you, please.'

I returned to the kitchen, found the bread container and handed it to Miss Malden, who prised the lid off and peered inside. 'Bugger, none of my ginger biscuits left. Have you been raiding my biscuits, darling?'

'No, no, certainly not Miss Malden, I didn't even know you kept biscuits in the bread container.'

'All right, darling. I believe you. I'm only joking.'

Miss Malden sat up and poured out the teas like a proper lady. I had milk in mine, but when she asked me how many sugar lumps I wanted, I really didn't know. Having a formal cup of tea was still something I had rarely experienced in my short lifetime. I sat nervously on the edge of my chair feeling inadequate and fearful of spilling tea on the carpet. I took a biscuit but found it stale and certainly not appetising. I waited for Miss Malden to open up the conversation.

'Now, young man, tell me all about yourself.'

Having only recently turned fourteen there was not a great deal to tell so the conversation soon lapsed and it was suggested I return to work, which I did. The remainder of the afternoon went well enough; the indoor tasks presented no more problems and at five o'clock I headed outdoors to tackle the gardening. There was a shed with some basic gardening tools and an old-fashioned lawn mower. I spent my last hour clipping the rosemary hedge along the front of the house so Miss Malden would at least notice I had done something. On the stroke of six, I knocked on the front door again to inform Miss Norah Malden I had finished for the day. She was full of appreciation for my efforts and then disappointed me by apologising because she did not have the money handy to pay me.

'Next week, darling,' she assured me, 'next week.'

Grandpa had never missed a payment and I'd been working for him for many weeks.

* * *

At dinner that evening I mentioned to my parents that Miss Malden had not paid me. Neither mum nor dad seemed particularly worried about this. Dad assured me many of his customers at the garage didn't pay up immediately for their repair work or vehicle servicing, but did so shortly after. Very few customers failed to eventually settle up with him. Dad reckoned he could count on one hand the number of defaulters he had had to threaten with prosecution over the years. 'She'll come good next week, you'll see...' said dad, encouragingly.

Next Saturday, I went through the same routine of ringing Miss

Malden around mid-day to remind her of my arrival at two o'clock. She seemed delighted. It was a hot, still day with the sun blazing mercilessly from an azure sky as I made my way to her station-master's house. Even the birds were quiet, sheltering somewhere in the shade. The only animal activities were the seething ant mounds and the occasional gecko scurrying out of my way. I was glad mum had insisted I take my hat. Despite the walk being short, I arrived sweaty.

'Hello darling, you're back again,' Miss Malden greeted me, 'come on in out of that bloody heat. I reckon its well over a hundred today.'

Mercifully, when they built the station masters' houses, they designed them to cope with heat; double brick exterior walls and generous verandahs so it was pleasantly cool inside. Nevertheless, Miss Malden must have been feeling the heat because she had not washed up and there was a sizeable pile of dirty dishes in the kitchen which she asked me to deal with first. This took me half an hour before I started on the dusting and sweeping routines that I had undertaken the previous week. Shortly before four o'clock I made the tea and brought the tray in to the lounge, as I had done the week before, making sure I had the biscuits this time.

Miss Malden was her usual cheerful self and was soon chatting about some of the famous people who had visited her fashionable dress shop over the many years she had run the business.

'Darling, you wouldn't believe some of the famous women I helped to dress. They would come to my boutique anticipating an exciting purchase and rarely would depart without total satisfaction. Naturally, I was always the epitome of professionalism. I could tell as soon as a smartly dressed woman entered, precisely what her particular taste would be. My shop became so busy, in fact, that I had to ask my clients to book their appointments. Would you believe it darling? Although I had well trained staff, I *always* insisted on serving the elite customers myself.'

'You must have been very clever, Miss Malden,' was all I could think to say.

'Well, I was, darling. I always made sure I was romantically attached to some incredibly wealthy gentleman, who I could then persuade to take me to the top fashion shows in London and Paris every year. I loved to go with them and stay in those posh hotels. Of course, I never married any of my suitors. It was far more profitable to have them competing for my hand, you see darling.'

I sat there nervously, not knowing how to react to these adult revelations, feeling inadequate and unable to contribute meaningfully to the conversation.

'Now run along dear, I think we've finished our…our…our…' Suddenly, Miss Malden's voice began to slur and then started to fade away. She raised a hand to her head as if stricken with a serious headache. Next, she tried to stand but crumpled, helplessly, to the ground. There she lay on her back, groaning and twitching, trying to speak. 'Dizzy…can't…I can't …I can't see…help me.' One hand came up to her head again, the other lay limply beside her as if no longer attached. 'Oh, my head…my head…it aches…'

I stood there horrified, clutching the tray, my body frozen, unable to move. Frightening thoughts rushed through my brain. She's dying, she's having a heart attack, she's desperately ill. I've got to do something. I have to save her.

I don't know how long I stood there gawping stupidly before something triggered me into action. I put the tray down and ran to find the telephone. I knew she had one because I'd seen it somewhere when cleaning the house, but where was it? I raced about through the kitchen, the dining room, back to the lounge, then found it in the hallway. I grabbed the receiver and trembling dialled triple O. It seemed to take for ever before someone responded.

'You have rung triple O, Emergency Services. Which service do you require, police, fire brigade or ambulance?'

'I need an ambulance,' I blurted out, 'it's really urgent, I think she's dying…'

'Now calm down young man. Let's take this one step at a time.

First, tell me about the patient and what the problem seems to be.'

'She's just fallen on the floor and she can't talk properly, she's groaning, she's...'

'Okay, did you see her fall over or did she collapse?'

'She suddenly fell off her chair and she's holding her head and mumbling. I think she's really bad.'

'Have you any idea how old the lady is?'

'She's very very old.'

'Is she a relative or a friend of yours?'

'No, she's my boss. I clean for her.'

'Are there any other adults currently in the house?'

'No, she lives alone.'

'Okay, I will send an ambulance, but I need to know exactly where you are. Give me the name of the town or village you are ringing from.'

'Rinsdorf.'

'Rinsdorf, good. Now the name of the street?'

'Harbottle.'

'Could you spell that please?'

'I'm sorry, I can't.'

'Very well. What number in Harbottle street?'

I don't know what number it is, but it's easy to find because it's the old station master's house.

'What's the patient's name?'

'Miss Norah Malden.'

'Is the patient breathing?'

'Yes, although she seems to be struggling.'

'Is she conscious?'

'What does that mean?'

'Is she awake, talking, moving at all?'

'Yes, she keeps mumbling things...'

'Right, the ambulance is on its way. It'll be at least forty minutes getting out to you in Rinsdorf. I want you to stay with the patient

10. Saturday Afternoons

and try to comfort her. Whatever you do, don't give her any food or drink. Do you understand?'

'Yes.'

'If she seems cold, cover her with a blanket. Now stay calm, the ambulance will be with you as soon as possible.'

'Thank you.'

I replaced the receiver and hurried back to Miss Malden. She was still lying on the floor rolling her head from side to side and making weird grunting sounds. It was then I noticed her face was distorted down one side. The poor lady had turned a ghastly ashen white. I took hold of her left hand and found it cold and limp as if there was no life there. I moved to the other hand which seemed normal and held it for her so she would know someone was there with her. The next forty minutes seemed to last forever. I kept wondering if the ambulance had crashed or lost its way.

Eventually, I heard the welcome sound of a vehicle pulling up outside and then loud knocking on the front door. I ran to open up, allowing a gust of hot steamy air to burst into the house. Two ambulance men stood there, one with a bag, the other, older man, with a stretcher. Hardly a word was spoken as they followed me through the house to where Miss Malden lay. I hovered around, staying out of the way as they attended to the poor lady. They were quietly efficient as they calmly went through medical checks and procedures. After ten minutes, they unfurlled the stretcher and carefully placed Miss Malden on it.

'You did a good job mate,' said the older man, giving me a comforting grin.

'Has she any family nearby?' asked the younger of the two.

'Sorry, I don't know. I just do her cleaning for her.'

With a heave, they lifted the old lady and headed for the door. As they moved outside, a concerned neighbour arrived. She was able to tell the men about Miss Malden's younger sister and promised to contact her to deliver the sad news that her sister was being taken to hospital.

'Looks like a stroke…' the older man declared, as they placed Miss Malden safely in the ambulance.

* * *

Once the ambulance left, I returned inside and continued with the house work. I was employed to do four hours of cleaning and gardening, but had lost over an hour with Miss Malden taking ill. I finished the indoor cleaning and thankfully skipped the gardening which would have been exhausting work in this heat. I took the spare house key with me, locked up, and headed for home.

Arriving home shortly after seven o'clock, I found mum in the kitchen preparing a salad for our evening meal. We possess only one portable fan and she had it going full blast in an effort to keep cool. I needed to talk about the ordeal I had been through so I unloaded on poor mum. After I'd finished describing Miss Malden's symptoms, mum nodded knowingly. As a trained nurse's aide, she quickly expressed agreement with the older ambulance officer's opinion that it sounded like a severe stroke.

'If it's a stroke she may not survive, Norman.'

'Crikey, you mean she could die?'

'Afraid so, dear. A stroke is a bleed on the brain. If they can't stop the bleeding, she could be a goner.'

Mum looked at me as she placed a pile of freshly washed lettuce leaves in a glass bowl and reached for some radishes.

'How terrible! Don't the doctors have ways of curing strokes? Grandma had a stroke and she's still alive.'

'It depends. If it's only a slight stroke, the person might make a full recovery. Miss Malden is an old lady though and the symptoms you've described sound severe; paralysis down one side of the body, inability to speak, weakness. It sounds to me, if she *does* survive, she'll need to be cared for in a nursing home. I doubt she'll be able to come back to her home.'

10. Saturday Afternoons

I shook my head, 'That's awful. She's a crazy old lady, but I was getting to like her.'

'Lay the table please dear, tea's nearly ready.'

As I grabbed the cutlery, it occurred to me I might now have lost two Saturday afternoon payments, no less than two pounds. Not much for an adult perhaps, but a decent sum for a fourteen-year-old. I mentioned this to mum, who shrugged her shoulders, 'These things happen sometimes dear; life's not always fair.'

She was right. It wasn't fair that poor old Miss Malden was fighting for her life, nor was it fair I might never get paid for eight hours work.

* * *

A few days later, mum had a phone call from a Mrs Carleton, the younger sister of Miss Malden. She had been visiting the hospital every day and reported things were not looking good. Miss Malden had had another couple of minor strokes and was not expected to survive. If she did pull through, she'd be virtually a vegetable and would have to be cared for in a nursing home. The station master's house was shortly going to be put on the market and Miss Malden's possessions sold. Mrs Carleton had heard that I had been doing the cleaning and gardening for her sister and wanted to pay for any arrears. So, I received my two pounds.

There was a pleasant twist in the tale for me too. Mrs Carleton thought it would be a few months before the station master's house sold and the new occupants moved in. She needed someone to keep the extensive gardens under control. She offered me five bob an hour to keep the lawns mown, the hedges clipped and carry out any general tidying up needed outside. Mrs Carleton imposed a limit of two hours of work a week. Nevertheless, it turned out to be quite lucrative for a fourteen-year-old because the station master's house didn't sell until late April and I made the grand sum of twelve pounds.

11. GRADUATION

I turned fifteen on November 7th. According to NSW state regulations, I was entitled to finish my schooling at the end of the term. Although I had quite enjoyed my time at the special school, I had made little progress and the teachers had given up trying to teach me to read and write. Being a friendly soul and kindly, I was popular with my peers. I was never disruptive in class so the teachers liked me too.

The staff always tried to give the students who were leaving a special send off. It was called "graduation" which struck me as an overly grand name for simply leaving school, however, that was the tradition and I was happy to go along with it. There were three of us graduating. My fellow graduates were Roger, who was deaf and dumb and Charlotte, who was legally blind.

Graduation was in two parts. There was a special school assembly for pupils and staff at which the graduates were required to say a few words. Later that evening, there was a more formal gathering at an outside venue attended by staff and the parents and close family of the graduates. At both occasions staff said nice things about us and wished us well. Graduates had to speak for two or three minutes at the school assembly, but a five-minute speech was expected at the formal evening function. I was used to saying things at school assemblies so a short speech there was not particularly worrying, but a five-minute speech in front of adults at a formal dinner was terrifying!

Mum and dad received their invitation three weeks before the graduation date. The invitation was extended to the parents and three "others". Mum, dad and Lynda were three definite starters which left two spare places. Grandpa seldom went out at nights nowadays, but he insisted on coming so we arranged for grandma to have someone to sit with her while grandpa was at my graduation. This left one spare place. Who to ask?

Mum and dad ran through the list of aunts, uncles and cousins, but they either lived too far away, were unwell or couldn't come that particular evening.

'Norman dear, you'll have to tell the school we want only five of our six tickets for the graduation dinner. I'm sure our spare ticket will be happily snapped up by the families of one of the other two kids who are graduating.'

'Mum, I've got someone I'd like to invite, please.'

'Really? Who dear?'

'She's not family, but she's a special friend.'

Hearing this, Lynda couldn't contain herself, 'Norman you're blushing, it's Janice, isn't it? You ought to see them on the school bus, mum. They're all over each other. Janice is a special friend all right!'

'Shut up Lynda, that's a lie. You can't talk anyway, I've seen you cosying up to Don Arnold...'

'Okay you two, wrap it up. Norman, if you'd like to invite Janice that's fine by me and I'll put her on the list. Pass me over the invitation please.'

Lynda looked daggers at me and stuck out her tongue. I ignored her and passed the invitation over to mum.

'You get along okay with Janice don't you Lynda?' inquired mum.

'I suppose,' my sister grumbled.

'Good, then that's settled,' and mum added Janice's name to the list of attendees, tore off the RSVP and passed it back to me. 'Put it in an envelope please, dear.'

* * *

Janice and my friendship had happily muddled along over the years, assisted by the fact we travelled together most days on the school bus. Now that I was almost fifteen and Janice a few months older, I knew I was deeply attracted to her. I loved her kindness and thoughtfulness, her open friendly personality and sense of fun. I found myself automatically seeking her out as soon as I jumped on the bus and nearly always, she kept a seat for me. When, I wondered, does a close friendship develop into something more?

A couple of other boys on the bus had yearnings for Janice too. Occasionally, I would find one of them sitting next to her when I boarded. One was a tubby guy called Fred Lomax. He was one of those people who is a born comedian and often had everyone sitting around him in stitches. What a gift! He never needed to tell jokes, he only had to start talking and play acting to turn any situation into a riot. Fred was extremely clever at mimicking his teachers, which was largely lost on me since I didn't attend his school. However, he would often have Janice squealing with delight at his antics. I envied Fred his talents and was fearful Janice might fall for him.

The other boy who was clearly interested in Janice was a tall handsome fellow called Dean Hartcher. Dean was a couple of years older than Janice, suave and somewhat aloof. Despite this, Dean commanded respect. I suppose you could say he had "presence". Talking to him, you gained the impression he was destined for great things in life; a politician perhaps, a fighter pilot or a millionaire. He was quiet and gentlemanly, never flustered or hurried and always seemed to have everything under control. Sometimes he would board the bus and flash a gobsmacking smile at Janice, who literally melted at this attention. Janice seemed besotted by this young man.

And then there was Colum Taylor, the boy Janice had invited to her fourteenth and fifteenth birthday parties; the sporty one, the one who played in the rugby team for his private school. He was a big hunk of a lad and pushy. One had the feeling he always expected to get his own way. Colum was never on our school bus because the Catholic school had its own transport. I confess, I wondered whether Janice was romantically involved with Colum Taylor. He was the mystery card in the pack.

On the day I planned to ask Janice to come to my graduation I waited for the school bus with some trepidation. Hopefully, I'd be able to sit next to her. My graduation would be a trifling affair compared to the one Janice would enjoy two years hence. She had told me around a hundred and fifty students graduated from her high school every year and it was a grand affair with a formal dinner, entertainment, speeches and presentations. Everyone dressed up, the boys in bow ties and evening suits and the girls in dazzling colourful dresses and jewellery. In comparison, only three of us were graduating from my little school and around fifty guests might be present.

On the day I planned to ask Janice to come to my graduation it was drizzling when the bus pulled up. I showed my bus pass to dear old Don who gave me his usual friendly wink and made my way down the bus. To my relief, Janice had kept a seat for me. I threw my port into the luggage rack above her head and plonked myself down.

'Yuk, you're wet,' she said, pulling away from me.

'Only a bit, it was raining and the bus was late.'

'Don told us he had had a problem starting the bus.'

I plucked up courage and looked at Janice sitting next to me so prettily.

'Janice, you know my graduation is coming up in a couple of weeks' time?'

She nodded.

'There are only three of us graduating but we still have a bit of a "do."'

'I'm glad, it would be so sad if nothing happened. Finishing school is a big thing, isn't it?'

'It is, I guess. Now I'm going to have to find full time work.'

'Wow, earning an income at fifteen! I wish I was.'

'Janice, my parents are coming to the graduation and we're allowed to invite another three people. Lynda's coming and grandpa and I have one spare ticket.'

Lynda turned to face me full on, searching with those lovely blue eyes.

'I was wondering…um…I was wondering…if you'd like to have the last ticket?'

'Norman, I'd love to come. Thank you for asking me,' her warm hand came over and squeezed mine gently for a brief moment, 'can I come with you?'

'It'll be a bit of a squeeze, six of us in the old Ford, but we'll manage. It's a good thing you're slim Janice,' I added.

She giggled. 'It's more friendly if we have to squeeze up, especially if I can sit next to you,' and she gave me a playful nudge in the ribs.

I felt a surge of excitement that Janice had so readily accepted my humble invitation and would be travelling close to me into town and back for my big evening.

'It'll be a bit tame in comparison to the graduations at your high school, I'm afraid.'

'Nonsense, everyone's graduation is special. It doesn't matter how many students are graduating.'

Janice squeezed my hand again.

11. Graduation

*   *   *

A couple of days after inviting Janice to my graduation, news came through that Miss Norah Malden had died peacefully at her nursing home. The massive stroke she sustained while I was there cleaning had been the beginning of the end. Despite her fighting spirit, she eventually succumbed. Some of the folk in town went to the funeral, but not me. Instead, I worked extra hard on her garden as a mark of respect and to bring the property up to the standard required for it to be listed for sale. Soon after the "FOR SALE" signs went up.

Some months after Miss Malden's death I was contacted by her solicitor, a Mr Straighten. Apparently, Miss Malden had left me something in her will and the solicitor wanted me to come to his office to talk about it. This was totally unexpected since I had known Miss Malden for only a few short weeks and never dreamt of being remembered in her will. I knew she had moved in fashionable circles and had counted a number of highly successful people among her clients, so it was humbling Miss Malden had thought of me when making out her will.

Mr Straighten turned out to be seriously obese and struggled to stand when I was ushered into his office. Dressed in a grey suit he gave a good impression of a balloon about to explode. I pitied the buttons trying desperately to hold him together. He was quite affable, however, and extended a flabby hand of welcome. Mopping his brow he waved the other hand about vaguely which I took to be an invitation to be seated. Settling himself back into his extra-large padded chair, Mr Straighten fixed his beady eyes on me, cleared his throat and began to speak in an unusually high-pitched voice.

'Well, young lad, Miss Malden must have taken a shine to you because she left a few things to you in her will.' He waited for my response.

'That was very kind of her.'

'Indeed. Would you like to know what will be yours?'

This struck me as a particularly silly question and for a moment I considered making a facetious comment in reply.

'Yes, please.'

Mr Straighten's sausage-like fingers flipped through the document sitting on the desk in front of him.

'Ah…' he said, pleased to have found the page he wanted, 'I'll read you the relevant sentence, "to my cleaner and gardener, Norman McDade, I leave my gardening tools and the lawn mower, together with the Ming dynasty piece of china we both so admired."'

I laughed, 'that's very generous of her.'

'Indeed. My assistant, Mrs Norwood, will be at Miss Malden's property between two and four o'clock next Saturday afternoon to supervise the proper disposal of Miss Malden's effects. If you can be there you can collect that which is rightfully yours.' The solicitor struggled to his feet again and held out a clammy hand, thereby indicating the brief meeting was over.

'Thank you, sir, I'll be sure to be there.'

How amazing! Even casual cleaning jobs can sometimes have fringe benefits.

* * *

My graduation day finally arrived and I found myself a nervous mess. I woke early and lay in bed rehearsing my five minute speech. I had to rely entirely on memory since written notes were of no use. My class teacher had been more than patient helping me frame my speech and practice it during lunch breaks. He must have been sick and tired of hearing my stumbling efforts to get it right.

Special arrangements had been made for my last day of schooling. I was to travel in on the school bus as normal. Mum and dad were to drive in later in time for the school assembly at eleven. As soon as assembly was over, I was free to go home with my parents leaving me the whole afternoon to get ready for the graduation dinner later that evening. At half past five our family were to journey round to pick up grandpa and then Janice and the six of us would drive back into town. The evening's graduation function commenced at seven o'clock.

On the bus going to school on my last day I was annoyed to find the over-weight Fred Lomax had grabbed the seat next to Janice and, as usual, was keeping everyone around him entertained. I was too far away to hear, but he carrying on about something to do with food and eating; a topic with which he was, no doubt, an expert. Whatever it was, on several occasions I heard Janice's distinctive squeals of glee. Once again I felt pangs of envy, if only I had Fred's natural ability as a comic and could make Janice laugh as much.

My last morning at school was a time of mixed emotions. As one of the three graduates I was seen as a bit of a celebrity and my peers went out of their way to be friendly and make my final hours enjoyable. At five to eleven pupils and staff filed into the school assembly hall and took their places for the school's graduation ceremony. It was at this point I was hit with a sudden sense of sadness and trepidation for the future. I hadn't benefitted much from my education, nevertheless, school had been a happy, safe and supportive place. Tomorrow I'd be out on my own in the big wide world to make a living and fend for myself. It was a daunting prospect.

Most of the teachers stayed with their pupils during assemblies to assist them when required. On the stage were the school principal, Mrs Radcraft, and her deputy seated together as usual. However, an additional seven chairs had been placed on stage, six for the parents of the three graduates and the seventh for the school's chaplain who was the special guest. Mum and dad were sitting up there on the stage looking self-conscious and gave me a wave as I walked in and found my seat.

I think I must have been somewhat overcome by the occasion because, looking back, my memory is blurry. Proceedings began when the school principal stood to welcome the guests, followed by the dozen or so children that made up the school's choir. Sadly, I can't remember what they sang. Next, the school's chaplain urged we three graduates to remember and practice the fine values with which we had been inculcated and stressed the importance of becoming good citizens. Then came the embarrassing part. The deputy rose to give a spiel about the good things I had done at my special school and called on me to come forward and say a few words. Many times, I'd been out front to announce things at school assemblies so this didn't faze me. When the other two graduates had also been accoladed and given their mini-speeches the event concluded with the national anthem. Finally, there was a special morning tea.

We three graduates were invited to the morning tea and were expected to stand about making polite conversation. I may not read or write but I *do* have a genuine love of the English language and I'm perfectly able to confidently discourse with adults. In fact, the deputy principal had made special mention of my exceptional use of vocabulary. The parents and senior staff were all there together with the chaplain. Three of the senior girls waited on us with sausage rolls, sandwiches and yummy cakes. I sailed through the school's graduation assembly and the ensuing morning tea without too much difficulty. The formal evening graduation ceremony was going to be considerably more challenging.

* * *

As a family, we "scrubbed up" remarkably well. Mum had a special hair-do and a new evening dress for the occasion and dad dragged out the suit he was married in twenty years ago, although he had to admit it was a bit tight in places. He had gone to great lengths to scrub his hands in an attempt to clean and remove the ingrained grease and oil in his pores. Lynda looked stunning in a pretty frock and had taken hours "putting on her face." For the first time I saw my sister as an attractive young woman. Mum had dragged me off a couple of weeks earlier to buy a dark suit and tie, 'You'll need a suit for job interviews,'

11. Graduation

she assured me. I even had a shiny new pair of black shoes, the soles of which I had to scratch because they were leather and slippery. Before we left, I found dad in the kitchen knocking back a quick beer. He claimed he needed, 'A bit of extra fortification.'

I had washed the car during the afternoon and we set off on time with dad driving. Grandpa was waiting for us and limped out using a walking stick. As I walked slowly down the driveway with him, he shoved something into the top pocket of my jacket. I pulled it out and discovered a folded ten-pound note, 'A special graduation gift, my boy,' he smiled. Ten pounds was a really generous gift! Grandpa squeezed in next to mum in the front seat and managed to get his walking stick to sit reasonably comfortably between his legs.

A few minutes later we pulled up outside Janice's home. Lynda had been nudging me and making silly comments ever since we left our house, relishing the opportunity for some girlfriend teasing. There was an expectant hush as I left the car and walked up Janice's driveway. They all knew I was smitten.

I rang the bell feeling excited even though I had seen Janice on the school bus that morning. An equally excited Mrs Fenton swung open the front door, 'Come on in my dear, Janice is almost ready. Are you feeling nervous, Norman?'

I had no chance to answer because Mrs Fenton barely stopped for a breath, 'I remember my graduation dear, quite some years ago now, of course. I was terrified! There was dancing too and I'm as clumsy as a hippopotamus. Wait here Norman dear, and I'll pop upstairs to see how things are going.' As before I had not managed to get a single word in as I watched Mrs Fenton move surprisingly adroitly up their stair case.

I didn't have to wait long. Janice appeared at the top of the stairs smiling down at me. She made her way down slowly and gracefully allowing me to feast my eyes on her slender figure, open friendly face and colourful dress. I had seen Janice in party dresses before but tonight she looked so special and I felt my heart beat faster. I resisted an urge to embrace her at the foot of the stairs and instead just said 'hi' rather limply. The magic moment was broken by Janice's mother storming down the stairs and launching into another of her spiels about this, that and the other. We were quick to escape with Mrs Fenton's voice still trailing along behind us as we walked down the driveway.

My family welcomed Janice warmly and, as expected, she slipped in next to me in the back seat. The journey to town was uneventful and my parents kept up a convivial flow of conversation. I had Janice sitting on my right and could feel her body warmth with my sister on my left keeping up a relentless series of nudges and digs in the ribs whenever she thought something remotely romantic happened. I promised myself I would get back at her mercilessly at the earliest opportunity.

The function was being held at the Returned Serviceman's League building where the large dining room had been reserved for our exclusive use. There were a number of formally set circular tables, each seating eight guests. One table had been labelled "McDade Family." After standing about for a short time we were asked to take our places. There were artistic place names on the table mats and I discovered I was seated opposite Janice. During the evening our eyes would often meet but conversation between us was impossible. The McDade family occupied six seats, the last two seats were occupied by one of the teachers and her husband.

This was the first time I had ever been to a formal dinner and I was nervous about my manners and how to behave properly. We were waited on first by a man who wanted to know what drinks we would like and then by a young lady who took our meal orders. There was quite some discussion centred round the menu. Mum quietly read out the selection of dishes for me. The five grownups shared two bottles of wine during the evening; we three teenagers were obliged to drink boring old lemonade. I was surprised to find there were three courses: entrée, mains and dessert. I noticed Janice seemed perfectly relaxed about such matters. Presumably her parents had been able to afford to take her out to more formal dinners occasionally.

11. Graduation

We three graduates had been timetabled to give our five-minute presentations after each of the three courses. I was scheduled to be the last one to speak following the desserts so I wasn't able to relax until my speech was over and I had received my certificate of graduation. Everyone gave me generous applause and I noticed Janice being particularly enthusiastic. Mind you, I think many of those present had drunk a fair bit by the time I gave my presentation and would have enthusiastically applauded a fly climbing up a window pane.

It must have been after ten o'clock when we made our final farewells and left the RSL Club. Mum, dad and grandpa had finished off two bottles of wine between them because the teacher at our table had turned out to be a teetotaller and her considerate husband drank only one glass of wine the whole evening. We were a noisy bunch as we headed for the carpark, mum and dad singing some silly old song I'd never heard before and grandpa waving his stick in the air pretending he was conducting. No longer steady on his feet, the combination of the wine and his failure to use his walking stick for its proper purpose meant grandpa soon landed in a heap on the ground and had to be helped up, all the while unleashing a string of uncouth language, I'd never heard him use before.

'Okay kids, get in the bloody old family bomb,' dad burped with one arm around mum's not inconsiderable waist.

'Fred, you're… you're pissed… you are. Do you know that?' giggled mum.

'Ere, give us a cuddle love…a kiss'll do for now but 'spect more later,' and dad descended into peels of raucous laughter. The two of them proceeded to have a big smooch in the middle of the carpark much to the embarrassment of us teenagers. Meanwhile, grandpa was down on the ground again swearing at his walking stick which he reckoned was buggered and didn't work anymore. With the help of the three sober juniors, grandpa was righted and with our help managed to lurch round to the front passenger door. Finding it locked, he looked around and spied my parents still busily groping each other.

'Hey you two, you're not on your bloody honeymoon, you know! Get the fuck over here and get this pile of shit back on the road. 'Tis past me bloody bedtime,' yelled grandpa.

Mum pulled herself away from dad's clutches and did her best to tidy herself up. Dad returned to the song he had been singing a few minutes earlier while fumbling through various pockets to find the car keys. It was while this key search was still underway that I felt Janice's soft hand slip into mine and she gave me a quick comforting squeeze. I squeezed back and then, just as quickly, her hand was gone.

'Dad, do you think you should be driving?' I asked.

He turned towards me with one hand hovering around the car door. Hoping the key was correctly positioned he pointed at me with the other arm. 'You mind your bloody tongue young Norman. I don't want no cheek in front of the girls 'ere. Get in and button up yer bloody mouth.'

A couple of times in the past, Lynda and I had witnessed dad drunk. We knew he was dangerous and not himself when intoxicated. He was liable to let fly with his language, but more disturbingly, to become physically abusive. There was one terrible night when dad came home drunk and started smashing furniture and crockery in the kitchen. We kids cowered, terrified, in our bedrooms not daring to come out. Next morning mum was uncharacteristically quiet and subdued, but was still there in the kitchen to prepare our breakfasts and school lunches. She said nothing about the incident and Lynda and I never discovered what had provoked such an outburst, apart from the grog. Tonight, it seemed, my graduation might also be remembered for all the wrong reasons!

Dad climbed into the driver's seat and the rest of us sat in the same places, mum next to dad and grandpa in the front also. I sat in the middle of the back seat with Lynda on my left and Janice to the right. Nobody was game to say anything but I believe we all realised dad was not fit to drive.

12. RANDALL'S CREEK

'Open all the bloody windows,' yelled dad, as he scuffled about trying to engage the key in the ignition, 'it's freaking hot in 'ere.' Those of us sitting by windows wound away and the dirty windows slowly descended except grandpa's window which stubbornly refused to budge.

'I'll do it for you grandpa,' volunteered my sister and lent over grandpa's seat to work the handle. Grudgingly, it obliged and grandpa mumbled a sleepy, 'Thank you, love.' Despite the erratic swerving of the car, the heavy mix of a late night with excessive consumption of wine, it was all too much for grandpa's fragile disposition and he soon lapsed into a heavy sleep. Dad was not concentrating fully on the driving and squeals of delight tinged with embarrassment from mum told us he was still touching her indiscreetly. We careered on through the near empty streets of town, more or less on the correct side of the road. Fortunately no police cars were in evidence, although I half wished they had been because, in all likelihood, they would have stopped dad driving and save everyone a petrifying trip home.

For the last week or two the weather had been hot and dry. The paddocks lay brown, an open invitation to grass fires. When we left the outskirts of town, we faced another thirty miles of narrow, winding dirt road with nasty surface corrugations. On the way to graduation jets of dust streamed out behind any vehicles approaching us and could be seen from miles away giving us early warning of their approach. But tonight, it was pitch black and these dust trails were no longer visible until our headlamps picked them up at the last moment. On some sections of the road the bull dust on the side of the road was inches deep and created a high risk of skidding or losing control for anyone not driving carefully in such unfavourable conditions.

Approximately half way home the road descends steeply down to the ancient single-lane wooden bridge that crosses Randall's Creek. Nobody is quite sure how the creek acquired its name, there are no Randalls living nearby, no explorers by that name or even a bridge engineer called Randall. Nevertheless, everyone has deep respect for the narrow wooden bridge that conveys travellers across Randall's Creek because it's notorious for accidents. Of course, if you stop to think for a moment, it isn't the bridge's fault that people have accidents there it's the poor driving. After every car accident at Randall's Creek the locals shake their heads sagely and blame the council for "not fixing that bloody bridge!"

I remember a feeling of foreboding as we arrived at the crest of the hill from whence the road begins its torturous, twisting downward journey to Randall's Creek. Apart from dad, who was still raving on and saying stupid things, everyone in the car was now quiet. No doubt they shared my feelings of apprehension. Somehow grandpa had remained sound asleep and we occasionally heard a laboured snore coming from his direction. It was no use asking dad to 'slow down' or 'take it easy' as this would only have motivated him to drive even more recklessly. I found myself reaching for Janice's hand as we began the steep descent.

'Hey-Ho we're on the big dipper, hang on for the ride of your life!' yelled dad as he swung the car first to the left and then to the right. He was clearly enjoying himself as we snaked our way round a series of sharp bends. 'I should've been a bloody formula one driver,' he boasted as his passengers were swung from one side of the car to the other. Somehow, we stayed on the road and avoided tumbling off the steep sides to certain death. As we approached the bridge itself, I dared to think the worst was over and perhaps we were going to be okay. I was wrong...

As dad straightened up to point the car in the correct direction to cross the narrow bridge another car suddenly came hurtling towards us. It crossed the bridge in the nick of time, narrowly missed us and careered on up the hill behind us leaving a massive cloud of dense dust in its wake. It was virtually zero visibility. We were going too fast to stop and shot across the bridge straight into the dust cloud. At this speed the only way we could avoid an accident was if dad knew instinctively which direction to take and at what point the road curved away when we exited the bridge. He must have driven this road a thousand times and knew it well, but not in a drunken state.

I will never forget the ghastly sounds of the crash. First came the screams and then the smashing, grinding, ripping of metal as we charged on blindly into the bush. It seemed to go on forever as we hit tree after tree while being thrown mercilessly and uncontrollably about. Then, we came to a standstill and there was a moment of total silence except for a weird hissing sound coming from the engine. It was as if the bush itself was holding its breath numb with shock.

I found myself spreadeagled on top of mum where the front seat should have been and aware of severe pain in several places. Mum was staring up at me from beneath the dashboard with panic in her eyes. A nasty gash across her forehead oozed blood and as I watched in horror, her eyes slowly closed and stayed close. Was she dead? I tried to raise myself and began to isolate my pains. My left wrist was limp and surely broken and my right knee badly bruised or worse. There was also a stabbing pain across my chest. But I was breathing and fully conscious.

We needed urgent help. The chance of another vehicle coming along the road this late at night was unlikely. There was no sign of grandpa or my sister. They must have been torn out of the car since the left side of the vehicle was totally missing, peeled off like the lid of a can. Dad was slumped over the steering wheel, groaning. Janice was still in the car lying on her back on the floor, seemingly unconscious. I couldn't see any obvious injuries she had sustained. I was the only person capable of getting out of this mangled mess and raising the alarm.

I scrambled out through the space where the front left-hand door had been and shouted out loudly that I was going to get help. There was no reply. I couldn't use my left arm but found I was able to stand and walk with a limp. The dust was clearing. It was a dark night, cloudy with no moon. I felt strangely light-headed as I groped my way around what remained of the car. There was still no sign of grandpa and Lynda so I limped painfully towards where the road should be. After about ten yards I met the edge of the dirt road and began to follow it up hill. My plan was to stay on the road until I reached a driveway leading to a farm house. I vaguely remembered there was a farm house perched on top of the hill. The occupants of the farm would probably have a telephone and I could ring for an ambulance.

I have no idea how long I struggled on up that hill driven by the desperate need to get help. I went through alternate bouts of dizziness and nausea all the time feeling acute pain from my injuries. I was able to support the broken wrist with my right hand but there was nothing I could do to alleviate the pain in my knee and across my chest. I prayed unsuccessfully for a vehicle, any vehicle, to come along the road.

At last, I reached the entrance to a property. It had a name up on a post which I couldn't decipher. I remembered to close the gate behind me and continued my painful journey along a well-used track that I presumed led to a farm house. I trudged on and on beginning to wonder whether I was on a track that led only to paddocks when I heard a dog barking somewhere up ahead of me. It must have sensed me coming and sprang into guard-dog duty mode. As I approached and the barking became louder, the occupants must have wondered what was going on because a couple of welcoming house lights came on. At last, I could see better where I was going.

12. Randall's Creek

I was relieved the noisy sheep dog was chained up because it was really going berserk as I hobbled along a concrete path that led towards the front door. The door opened before I reached it at the same time as an outside light came on and shone brightly in my face. A large man stood in the doorway in his pyjamas, glaring and confronting.

'Please sir,' I blurted out, 'there's been a terrible accident down at Randall's Creek.'

13. THE AFTERMATH

The first of three ambulances arrived at Randall's Creek a little over an hour after the accident. I was sitting in Jim Negune's ute, the farmer I had disturbed in the middle of the night. Sadly, smashes at Randall's Creek were all too common and Jim had attended several over the years. He told me he never took food or drinks down to the injured in case they needed urgent surgery, but blankets were always most welcome. By now, I was suffering serious delayed shock and couldn't stop shaking and shivering. I was grateful to have one of Jim's warm army blankets wrapped around me. I kept passing out and then waking suddenly to re-live those horrifying few seconds when we careered off into the bush. Jim wouldn't tell me how everyone else was faring, except to say it was serious and he was doing his level best to keep up their spirits. In my few lucid moments I longed to hear more.

Passing in and out of consciousness made it difficult to understand what was going on around me. I vaguely remember a friendly policeman telling me the road was closed and when the ambulances came they would take me to hospital. He also said something about me being brave to have walked so far to get help. Then I must have passed out again. The next time I woke I found an ambulance officer leaning over me asking what pains I had and how bad they were. He seemed most concerned about the pains in my chest. Later, I over-heard a conversation between two of the ambulance officers.

'I've finished the triage. We'll take the most urgent first; that's the man and the woman in the front seat. We're going to require gear to get the bloke out though. He's sustained major chest injuries and probably a punctured lung. He's also trapped by the legs. They're both badly smashed up. They can both go in Dave's ambulance asap. Next priority is the two young ones. They've got some nasty injuries too but not life-threatening as far as I can tell. You can take those two, Neil. Tell Martin to collect the two deceased after he's finished helping us remove and stabilise these four.'

'Okay mate, I'll radio base and warn the hospital to be on standby to receive four emergency patients. What time shall I give for the ETA?'

'Tell the hospital the ambulances should start arriving in a couple of hours. That'll make the ETA around half past two. Stress the patients are pretty badly smashed up, so they'll need every one of their trauma teams on stand-by. Two may need transferring to Sydney.'

I must have passed out again, because I don't remember anything more until I found myself lying in an ambulance. Somebody else was being gently stretchered in to join me. I recognised a pretty party dress. My fellow traveller was Janice. It was at that moment I realised with a jolt that it was entirely my fault that poor Janice was now on her way to hospital. If I hadn't been so selfish and invited her to come to my graduation, she would be safely tucked up in her bed at home. I gently called her name but there was no reply. Then I noticed Janice had a neck brace on and her head was swathed in bandages. She wasn't moving.

'Okay Norman, we're leaving now. We'll have you at the hospital in an hour or so.' I recognised the voice of the ambulance officer called Neil.

'How's Janice?' I called out.

'Is that the name of the young lass I've just brought in?'

'Yes.'

"Is she your sister, Norman?'
'No.'
'Girlfriend?'
'I dunno.'
'She's unconscious at the moment, mate. Had a nasty knock on the head. Now, just you try and relax, we need to be on our way.'

I heard the doors at the back of the ambulance slam shut before once again passing out.

* * *

My memories of arriving at the hospital are vague. There were nurses, doctors, bright lights, weird machines, beds and needles everywhere. I do remember vomiting all over the floor and feeling acutely embarrassed about it.

Things began to return to some sort of normality the next day. I emerged from a deep sleep to find a nurse holding my arm checking my pulse. She smiled comfortingly.

'How are you feeling Norman?'
'Groggy.'
'Do you know where you are?'
'The Base Hospital?'
'That's right. Do you remember what happened?'
'Yeah, a car accident.'
'That's right.'
'What happened to the others in the car?'
'Okay, that's all I need to do for you now.' The nurse smiled sweetly and left abruptly. Clearly, she didn't want to tell me anything more. Not a good sign…

I must have fallen asleep again, because the next thing I remember was a doctor and another nurse standing at the end of my bed.

'Hello Norman, how are you feeling?' asked the doctor.
'Not too bad, thank you.'

13. The Aftermath

'That's good. It was a very nasty accident you were involved in, but the good news is that your injuries are not too serious. You have a broken left wrist and you messed up a few of your fingers. We've straightened everything up for you. You'll need to keep the wrist in plaster for six weeks. You also have three broken ribs. There's not much we can do for them I'm afraid and they will give you quite a bit of pain for a time. I'll prescribe you some strong pain-killers to last you for a few days. You also bashed your right knee. We x-rayed it for you. No break, just severe bruising. Any questions?'

'What happened to the rest of my family?'

'Matron, may I leave that to you please?' the doctor responded and the two of them moved off leaving me alone and fretting.

I concluded there must be some awful news and nobody wanted to be the one to have to break it to me. Perhaps, I thought, if I can get out of this bed, I'll be able to find out for myself. Sitting up, however, proved horribly painful. Sharp stabbing pains shot across my chest and almost every muscle in my body complained. I sank back into a prone position, which relieved the chest pains and hoped like hell the matron would be back soon.

'Norman? Are you awake?'

I opened my eyes to find the same plump matron was, indeed, back and standing at the side of my bed. There was a sternness about her demeanour and she looked formidable in her clean, starched matron's uniform.

'Hello, matron.'

'Norman, I want to talk to you about the others who were in the car with you. May I sit on the bed?'

'Yes, yes, of course.'

Matron surprised me by perching on the side of the bed and taking hold of my good right hand which she gently caressed. Gone was the stern, officious matron; this one was a kindlier, mother-like figure.

'Norman, I have some sad news to share with you. Both your parents were badly injured and have been air-lifted to a bigger hospital in Sydney. Your father is on the critical list. That means, it's touch and go whether he will recover from his injuries. We must hope and pray for him. Your mother is also in a bad way, but with expert medical attention should make a good recovery. It's likely to be many weeks or even months before they can return home.'

I had expected to hear something like this, since I had seen they were in a bad way before I went off to get help. The good news was that they had both survived.

'So, Norman, there won't be anyone at home to look after you when we send you home in a couple of days.'

'What about Lynda, my sister? She should be there.'

Matron was gently shaking her head, 'I'm so sorry Norman, Lynda passed away.'

'Oh God, no…surely not?'

Matron nodded, 'Your grandfather didn't make it either, I'm afraid.'

'Grandpa died too?'

'Yes.'

'What about Janice?'

'She's going to be fine,' matron smiled, 'she's still unconscious and has a badly sprained neck, a broken right arm and a heap of bruises but nothing that won't mend with time.'

'I shouldn't have invited her to come to my graduation.'

'No point worrying about that now, Norman. Just you concentrate on getting yourself better.'

'Can I go and see Janice?'

'Not today. You still have concussion yourself. Perhaps tomorrow. By then, Janice might be conscious again too and you'll be able to speak with her.'

I managed a trace of a smile. Matron stood and metamorphosed back into the strict looking boss of the ward and I was left to process the grim news she had imparted.

Later that afternoon, I had an unexpected visitor in the form of

13. The Aftermath

Mrs Fenton, Janice's mother. She was her usual non-stop talkative self.

'Hello Norman, matron said it was okay for me to come and see you for a short time, but not for too long, mind,' she beamed and dragged a chair to the side of the bed. She dived into a large wicker basket and dragged out a bunch of dark-coloured grapes, 'these are for you, dear…I hope you like grapes? I've just been to see Janice but she hasn't come round yet. She had a bad knock on the head, you know, but the doctor says she will be fine. And what about you, dear? It looks like you broke your wrist? Janice has a broken arm too…'

'Excuse me, I need to do my hourly checks,' interrupted an elderly nurse, 'I'll only be a few minutes.' Reluctantly, Mrs Fenton vacated her chair, moved away to the end of the bed and hovered there like a hawk ready to dive in on its prey.

'All good,' smiled the nurse a few minutes later and left me in the hands of the ever loquacious, Mrs Fenton, once more.

'Now dear, you won't be able to go back home for a long time because there'll be nobody there to help you while you recover. Sadly, you can't stay with your grandparents either. So, if you have nowhere else to go, you are most welcome to stay with us until you are completely better. We have a nice spare bedroom for guests. I know you have been good friends with Janice for many years. My husband won't mind you staying, I'm sure, although I had better ask him first…'and she giggled, guiltily. 'So, what do you think?'

The thought of trying to co-exist for a number of weeks with the ever-talkative Mrs Fenton did not appeal, but the wonderful opportunity to live in close proximity to Janice trumped any such concerns.

'Thank you, Mrs Fenton, that's extremely kind of you,' and I managed a weak smile.

'By the way, dear, did you hear who was driving the car that forced your dad off the road and then never stopped after the accident? I couldn't believe it when I heard. Apparently, the police got onto him straightaway. I don't know how they found out who was behind the wheel. Anyway, they reckon the young man was driving recklessly and far too fast for the night-time conditions. I was really shocked because he has had a bit of a crush on our Janice, you know…'

'Really? Who was it?'

'Colum Taylor, the young lad who goes to the Catholic college in town. He's a top rugby player, I understand. I must say, I was a bit uneasy about him being so interested in our Janice. He was just a bit too cocky for my liking. You know, over-confident and always bragging about how marvellous a sportsman he was.'

14. RECOVERIES

Accidents happen in a split second, but recovery can take months or even years and is not always complete. Our crash at Randall's Creek was a typical example.

The full enormity of what had happened at Randall's Creek took time to sink in during the first couple of days as I lay in a hospital bed in too much pain to get up or do anything. I had lost two people I loved dearly, Lynda and grandpa. They had had the misfortune to have been sitting on the left-hand side of the car when we careered off into the bush taking out five or six small trees and ripping out the whole of their side of the car. I learnt later their mangled bodies were found yards away. Death must have been instant. Lynda and I were close. She had never teased me about my learning disabilities. At sixteen, Lynda was already making exciting plans for her future. Dear old grandpa had always been someone I looked up to forever kind and supportive. I wondered what would happen to poor grandma now that grandpa was no longer there for her. How would she manage?

On the third evening, when I was playing about with a less than appetising looking hospital dinner, a different nurse came to see me. She said she was from ward 4F, a ward for female patients. There was a girl there she said, called Janice, who was asking about me. Apparently, Janice had regained consciousness but was not allowed out of bed yet. I asked the nurse to tell Janice I was fine and that I would come and see her as soon as I was permitted, perhaps as early as tomorrow.

I endured a restless night. My aches and pains stopped me from getting comfortable and there were a couple of horrendous snorers in the ward. And if that wasn't enough, every hour or two a nurse would suddenly appear at my side to give me a pain-killer or carry out the regular health checks. I doubt whether I managed to scrape together more than two or three hours of sleep. Breakfast next morning, was little better than last night's dinner, but at least I felt more like eating. Matron and the doctor were back to see me again after breakfast.

'How are you feeling today, young man?' asked the doctor.

'A bit better thank you, doctor.'

'Good. I'll check that chest again to make sure we haven't missed anything.'

I went through the painful process of sitting up so the doctor could use his stethoscope.

'You're doing well. Being young and fit is in your favour. Let's get you up and about today and if everything is still good tomorrow morning you can be discharged.'

'Do you know how my parents are doing in Sydney, please?'

'Your father is in an induced coma. Both have had major surgery. I don't have any further details. They certainly won't be coming home for weeks. Do you have someone who can look after you if we discharge you tomorrow?'

'Yes, I think so.'

About an hour later, at my request, matron gave permission for a nurse to escort me to ward 4F to visit Janice. Mrs Fenton was also there when I limped slowly up to Janice's bed. As usual Janice's mother was talking flat out, but my arrival stopped her mid-sentence and there was a precious moment of quiet.

'Hello Mrs Fenton, hi Janice.'

'Norman, lovely to see you up and about,' beamed Mrs Fenton, 'Janice is coming along nicely too. The doctor thinks she may be ready

14. Recoveries

to be discharged tomorrow. But look at all her terrible bruises! It looks like she's had fifteen rounds in a heavy-weight boxing match. If everything goes according to plan, I might be allowed to take both of you home with me tomorrow morning. You'll have top care at my place Norman and I'll soon have you fattened up and looking well again. Janice, darling, did I tell you I've invited Norman to stay with us until he's found somewhere else to live? You can keep each other company while you convalesce, won't that be nice? You will be coming won't you Norman, dear?'

At last Mrs Fenton stopped to draw breathe and I was able to properly accept her kind invitation. Janice and I exchanged painful smiles through our bruises.

* * *

Colum Taylor escaped physical injury, but nonetheless paid a heavy price for his foolhardiness. The police targetted young males who behave like idiots on the roads and certainly threw the book at Colum. As he was still only sixteen, he ended up being convicted in a juvenile court for dangerous driving and failing to stop to offer assistance following an accident. He was fined two hundred pounds and had his learner's licence cancelled for three years. The police were never able to ascertain for sure who caused the accident at Randall's Creek, but suspected it was Colum's fault. This meant dad was never taken to task for his drunken driving. My father was more than fortunate to avoid serious legal repercussions.

Colum's misfortune was my gain. Mr and Mrs Fenton and Janice dropped him like a hot potato and Colum was never invited to their house again. One of my three competitors for Janice's attentions was now out of contention and assigned to the sin bin. It seemed inconceivable that Colum would ever be welcomed back.

I heard later that Colum was remorseful and quite devasted by what had happened. Overnight he had earnt himself a bad reputation around town and was no longer to be trusted. Forbidden to drive, Colum was effectively "grounded." His father, who ended up paying most of the two hundred pound fine, was furious with him and even threatened to take him away from his Catholic high school. Rumour had it that Colum was to be made a school prefect in his final year at school, but that never happened. He did, however, continue to play rugby for the school. I'm not sure about the intensity of Colum's feelings for Janice. Any chance of furthering that romance was now surely snuffed out.

* * *

Four days after the accident mum came out of intensive care and was moved to an ordinary ward. Dad spent an entire week in intensive care. It was difficult for me to get updates on their progress. Thankfully, our GP kept in touch with the hospital in Sydney and rang me when there was some news. I desperately wanted to go down to Sydney to see them but had no means of doing so. Accepting the kind hospitality of the Fenton's was wonderful, however, I didn't feel I could ask them to drive all the way to Sydney on my behalf.

Surprisingly, it was Mr Fenton who arrived to collect Janice and me from the hospital. I had seen very little of Janice's dad until now. He always seemed to be away working somewhere. Mr Fenton was a soil scientist and spent much of his time visiting farms in the neighbourhood advising farmers on such things as the most suitable crops to grow, crop rotation, contour ploughing, reducing erosion and how to upgrade their soils.

It was difficult to imagine two married people so unalike. Mrs Fenton, generous, warm, welcoming, gregarious, unable to stop talking, short and plump. Mr Fenton, on the other hand, was a tall taciturn man of few words. Strongly built, it was easy to see how he would be well received amongst the hardened, no fuss men on the land. His aloofness towards me may have been due to shyness or simply disinterest. It was hard to know.

14. Recoveries

Mr Fenton picked Janice up first, then came to my ward. I was dressed in my dirty, torn graduation gear and ready to leave, sitting alone outside the entrance to the ward.

'Norman,' was his curt welcome, accompanied by a nod.

'Hello Mr Fenton, its very kind of you to allow me to stay with you.'

No reply. Perhaps he didn't want me to stay or was angry I had invited Janice to my graduation? He picked up the plastic bag the hospital had given me containing the meagre collection of items I had with me: my graduation certificate, a pair of pyjamas the hospital had supplied, a book someone had given me that I planned to give to the Fentons, a couple of spare bandages and a container half full of pain-killers. He was already carrying Janice's luggage which was more substantial than mine, since her mother had brought several items from home. Janice and I traipsed slowly along the hospital corridors behind Mr Fenton, still badly bruised and me limping heavily.

Very few words were exchanged on the way back along the same road on which we had come to grief. As we approached the infamous Randall's Creek, Mr Fenton slowed and pulled over to the side of the road. The flattened saplings and trees were easy to see, but there was no sign of our car which, no doubt, had already been dumped at someone's scrap metal yard by now.

'You were lucky,' Mr Fenton remarked, 'could've been much worse.'

Janice and I re-lived those horrifying seconds when we knew we were totally out of control and staring death in the face. We were glad to leave the site.

Half an hour later we arrived at Janice's home to be smothered by Mrs Fenton's warmth and care. She had cake and soft drinks ready and wanted a full report on how we were feeling and what special care we needed with regard to pain killers and other medication. I decided to try and manage without pain killers any more.

* * *

I spent six weeks with the Fentons. I had a small sum of money saved up in my bank account as a result of the two jobs I had had over the last few months and I offered to pay something towards my board. 'Thanks, but no thanks,' was Mr Fenton's response, 'you're going to need that money, Norman,' he added.

Living in Janice's home didn't turn out to be quite the opportunity to get closer to her that I had hoped it would be. The day after we returned from hospital, Dean Hartcher, the tall suave lad in year twelve turned up and was welcomed with open arms. I watched, gobsmacked, as Janice and Dean had a long and loving embrace. How stupid I'd been to ever imagine *I was* Janice's favourite! Dean and Janice must have been a dating couple for months. All those times Janice had kept a place for me on the bus meant absolutely nothing. She was just being kind and nothing more. Coming to my graduation was the same; being supportive of the poor little bugger who can't read or write and has to go to a special school! Janice pitied me and nothing more than that.

That night I cried until my pillow was wet. How could I have been so wrong? I had seen Janice and Dean exchange a quick smile on the bus sometimes, enough to make me think he could be interested in her, but that was all. Now it was clear they had been quietly dating for months. I felt cheated. Janice could have had the decency to tell me she was going out with Dean so I knew where I stood. How could I have been so naïve as to imagine Janice and I were special together? The angrier I felt about the whole situation, the more I realised I was in love with Janice.

I felt miserable for days. The Fentons were most understanding, believing my depressed mood to be the result of the car accident and the nasty bash on the head. 'Concussion,' Mrs Fenton assured me, 'can last for quite a long time and you never know how it will affect you.' Dean often called around after school and he and Janice would sit about in the garden laughing and flirting while I moped around elsewhere.

14. Recoveries

After two weeks, Janice was well enough to go back to school leaving me and Mrs Fenton to keep each other company. Mr Fenton was away for days at a time running workshops, attending agricultural shows or advising farmers. I could only use one hand, but did what I could to help in the garden, putting away the dishes and assisting Mrs Fenton with housework. I soon became bored and as my knee improved, started walking. At first, I managed only half a mile, but as the healing continued, I lengthened my walks until I was doing around five or six miles a day. I had a number of favourite walks, mostly around town and it was on one of these walks that I picked up a new job.

I was sauntering past our small community hospital one day and decided to call in to see my grandma. She had been admitted to the nursing home section of the establishment because with grandpa deceased, she had no way of coping on her own at home. The dear lady had deteriorated further and the nurse told me she now suffered dementia on top of her history of debilitating strokes. I did my best to have a conversation with grandma but it was hard work. In the bed next to grandma was another elderly lady, who was reading and quite lively and perky.

'Excuse me young man, are you the grandson who used to clean and garden for Mr and Mrs McDade?'

'Yes, I am.'

'Come over here and sit with me for a moment young man, I want to talk to you.'

I looked at grandma who had fallen asleep again. Discretely I moved my chair over to the other lady's bed.

'I'm Mrs Bassington,' and she extended a long white bony arm full of blue veins for me to shake her hand.

I smiled, 'I'm Norman, Norman McDade.'

Mrs Bassington hoisted herself up onto her pillows more comfortably and said, 'Yes, I know all about you, young man. For months you did the cleaning and gardening for the McDades. So sad about poor Mr McDade passing away after that terrible crash down at Randall's Creek. Are you nearly better?'

'Yes, thank you. In another week I'll have my plaster off and be ready to resume work.'

Mrs Bassington seemed delighted to hear this news and came out with a startling suggestion.

'My legs are buggered young man and I'll be in a wheel chair for the rest of my life. I have a large house that I love dearly and don't intend to ever leave. I'm a widow and now that I'm wheel-chair bound need a cleaner cum gardener who I can trust. Your grandpa raved about you. He said you were a hard worker, used your nous and were always pleasantly mannered. So, would you like a job with me?'

I was taken aback by this sudden work offer and unsure how to respond, 'Where do you live, Mrs Bassington?'

'Greystones. The large house at the top of the hill. My husband was in real estate and very successful. I can offer you fifteen hours a week for starters. After a couple of months, we can review that to see if it's enough or too much. What do you think?'

'It sounds wonderful, Mrs Bassington. Will you be out of hospital soon?'

'Next week, I expect. My bones are getting crumbly and I keep having falls. I'm having lessons on how to manage with a wheel chair and my house is already wheel-chair friendly.'

Mrs Bassington gave me a friendly smile and somehow, I just knew she would be good to work for.

'Now, what about your parents? How are they going?'

'Mum is expected home next week and I'll have to do everything for her at home for a time. Dad still has a couple more operations to endure so there's no date yet for his return.'

'A bad business all round,' empathised Mrs Bassington, 'how about you call at my house at ten o'clock on February 18th, ready to start work? I'm happy to pay you the basic wage. I'll get my solicitor to draw up a contract so everything is done properly.'

'Mrs Bassington, I do have a small problem that I should tell you about.'
'What's that young man?'
'I'm illiterate.'
'Oh, we can get round that. Don't you worry, my dear boy.'

Grandma was stirring again and I moved back to her bed. She looked at me blankly for a moment then fell asleep again with a lingering grunt.

Ten minutes later I left the hospital in high spirits. For the first time since graduation something positive had happened!

15. GREYSTONES

Over the next few months my time was divided between home and working for Mrs Bassington at Greystones. Mum came home as planned but her recovery proved to be painfully slow. The doctors considered her mended, however, living with her back in our home I knew she was struggling. Lying for weeks in a hospital bed seemed to have drained her strength and vitality. It was as if the accident had changed her personality. Getting up in the mornings was a big effort and she lacked the motivation to do much during the day. Randall's Creek had well and truly knocked the stuffing out of mum.

Inevitably, I became more domesticated while mum's extended convalescence dragged on. I virtually did everything: shopping, cleaning, gardening, preparing meals, laundry and anything else that needed doing around the house. Dad remained in Sydney recovering from further surgery to his legs. The surgeons were at last confident they had put sufficient rods, bolts and screws into his limbs to enable him to walk again, aided by walking sticks to help with balance. Now he was undergoing months of rehabilitation at another hospital in Sydney.

Part of mum's problem was depression. The accident had taken away her father-in-law as well as Lynda her one and only beautiful daughter. The family business had had to be sold for what was a disappointingly low price and my parents had only a small on-going income. Dad looked like being an invalid for the rest of his life and would be difficult to manage. In the meantime, mum felt physically and mentally spent. Realistically, what was there for her to look forward to?

In an attempt to help mum, I encouraged her to invite some friends to come over and spend time with her. Mum had been a member of the Country Women's Association (CWA) before the accident and their members proved a great support. The CWA organised a roster of folk to visit twice a week and bring something tasty to share with mum. It was the company that was most important though. This steady flow of visitors seemed to help.

I'll never forget the first day I cycled up the steep hill to Greystones because my knee was still sore. The house was indeed grey, having been constructed of grey sandstone blocks from the local quarry. When Mr Bassington retired from his prominent job in Sydney, he and his wife decided to move to the country and had selected our small town because the land was cheap and they could purchase ten acres on top of a hill offering stunning views. Some of the locals were, initially, suspicious of these "Sydney millionaires" with their snobby airs and graces when they first descended on the town, but they mellowed when the building of the mansion and the extensive garden landscaping created jobs for many of the tradesmen about town.

Greystones was the largest house I had ever visited; no expense had been spared. The ten-acre property was completely surrounded by a grey stone wall and when I finally puffed my way up to the impressive wrought iron gates, I looked back and gazed across the valley with our township nestled snugly below. I stood for a moment or two picking out special places: my home, the garage, the school, the hospital, the park, Norah Malden's station master's cottage, my grandparents' old house and, of course, Janice's home. Bathed in sunshine, my town looked a peaceful paradise.

I turned around to face the shiny black iron gates held in position by two massive grey stone pillars with splendid carved lions atop, challenging all those who entered. A gardener saw me waiting and walked over to open the gates. A moment later Mrs Bassington, resplendent in her new wheelchair, welcomed me at the grand entrance to Greystones.

The elderly Mrs Bassington looked surprisingly fitter than when I had last seen her in a hospital bed the previous week. She sported a smart purple hair-do, was wearing a colourful floral dress and had sparingly used lipstick and make up on her face. Even her fingernails were painted. She sat bolt upright in her new wheel chair and greeted me with a broad smile. She was still thin but was very much in command of her faculties.

It was soon agreed I would work three five-hour shifts on Mondays, Wednesdays and Fridays. Mrs Bassington had gone so far as to list the jobs I should do on each of these days. Together, we moved around the house with me pushing her wheel-chair and she doing the explaining. Before he died, Mr Bassington had also experienced mobility problems which had necessitated a lift, large enough to accommodate a wheelchair, being installed. So, getting up and down floors was no barrier for Mrs Bassington.

As we moved about the house a number of things impressed me. The furniture was stylish and expensive and the walls displayed many works of art. Mrs Bassington saw me looking carefully at one of her paintings and remarked, 'Nearly everything on the walls is a print, my dear, although we do have a couple of small originals. My husband, being English, was an enthusiastic collector of British art. If you look around you'll see prints of works by Constable, Turner, Stubbs, Blake and many others. Do you like art?'

'I don't really know. I haven't had much chance to find out,' I confessed.

'Well,' she said, 'I'll have to complete your education, then.'

'Mrs Bassington, what's the music playing throughout the house?'

'My dear boy it's Beethoven, the Pastoral Symphony to be precise. I love classical music and it's piped throughout the house so I can listen without interruption wherever I happen to be.'

'Wow,' was my sadly inadequate response.

'I suppose you're going to tell me you don't like classical music?' she commented, 'not many people of your age listen to the classics, more's the pity.'

'I'm sorry,' I stuttered, 'I don't think I've ever heard any classical music.'

'Here we go again,' Mrs Bassington sighed, 'I don't know what's becoming of the younger set these days.'

I didn't know how to answer that so I kept quiet.

* * *

It didn't take long to get into a cleaning routine at Mrs Bassington's mansion. We got along well and I found her kind and considerate. Before long, under Mrs Bassington's tutelage, I could recognise the artist responsible for many of the prints on the walls and even knew the titles of a few. Most surprisingly, I began to like some of the classical music Mrs Bassington constantly played in the back ground. Whenever I had the chance, I would ask her who the composer was so that I started to "have an ear" for certain composers. We played a sort of game. Mrs Bassington would bombard me with the music of only one composer for the whole morning and before I left, I had to tell her the name of that composer. Soon I found I was able to recognise Mozart, Tchaikovsky, Beethoven, Brahms, Haydn, Bach and several others. Mr Bassington's English bias meant we sometimes listened to Vaughan Williams, Purcell, Britten, Holst, Elgar and the light operas of Gilbert and Sullivan. Mrs Bassington did much to widen my education.

Dad finally came home six months after the accident having made good progress in the rehabilitation hospital. He could get about with a specially designed walker. Dad's return encouraged mum to resume her domestic duties and play the role of the faithful housewife again. This was great for me. As mum took on more of the domestic work, I steadily pulled back so that by the end of the year, when I turned sixteen, we had arrived at a far more satisfactory arrangement.

Coinciding with mum's increased activity at home was a slow deterioration in Mrs Bassington's health. She confided in me quietly one morning. For many years she had smoked and now she was paying the price, suffering from a nasty respiratory illness called emphysema. She explained that the prognosis was not good and she would gradually get worse. There wasn't much the doctors could do for her, she admitted. As Mrs Bassington found carrying out her normal duties was becoming increasingly difficult, she employed me for longer hours. This suited me fine. By the end of the year, I was working thirty hours a week including two hours for shopping. It was harrowing, however, observing Mrs Bassington's gradual decline.

It was while out shopping for Mrs Bassington one afternoon that I ran into Janice. I hadn't seen her since I had left the Fenton's home when they had so kindly taken me in. Janice was often in my thoughts, though, despite the fact I knew she was going out with Dean Hartcher. I still had strong feelings for Janice and hoped that somehow, we two might get together as a couple. Dean Hartcher seemed destined for great things; he had been accepted to study law at the University of Sydney. In my darker moments I asked myself if I was stupid to dream that Janice would ever be interested in me. Compared to Dean, I was a "nothing;" illiterate, poor job prospects and not particularly good at anything. Any sensible girl would surely look for better prospects in a future partner.

Janice was standing at the end of a short queue waiting to be served in "Charlie's, Your Friendly Family Store." As I came round the kitchen utensils section, I had a moment to have a good look at her without her knowing. She was as pretty as ever. Although still dressed in school uniform, I admired Janice's shapely figure and the wave of her blonde hair. She was standing patiently with her arm through the handle of a wicker basket. Schools insisted on modest dressing, so Janice wore no jewellery. I moved quickly to be next in line behind this lovely girl.

'Janice?'

She turned and smiled broadly, 'Hello Norman, I haven't seen you for ages. How are things?'

'Not too bad, thanks.'

In the last few months, I had shot up another couple of inches. I was now looking down slightly at the girl of my dreams and marvelling at those blue eyes and the honest, open face.

'I was hoping you'd call round sometime to tell us how your parents were doing?'

I blushed. 'I've been too busy looking after them and working up at Greystones.'

'That's no excuse,' she pouted, 'anyway, how are they?'

'Next please…' called the shop keeper.

Janice was now at the head of the queue and I had no chance to reply. We both made our purchases. Anxious to enjoy every minute with Janice, I suggested we have ice creams. I bought them and we went outside to sit on the one long wooden seat that Charlie offered his customers. It was hot out there in the full sun and we were forced to quickly lick our dripping strawberry cones. I needed to get back to Mrs Bassington since she was actually paying me to sit here and scoff an ice cream with the girl of my dreams. As I rose to leave, Janice said, 'Norman, can you come round to our place tomorrow? Mum would love to see you and catch up on your news.'

Tomorrow was a Saturday and it was quickly arranged I would come round for afternoon tea at three. Suddenly, in the space of a few minutes, the world seemed a better place!

16. BRANCHING OUT...

On Saturday morning I surprised mum by making a double batch of date slice; one batch for home consumption the other to take round to the Fentons as my contribution towards the afternoon tea. The upside of spending weeks caring for mum was that I had further developed my cooking acumen, although still under the watchful eye of my convalescing mother. That afternoon I donned some respectable clothes, strapped my tin of date slices to the carrier on the back of my bike and arrived at the Fentons a few minutes past three.

Not unexpectedly, it was the loquacious Mrs Fenton who came to the front door to welcome me. I moved through the house to the accompaniment of Mrs Fenton's views on the weather, the test cricket and teenage crime. When we reached the dining room I was surprised to find Mr Fenton was home for the weekend sitting at the dining room table with his daughter, both eying off a large plate of sandwiches. We were rather formal and I sat in the same place allotted to me when I stayed with them months back. Mr Fenton launched into his predictions about the prospects for merino sheep this year until interrupted by Mrs Fenton who sailed in from the kitchen carrying a plate bearing my date slice.

'Look what a clever young man Norman is,' she chuckled as she carefully lowered the plate of date slices in front of Janice, 'you two will have to have a bake off one day to see who cooks the yummiest date slice and Mr Fenton and I will be the judges.' She peeled into laughter at her creative suggestion. I glanced at Janice to see her blue eyes studying my face. I tried to read those lovely eyes. Were they admiring, mocking, disbelieving, doubting, loving? I couldn't tell…

We chatted comfortably about a range of topics while we polished off almost all the sandwiches, a substantial piece of Mrs Denton's rich fruit cake and finally raided my date slice. Mr Denton then politely excused himself, professing some office work awaited him, while Mrs Denton promised to do the cleaning up, which left Janice and me to our own devices. At her suggestion, we went out to the back garden and sat down on the easy chairs in the deep shade of their healthy mulberry tree. Here, away from her parents, we felt more relaxed and spent the time catching up on our separate doings.

Now that Janice was sixteen, she had commenced driving lessons, going out mostly with her mother, but having a proper lesson with a driving instructor once a week. School was going well she assured me. Next year she would be in her final school year and in November would sit for her leaving certificate. She was still intent on going to a Teachers' College to become an infants or primary school teacher. I felt I had little to report to Janice, apart from updating her on the slow recovery journeys my parents were still making. Janice was interested, though, in hearing about Mrs Bassington and the palatial Greystones.

'Norman…forgive me asking, but what are *your* plans for the future?'

I was ill-prepared for such a question and fumbled around to come up with some sort of a credible answer. In desperation, I told a harmless white lie. I was so anxious to impress.

'I'm going to start a business.'

'Really? What sort of a business?'

'A cleaning business.'

Having told the lie, I reckoned I might as well keep building on the idea, make it appear as though I had been planning this for a time. Those beautiful blue eyes were sparkling; Janice was genuinely interested.

'But Norman…how can you start a business if you can't read or write?'

'Easy, I'll get mum or dad to do that part of it. I'll do the cleaning work and they can do the paper work. It's a cinch.'

'Have they agreed to help you?'

'Not yet, but I'm sure they will.'

'You'll have to move from here then.'

'Why?'

'Oh come on Norman, there aren't many people in this little town who are going to want your cleaning services are there? You'll need to move to a bigger place, you'll have to branch out, spread your wings.'

'Yes, I suppose so…'

'I'm really proud of you, Norman. It's a great idea and I think it might work.'

Janice was genuinely impressed and I glowed with false pride. Perhaps I had stumbled onto something? Perhaps, if I continued with this crazy idea of setting up a business, Janice would see me in a better light and become my girlfriend? I decided to add a little cream to the mix.

'I've been thinking about what my trading name will be…'

'Really?'

'Yes, I've got a few ideas floating around in my head.'

'Do tell me, Norman.'

'I'll buy one of those groovy little white panel vans and have my trading name emblazoned on the sides and on the back. The signs might say, "Norm's Cleaning Services, No Job Too Dirty!" or," Clean Up Your Act with Norm!"'

'How exciting, Norman. When are you going to start?'

'Sometime soon,' I said, leaving my answer deliberately vague, 'sometime soon…'

That night, as I lay in bed, I turned our conversation over and over in my mind. Quite by chance I had hit on an exciting possibility for the future. Could I really turn my little white lie into a little white van? Could I actually open a cleaning business, something real, something substantial, something that would raise my stakes in Janice's eyes? The more I thought about the idea, the more enamoured I became. Janice was right though. This little town could never support a cleaning business; I needed to branch out and move to a larger place. In three weeks, I would turn sixteen and be permitted to start learning to drive. Getting my driver's licence had to be my number one priority.

* * *

Dad stayed in bed in the mornings and mum took his breakfast to him. We were both worried about his mental health. If anything was not exactly as dad wanted it he flew into a rage and would shout and swear and threaten us with all kinds of horrible outcomes. The doctors advised us that dad had suffered brain damage in the accident and this was causing his uncontrolled outbursts. Other than drugging him with tranquillisers, there was nothing more they could do. I could see the temper tantrums were particularly distressing for mum since this was not the man she had married twenty years ago. Dad had a brass bell sitting at the side of his bed which he rang whenever he wanted attention. On this particular morning, he rang it angrily just as I was about to open up to mum about my new found business plans. Mercifully, dad only needed our assistance to move from his bed to his wheelchair, but five minutes later he was ranting again.

'Where the hell's my bloody breakfast? You fucking loafers are sitting in there scoffing yours and leaving me, a bloody cripple, to bloody well starve. Get off your arses and do something for a change!'

Mum rolled her eyes and hurried over to the sideboard to pick up the tray she had prepared some time earlier with everything laid out ready for dad's breakfast. I opened the bedroom door so mum could sweep in with the tray without a moment's delay.

'I'm coming dear,' mum called out as the bell was shaken violently a second time.

'About bloody time,' dad snarled.

'Did you sleep any better?' mum inquired as she placed the tray before him.

'I need a pee. Quick, get that bloody bottle for me.'

Mum moved the tray and passed dad the bottle. With no attempt at modesty, dad yanked back the opening in his pyjamas and urinated loudly while mum stood meekly by. Job done, he thrust the bottle at her as if she was a lowly servant. Embarrassed by this oafish behaviour, I took the bottle from mum, with dad still carrying on as I left the room. Mum also beat a hasty retreat as soon as she was able.

'Mum, this can't go on like this, dad's a total pain. Either he has to be more heavily sedated or he has to go into some kind of care where there are people trained to look after patients with severe brain damage. It's not fair on you trying to look after him.'

Mum reached for the teapot, refilled her cup and sat down at the kitchen table.

'He's getting worse, not better. Whatever medication they've put him on it's not working. I'm at my wits end, Norman. We have no money coming in, except for a small invalid pension for dad and the contribution you're so generously making towards our weekly expenses. I really need to get a job at the hospital again but there's no way I can work while looking after your dad full time. I don't know what to do.'

'We *have* to get the brain specialist to examine him again and bump up his daily dosage or find a place for him in an appropriate hospital somewhere.'

'Dad would never forgive me if I allowed him to go into an institution.'

'Face facts mum, if we don't get something done soon, you'll end up in an institution!'

I could see mum was close to tears, so I backed off.

'It's so frustrating. Did I tell you matron rang me yesterday asking if I could come back to work? They're short staffed. I'd love to go back and we desperately need the money.'

'Okay, that's it, get on the phone straightaway and ring the specialist. Demand a reassessment for dad. If we don't...'

My sentence was cut off by the furious ringing of that awful bell and the sound of dad yelling obscenities from his bedroom.

* * *

We were fortunate. A cancellation came through, unexpectedly, allowing dad to be re-admitted to the trauma ward in Sydney to be reassessed by his brain specialist. Following another battery of tests, with dad totally uncooperative, the specialist agreed that dad's condition had deteriorated significantly and he needed to be admitted to a special ward at another hospital. Here, we were told, the staff would try electric shock treatment, a revolutionary and controversial new therapy used for a limited range of brain injuries. The specialist made no promises. It worked amazingly well, he claimed, in some cases. Initially, dad's course of treatment would last six weeks.

This was the respite mum desperately needed. For the first two days she simply slept. Then, feeling a new woman, she rang matron and was back fulltime the very next day. Now that mum was less stressed, I decided to approach her again about my own plans. My opportunity came shortly after she returned from her day shift.

'Mum...can I chat to you about an idea I have?'

She was sitting in the lounge with her feet up, enjoying the curried egg sandwiches I'd made for her.

'Of course, dear. My feet are killing me. I'm taking longer than I expected to get used to being on my pegs for eight hours every day. I still get muscular pains from the accident, you know. Anyway, what's the great idea?'

'I want to move to a much larger town for work.'

'Really?'

'Yup, there's not much cleaning work for me here. Mrs Bassington's great, but I don't think she'll be able to stay in that huge place much longer. She's in her eighties, you know. Nobody else around town is likely to need my cleaning services. That means I have to go to a bigger place where I can get heaps more work. So, I'm planning to start a business of my own, if you could help me with the paper work, please?'

'But you're only sixteen Norman! How can you possibly run a business when you haven't even got your driver's licence yet, let alone a car...'

'I'll use my bike to get about.'

'Oh, yes? I don't want to sound like a wet rag dear, but how will you carry your cleaning gear about if you're on a bicycle?'

'Easy! I'll fix one of those trailers on the back.'

'Okay...let me think about this for a minute. Where are you thinking of going? Where will you live? And you'll have to find yourself accommodation. I don't know how you'll manage on your own with your reading problem?'

'I can't answer any of your questions yet mum, but I really want to give this a try. I have to find a town that's nearby so I can get your help when I need it. Do you have any friends in the towns around here where I might be able to get board?'

Mum wiped her fingers slowly and thoughtfully on her serviette and had a slurp of her tea.

'Did you put sugar in this, Norman?'

'Yes, perhaps I forgot to stir it.'

'All our relations live interstate so that's no help. I do have a good friend who lives in Shelford who I worked with for several years. She recently went through a messy divorce and her husband moved out. She has three kids, but I know two have flown the nest. The youngest daughter, Celeste, is still at home I think.'

'Do you think your friend might be interested in having a boarder? Shelford is quite a large place and my job prospects would be far better there. There are even a few factories in Shelford and that new open cut gold mine has recently opened a few miles out of town. Big places need cleaners, don't they…'

'Get me another cup of tea will you, love. And this time, be sure to put in two spoonfuls of sugar and stir them in properly.'

I grabbed mum's mug and retreated to the kitchen, feeling mildly hopeful. When I returned mum was already on the phone and gestured for me to leave her tea on the side table. I picked up the gist of her conversation; she was speaking to her friend in Shelford. Mum spent the first ten minutes catching up on old times, sharing a laugh about a couple of cranky old matrons they had both endured many years ago. Then mum came round to the real reason for her call. I listened more intently.

'Norman's very tidy, Jayne…and as honest as they come…lovely manners…happy to help around the house…works hard…'

At the end of the call mum replaced the receiver and looked across at me.

'Well?' I asked.

'Jayne's going to think about it, Norman. She's still adjusting to her new life with no husband and only one child still at home. She wants to discuss the idea of taking in a boarder with her daughter, Celeste, before deciding. She's promised to ring back within the week.'

I went to bed that night hopeful my attempt to branch out into pastures new was a real possibility.

17. MOVING ON...

I didn't have to wait long. Mum's friend, Mrs Jayne Franchanji, rang back three days later with a firm offer. I could have one of the boys' bedrooms and full board which meant all meals included. She was happy for the arrangement to start in two weeks' time on a trial basis for a period of three months. She suggested mum and I come over sometime next weekend to have a look before we accepted. This we did.

Mrs Franchanji was friendly and enthusiastic about the idea of having me as a boarder. Jokingly, she suggested it would be like having one of her own boys about the place again since the three men in her life had all left during the last twelve months. She even went as far as asking me what meals I liked and disliked. Celeste, Mrs Franchanji's daughter, was out playing netball but I saw a school photograph of her and noted her remarkably good looks. It was arranged that mum would drive me over on Sunday week and I would pay my board a week in advance. The only restrictions were no smoking or alcohol in the house.

Mum was supportive but did have one major concern. How was she going to cope with dad on her own when he returned home in a month's time? She had already signed on as a casual nurse's aide at the hospital; work she was enjoying. Dad would probably need round the clock care, forcing mum to stop work again. There appeared to be no other solution. We both hoped like hell that a miracle would happen and dad would come home virtually cured.

My immediate challenge was having to break the news to dear old Mrs Bassington that I would be resigning in a little over a week's time. I decided to tell her on Monday morning which would give her time to find a replacement. As I sweated up the hill, peddling frantically, I turned over in my mind the words I might use to explain my decision and what I could do to make the transition to a new cleaner easier for her. Mrs Bassington was a delightful human being and I felt bad about deserting her. I had learnt much about the English artists and classical music in the few months I had worked at Greystones.

The large wrought iron gates were wide open as I crested the hill and was surprised to find an ambulance parked outside the main entrance. The gardener, who was hovering around, told me Mrs Bassington had had a nasty fall in the kitchen that morning. He had found her lying on the floor unable to get up. The ambulance officer had confirmed she had a broken wrist and had possibly broken a bone in her leg.

Anxious to do whatever I could to help, I bounded up the entrance steps and made my way to the spacious kitchen where I found Mrs Bassington shaken, but smiling, sitting up on one of those special ambulance trolleys. The ambulance officer was tidying up the last of his gear and preparing to wheel Mrs Bassington out to the ambulance.

'Oh Norman, I'm so pleased you've arrived before this nice young man whisks me off to hospital. I have a terrible confession to make.'

Mrs Bassington was still in her nightclothes and started shivering as she spoke. Seeing this, the officer wrapped a blanket around her shoulders and remarked, 'You'd better make your confession straightaway Mrs Bassington because we're ready to go.'

'Oh, dear. I don't feel very well either. Norman dear, when you leave, please turn off the lights and lock up. I really do need to speak with you as soon as possible. Can you come down to the hospital later this afternoon please? I fear they might keep me in overnight.'

'Yes, of course…'

And, with a weak wave of her good arm, she was gone. Perhaps fittingly, the music playing as she disappeared was "The Four Last Songs" of Richard Strauss.

I completed my usual five hours of cleaning and gardening before circulating around the house to check every light and gadget was switched off, windows properly closed and doors locked. The bad news about my resignation would now have to wait until the afternoon.

* * *

Later that afternoon I picked a bunch of colourful roses from Josie's garden next door. I wrapped the stems up well in old newspaper and headed off to our small local hospital. Mum had been on duty there during the morning when Mrs Bassington had been admitted and confirmed she was being kept in overnight for observation.

I found Mrs Bassington sitting up in bed trying to drink a cup of tea with one, unsteady hand. She was looking considerably better than when I had last seen her and managed to give me a pleasant smile. One arm was now in plaster and supported by a sling. There was a small plaster on her forehead where she had bashed her head on the side of the kitchen table. I inquired how she was feeling and asked one of the nurses if the flowers could be put into a vase. Thankfully the x-rays had shown her leg was not broken, just sprained.

'Norman, that is so kind of you to bring in such lovely flowers. Are they from my garden?'

I had to admit I had raided Josie's place next door.

'Can you find a chair somewhere, Norman?'

I returned a moment later with a well-used chair from the corridor and sat down slowly, stealing myself for the task of informing Mrs Bassington that I was about to desert her. However, she spoke first.

'Norman, I have some bad news for you I'm afraid. Greystones is too large a property for me on my own nowadays so I have put it on the market. There'll be an auction in a fortnight. I couldn't tell you earlier because it was only yesterday that I agreed the terms with the real estate people. It means I'll no longer require your services after next week. You have done such an excellent job and I'm hugely grateful to you. Because this is such short notice, and I feel awfully embarrassed, I promise to pay you for an additional six weeks. I hope in a small way this will make up for the lateness of this advice?'

Mrs Bassington was looking at me pleadingly and I melted. Without thinking whether it was appropriate or not, I reached out and gently held her good hand.

'I'm so sorry you feel you must sell but I understand your reasons. More to the point, how are you going to manage when the hospital discharges you?'

'That's all taken care of, my dear. My niece in Shelford is coming to stay with me for a couple of weeks until I'm better. Then I plan to go into one of those "three in one" places.'

'Three in one place? What's that?'

'You buy a unit and live independently on your own for as long as possible. Then, when you find cooking and looking after yourself is getting too difficult, you move into the second stage, an assisted care unit. The third stage is when you are bed-ridden and need full time nursing. The three stages are located on the same site which is why it's called a "three in one". Clever, isn't it?'

I nodded.

'Mrs Bassington, I don't think you should pay me the additional six weeks of wages.'

'Why ever not?'

'Because today I was going to give you, *my resignation. I'm moving in two weeks' time to Shelford. I was going to tell you this morning but when I arrived you were being carted off in an ambulance.*'

'Well, isn't life full of unexpected tricks! It has all worked out beautifully in the end, hasn't it? I'd still like to give you the extra six weeks of wages though Norman as a special thank you. You deserve it! If you hadn't come along when you did I would have had to leave six months ago.'

'That's really kind of you, Mrs Bassington. It will be a huge help because I want to set up my own cleaning business in Shelford.'

'What a wonderful initiative, good luck with it! One more thing, Norman. Now that I've introduced you to some art works, I want you to have two of my prints. Everything has to be sold, except for a couple of my favourite prints which I'll keep for my retirement unit. The prints won't fetch much, but some of my furniture is excellent quality and should sell well.'

'That's very kind of you.'

'So, you know where the key is. Have a good look around Greystones and select the two prints you would like. Now, if you'll excuse me, I think I might have a nap.'

'Yes, of course Mrs Bassington. I hope you get home soon and start to feel yourself again.'

* * *

A few days later I was going through my belongings trying to decide what to take to Shelford. I had seen the room that Mrs Franchanji had allocated for me and realised it was quite small. It contained a wooden cupboard, large enough to hold my clothes and footwear and a desk that was no use to me, except as a table. Dad had a large old trunk that I planned to take if it fitted into mum's car. I would keep my cleaning gear in the trunk. I didn't think Mrs Franchanji would allow me to put my two prints up on her walls so they would have to stay with mum. I had been to Greystones and selected two prints of J.W. Turner's marvellous impressionistic seascapes.

Mum had popped home to have lunch with me and we had just sat down when the trauma specialist, who had been treating dad in Sydney, rang. The news was mixed. Dad had shown slight signs of responding to the electric shock treatment and the specialist recommended he remain in hospital for a further six weeks for a second complete round of the treatment. In essence, the specialist wanted mum's permission to repeat the treatment. Mum was more than happy to give the green light and assured the specialist that the two of us would come down to visit dad again soon.

All was now in readiness for me to make my much anticipated move to Shelford.

18. SHELFORD

Mario Franchanji migrated to Australia during the 1930s depression and threw himself into market gardening along the fertile river flats where the town of Shelford was situated. Soon he owned a couple of small plots of land and began to make money. A few years later he opened a small but lucrative business in town where he successfully sold his local produce. Along the way he married Jayne, a pretty young nurse who had migrated from the United Kingdom. The marriage was a happy one for twenty years until Mario became restless and fell hopelessly in love with another much younger woman. Mario and Jayne had divorced six months before I came to stay as a boarder.

When I arrived Jayne was still getting over the pain of the divorce. Her two older children, Paolo and Antonio had recently left home, one to join the navy and the other to study medicine at the University of Sydney. With only her daughter, Celeste, still at home, Jayne had returned to nursing. After the noise and bustle of five energetic people in the house for so long, it now felt empty and Jayne confessed to sometimes being lonely. Another person in the house, in the form of a paying boarder, might just help fill the void.

It was a hot Sunday afternoon in January when mum and I arrived at Mrs Franchanji's home and sweated our way into Mrs Franchanji's house lugging dad's heavy trunk and two old suitcases.

18. Shelford

Heaving my belongings upstairs without scratching the walls was a tricky operation and we were pleased when Jayne invited us into her relatively cool lounge for refreshments afterwards.

Jayne, for that is how she asked me to address her, was probably nearing fifty and losing her good looks. She made no effort to dress smartly, or even attractively, and wore a lose-fitting plain patterned dress, no stockings and sandals. Her hair was roughly brushed back with the occasional greying hairs showing through. Sun-tanned hands and face were sure signs of her passion for gardening, an interest she had shared with her ex-husband, Mario. I could imagine her as a no-nonsense nurse, efficient and competent.

The double storey house was large but tidy. Mario's Italian background was in evidence in the choice of heavy dark furniture and several enlarged photographs of Italy: the Coliseum, the Leaning Tower of Pisa, the Vatican and various Venetian canals. Another wall contained a collection of family photographs that had recently been re-arranged and reduced in number as a consequence of the marriage break-up. There were no pictures of Mario anywhere but heaps of mum and the three children. Again, I was struck by how pretty Celeste was, the youngest member of the family, whom I was yet to meet.

Jayne did us proud with her refreshments, producing large bowls of gelato with a halo of raspberries freshly picked from the garden and accompanied by thirst-quenching lime sodas. If these refreshments were anything to go by, I could look forward to being well provided for in the food department. Mum and Jayne fell naturally into nursing talk for before Jayne turned to look at me.

'Now Norman, do you have any violent dislikes with particular kinds of food?'

'Not really.'

'Yes, you do,' mum interrupted, 'you won't eat oysters for one and you always complain if I put coconut on anything.'

'Do you like Italian food?' asked Jayne.

'I don't think I've tried any.'

'What? Never tried pasta, spaghetti, or pizza?'

'I've had spaghetti a few times, mum does it sometimes.'

'Well, we have to broaden your horizons then…'

The conversation was cut short by the sudden entry of Celeste, back from playing netball. She looked even more vibrant and attractive than her photographs. She ran over to her mum, bent over to give her a kiss revealing a gorgeous pair of slim toned legs. Then she turned and flashed a happy smile at mum and then me.

'Darling this is Mrs McDade, with whom I once nursed and our new boarder, Norman.'

'Hello, Mrs Mc Dade, hi Norman.' Celeste held my gaze for a moment. 'Mum, some of the girls are going to the movies tonight. Can I go, please?'

'What's on?'

'I've no idea but Susan said it was a scream and well worth seeing. Please mum…there's about six of us going.'

'And what are you all doing afterwards?'

'We'll probably go to Sammie's Bar for a milkshake.'

'As long as you are back home by ten at the latest,' Jayne insisted.

'I promise mum. Now I really need a shower. Good bye Mrs McDade. See you later Norman,' and with a little skip she turned and was gone.

I'd never seen such a lovely girl. Celeste had barely been in the room thirty seconds yet I was smitten. Incredible legs…a beautiful face…vivacious…Wow!

* * *

That first evening there was only Jayne and me for the evening meal. Mum had returned home and Celeste had left to go to the movies with her netball friends. I found Jayne easy to get along with and I'm sure she was pleased to have my company. I still remember that first meal. It was lamb chops and heaps of vegetables, desserts were stewed plums from Jayne's garden with custard. I volunteered to help with the washing up and my offer was welcomed. When we finished, Jayne found the local newspaper.

'Norman, your mum told me you have a problem with reading and writing and asked me to help looking for job vacancies in Shelford for you.'

I blushed. It was still embarrassing to be reminded of my disability.

'The weekend paper usually has heaps of job ads so let's have a look and see what's available.'

She thumbed through to the back of the paper to the section headed "JOB VACANCIES".

'Now Norman, are you only looking for cleaning jobs?'

'Yes.'

'Ah…here we are. There are three jobs listed under "Cleaners" this week. One is in a private home, one is in a factory and the third is up at the hospital where I work. How about that! The private home is only for a few hours a week but the other two are probably full-time positions. If you get the hospital job, I might be able to drive you there and back sometimes. What do you think?'

'I think I'll try for both the factory and the hospital jobs.'

'Good thinking. Both ads have phone numbers to ring so use my phone first thing Monday morning. I'll circle the numbers for you… pass me that pen will you. There…the top number is the hospital job. Okay?'

'Yes, that's great, thanks.'

I tried the hospital's cleaning job first. The woman who answered took my phone number and promised someone would ring me later. Next, I rang the factory, which manufactured white goods such as refrigerators and washing machines.

'Sorry mate, job's gone,' was the factory's curt reply.

So, I was obliged to hang around at home waiting for the hospital to call back. They never did. Shortly after four o'clock Jayne arrived home, tired after her eight-hour shift.

'Ring them again,' she urged, 'you have to chase jobs. Jobs won't chase you, be pro-active.'

I did as Jayne suggested and this time spoke to someone called the employment officer.

'Any experience?' the employment officer asked.

'Yes,' and I told her of the three private homes I'd worked in.

'Only casual part time work, then?'

'Yes, but I have excellent references.'

There was a long pause before the employment officer responded. 'Okay, I'll slot you in for an interview tomorrow morning at mid-day. Bring your references with you. Bye...'

* * *

I fronted up at the hospital's administration office at a quarter to twelve. Jayne had kindly allowed me to ride one of the boys' bikes to the hospital for my interview. Never having been formally interviewed before, I was really nervous. Jayne had given me some tips on how to be a successful interviewee, while Celeste sat the whole time listening and watching me with those luscious eyes.

'You must appear confident. Look the interviewer in the eyes, smile and make sure you are nicely dressed. Always be polite and most importantly, give full answers to their questions. It's no good just saying "yes" or "no."' I kept going over Jayne's tips as I cycled to the hospital.

The hospital's receptionist took me along a long corridor and told me to take a seat. 'They'll call you when they're ready,' she assured me.

I sat down on the nearest chair, fiddling nervously with my treasured references from Mrs Bassington and Grandpa. There were three other people sitting on chairs on the opposite side of the corridor to me. I observed them discretely, assuming I was competing against them for the cleaning job. One was an older man, who looked scruffy with a three or four-day stubble and unkempt hair. Mentally,

18. Shelford

I dismissed him for his poor presentation. If he couldn't present a clean, washed appearance, how could he possibly keep hospital wards clean? Next to the scruffy man was a youngish woman who, even to my unpractised eye, appeared to be heavily pregnant. I eliminated her too on account of the fact that she would have to leave work soon to give birth to her baby. This left the third candidate, who was middle aged and clearly a new Australian from somewhere in Eastern Europe. Quite possibly she didn't speak English, which would be to my advantage.

It was at least half an hour before I was called, the other three having already left. Even though Jayne had given me her tips, I was not sure what to expect. The door opened suddenly and a smartly dressed lady looked at me, 'Mr Norman McDade?'

I jumped to my feet, 'Yes, that's me.'

'Come in please…'

It was a large airy room with ground to ceiling windows letting in the sunlight. To my horror there were *three* people sitting in a row behind a couple of tables watching my entry. I had expected a one-to-one chat. The smartly dressed lady pointed to where I should sit and joined her three colleagues on the other side of the tables. A large suited man with a moustache spoke first. He looked as though he was in charge.

'Good afternoon, my name is Mr Drebden and I'll be chairing this interview. Now, what's your name, please?'

'I'm Norman…Norman McDade, sir.'

'How old are you, Norman?'

'I'm sixteen and a half, sir.'

'Why do you want to be a cleaner?'

"I'm good at it, sir.'

'Is that so? Have you had any experience as a cleaner?'

'Oh, yes sir, lots.'

'Really?' The chairman appeared amused.

'Yes, sir. I've brought references for you to see.' I jumped up and placed my two precious references on the table in front of the chairman. Mum had read then to me a few days ago, so I knew they were most complimentary. The chairman glanced at them and passed them to the thin lady sitting on his left.

'Have a read of these will you Dorothy, please. My colleague, Mr James, who is the head cleaner at the hospital will ask you some questions.'

Mr James was a tall angular man, strongly built but with a kindly face. He smiled at me revealing a gap in his teeth. There was a lengthy scar on the side of his face and I wondered if it was a war wound.

'Norman, what do you know about keeping hospitals clean? Germs spread quickly if cleaners don't do their jobs thoroughly.'

'I don't know much about hospital cleaning, Mr James, but I had to wash the kitchen and bathroom floors at my other jobs.'

'Have you used disinfectants?'

'Oh yes.'

The lady called Dorothy passed my references across to Mr James and asked me the next question.

'Your references show you have only been doing part-time jobs. This job requires a forty-hour week, that's five eight-hour shifts. How do we know you can work that long every week?'

'I'm young and fit.' To emphasise this, I flexed my right arm and thumped my muscles. This amused them all.

Mr Drebden cleared his throat and took control of the interview again.

'If we employ you, when can you start?'

'Today!' I responded with enthusiasm. Again, the panel seemed amused.

'Thank you for coming in Norman. We'll let you know in the next day or so if you've been successful. Miss Hargrove, would you please photocopy these references and get Norman's contact details before he leaves.'

The smartly dressed lady, who had been taking notes throughout my interview, rose to her feet and asked me to follow her into the office. There, she did the necessary paper work and told me she thought the panel liked me. Ten minutes later I jumped back on the bike and rode back to my new home feeling pretty good about my first interview. My move to Shelford already looked promising!

19. THE HOSPITAL JOB

I felt well pleased with myself as I rode the Franchanji's bicycle out of the hospital grounds and onto the road. The smartly dressed lady had told me, confidentially, that the panel "liked me" and I believed that was a good omen. Amazingly, my inability to read or write had not been a problem since there had been no papers to read or forms to complete. I hadn't even had to put my signature anywhere. To celebrate my promising interview, I stopped at a corner shop and bought a strawberry milk shake. I had nothing to do for the rest of the afternoon and took the opportunity to look around Shelford. It was a busy town, attractively laid out with a number of churches and a large well-established Botanical Garden in the centre of town. Schools finished around three o'clock which meant Celeste might return home soon. I headed off, determined to be back in time to welcome her.

I timed it well. Returning the bicycle to its rightful place at the back of the garage, I used the key Jayne had given me to let myself in and was in the kitchen putting the kettle on when Celeste breezed in.

'Oh…hello,' she said and ran upstairs. A few minutes later she re-appeared having changed out of her school uniform into a blouse and slacks. With a shy smile, Celeste headed straight for the fridge and took out a large plastic container of choc-chip ice cream.

'Want some?' she asked.

'No thanks.'

19. The Hospital Job

Celeste dished out two large scoops, licked the spoon and sat down opposite me. She looked even more attractive in casual attire than her school uniform.

'So, how did the interview go?'

'Okay, I think. They're going to let me know in a day or so.'

'How exciting. Were you scared?'

'A bit.'

A blob of ice cream dropped onto her blouse. Embarrassed, she wiped it off with a finger. The movement was enough to show me that beneath the blouse she had well-formed breasts for a fifteen-year-old.

'Norman... can I ask you a personal question?'

'Depends what it is.'

Celeste was looking at me again with those gorgeous twinkling eyes. She took another mouthful, but kept her eyes on mine.

'Is it true you're illegitimate?'

'No way!' I exclaimed.

'Oh, I'm such a twit! I didn't mean illegitimate, I meant illiterate.' This time she coloured deeply. 'I'm so sorry Norman, that was really stupid of me.'

I laughed, 'As far as I know I'm not illegitimate, but I do confess to being illiterate.'

Without warning, she completely changed the topic, 'Do you have a girlfriend?'

It was my turn to look rather sheepish, 'There's a girl back home I really like, but she's going out with another bloke. I guess the answer is, no.'

'I'd love you to be my boyfriend,' Celeste leaned across the table, invitingly.

I had no idea how to respond to such a frank suggestion. Fortunately, at that precise moment there was a call from the hallway.

'Anybody home?' It was Jayne. Our magic moment was broken.

* * *

Next morning Celeste and Jayne went their separate ways leaving me at home alone hovering anxiously around the telephone like an animal waiting to be fed. To be helpful, I had picked a large bucketful of Jayne's broad beans early that morning. After they left, I sat down near the phone to begin removing the beans from their pods in readiness for Jayne to freeze when she came home in the evening. It took me the best part of an hour. I was just cleaning up when the phone finally rang. I grabbed the receiver, only to discover it was the local butcher wanting to get Jayne's weekly meat order. Half an hour later the phone rang again. Again, I charged over to pick up the receiver.

'Good morning, this is the Franchanji residence. Norman speaking.'

'Good morning, Norman. This is Miss Hargrove from the hospital.'

'Hello, Miss Hargrove…'

'Good news, we are offering you the cleaning job. Initially, you'll be on probation for three months. If you meet our requirements during those three months, you'll then be offered a permanent position. How does that sound?'

'Fantastic, thank you so much!'

'Can you come over this afternoon to do the paperwork?'

'Yes, what time?'

'Let's say… two o'clock? If we get everything organised this afternoon you can start work at seven tomorrow morning. Sound good?'

'Definitely!'

'See you at two o'clock then…'

Once again, I borrowed the bicycle from the garage and pedalled up to the hospital. Miss Hargrove was in her office waiting for me and looking as smart and professional as when I was interviewed. Laid out on her desk were several forms and documents.

'Okay, Norman. This shouldn't take us long. I have here your cleaning contract, a copy of the hospital guidelines, which you need to take home and read, and a form for you to become a member of the Allied Workers' Union if you wish to join.'

I looked crestfallen, 'Miss Hargrove…I…I…I'm illiterate.'

'I beg your pardon?'

'I can't read or write.'

Miss Hargrove looked as though I'd hit her with a sledgehammer, 'Are you fooling with me?'

'No, I'm not. I'm sorry but it's true. I've never been able to read or write.'

'You never mentioned this at the interview.'

'Nobody asked.'

'So, how on earth are we going to do all this paperwork then?'

'I don't know,' I muttered, desperately wishing the floor would open up and swallow me.

'But you're such an intelligent young man, Norman. How come you can't read?'

'It's a long story, Miss Hargrove…'

She looked long and hard at me, then abruptly sat at her desk. 'Sit down Norman, you don't need to be able to read to sweep the floors or do the polishing. I'll help you with these forms. Can you do a signature?'

'Oh yes…I'm really good at doing signatures but you'll have to point to where I have to put them.'

And so, it was. In the next hour my papers were fixed up and it was arranged I meet Mr James, the head cleaner, at seven next morning. I decided against joining the union. Miss Hargrove was instantly promoted to be my favourite human being!

* * *

Celeste, Jayne and I had a bit of a celebration that evening. I was despatched to buy three buckets of hot chips while Jayne opened a bottle of non-alcoholic apple cider. Instead of just having choc-chip ice cream, Jayne picked a heap of soft sweet raspberries from her garden. Although Celeste had homework to finish we found half an hour for the three of us to have a couple of fun games of "Pick-A-Stick." I went to bed early excited about my first real job starting the next day. Jayne lent me her alarm clock set for the unbelievably early time of five-thirty.

It was drizzling next morning when I left in the half-light of pre-dawn. The roads glistened and heavy drops splattered me whenever I rode under trees. My thin plastic raincoat did little to keep me dry. Despite the inclement weather and arriving unpleasantly damp, I felt full of energy and enthusiasm as I parked the bicycle in the bike shed provided for hospital staff. I removed my trouser clips and raincoat and entered the main entrance of the hospital carrying my backpack containing a picnic box of sandwiches Jayne had made for me. My wet shoes were slippery on the highly polished floors as I made my way to see Mr James in his office.

It was still only ten to seven when I knocked tentatively on Mr James's half-open door. In the short conversation we had time for he congratulated me on getting the position and informed me I'd be solely responsible for cleaning wards three and four. He said he would come with me to show me the ropes and warned he would be round once or twice a day to check I was doing everything correctly. Then he looked at his watch and announced it was time to go to the staff room next door to meet "the team". It was customary, he explained, for the seven cleaners the hospital employed to meet and socialise until a quarter past seven every morning before the day's work officially started. This pre-work gathering was excellent for staff morale, he stressed.

I followed my boss into the staff room and was introduced to the six other hospital cleaners. They were a mixed bunch, all blokes and coming from a range of different ages and nationalities. However, I didn't think they were particularly welcoming. They were summing me up too and one of them bluntly expressed his surprise that I was, "Just a kid." Apparently, Mr James seldom joined them in their staff room because they felt constrained by his presence. I was relieved when Mr James took me away to start work in wards three and four.

There was nothing overly challenging in my cleaning duties. Basically, during the morning I was required to mop the floors with a green coloured disinfectant, wipe all the hard surfaces down with a different kind of disinfectant, remove rubbish and waste materials and immediately attend to any spillages. This whole process was repeated in the afternoon. If I ran short of cleaning materials, I had to see Mr Jones, who would replenish. There was nothing to it! I could foresee boredom would soon haunt me unless I punctuated the day with some chats to either the patients or staff. We had forty minutes for a lunch break and this, Mr James instructed me, was to be taken in the cleaners' staff room at noon.

At mid-day, armed with my picnic box containing Jayne's sandwiches, I quietly entered the cleaners' staff room and headed over to the urn to make myself a cup of coffee. The members of the "team" must have arrived early since they were already sitting at the table with steaming cups of tea or coffee.

'Well, look who's here, it's the school kid. Lost your bloody way, have ya? This isn't the school playground you know.'

There was a ripple of laughter from the others sitting around the table.

'Hope you've got mummy's permission to get out of class?' remarked another.

Further sniggers from "the team."

'Don't forget to put your hand up when you need to go to the toilet.' More giggles...

'It's okay, he's still in nappies.' This last comment was met with peals of laughter.

My coffee made, I sat on a seat by the window, on my own. There was a spare seat at the table but I didn't feel like joining them.

Occasionally, on the school bus, I had been ribbed about my learning difficulties but it never lasted and usually someone stepped in to stop it. Never had I experienced anything quite like this. I was now being teased for my youthfulness. What would these men do, I wondered, if they ever discovered I had a serious learning disability?

Sitting on my own and out of the way, the group forgot about me and launched into a spirited discussion about the upcoming footy season and which teams were likely to dominate. I finished my sandwiches and coffee and sat there contemplating what to do next. There was another fifteen minutes of lunch break remaining and I felt silly sitting alone by the window doing nothing. I decided to unobtrusively go to the sink to wash out my cup and quietly leave the room. However, as soon as I moved, my tormentors noticed me and started up again.

'Make sure you go to the toilet before returning to class, Norman.'

'Which one do you go to? The boys or the girls?'

This last comment sent them into hysterics.

'Perhaps we should check whether he's got any balls,' squealed another.

I left my washed cup on the drainer and walked out, accompanied by a cacophony of further derisive comments I couldn't make sense of.

I wandered back to my two wards and began pushing my mop around ten minutes early. I was shaken by what had happened in the staff room and the cruelty of my fellow cleaners. I had to admit I was probably at least ten years younger than any of them. Perhaps, I thought, this sort of thing happened to new employees everywhere? Maybe the most junior person in a group always has to put up with teasing and nastiness? I hoped it would only last a few days until they got used to me and then everything would quieten down. Somebody once told me if you're teased you should never react because that's what the bullies want you to do. It's like baiting a bear; the more you do it, the angrier the bear gets and as a consequence, the more the audience enjoys the spectacle. I decided my best strategy was to totally ignore the taunts. Eventually the fellows would lose interest and I'd be accepted.

At the end of the day, I signed off and cycled home. The rain had lifted and a cool southerly was blowing making it a more pleasant trip. Jayne and Celeste were eager to hear how my first day at work had been. 'Excellent,' I lied.

20. CELESTE

During my third weekend staying as a boarder at Jayne's, my mother came over for the day. It was great to see her. The news about dad was not good, however. He remained at the Sydney Rehabilitation Hospital having scarcely made any progress. It was almost as if he had given up learning how to walk again. The doctors were also still concerned about his chest. The steering wheel had broken several ribs, punctured a lung and caused extensive soft tissue damage. The staff at the Rehabilitation Hospital agreed to persevere with dad for another few weeks, but if he didn't start to make significant progress soon, they would have to consider where he should be moved to on a permanent basis. Mum planned to visit dad next weekend.

At work, I fell into a "survival for sanity" routine. Rather than endure the lunch time abuse, I took to eating my picnic lunches elsewhere. There were plenty of places out of doors under shady trees where I could enjoy my lunch in peace. Sometimes I would meet up with a couple of the maintenance blokes for a bit of company. I rarely set eyes on the other cleaners nor did I want to.

It was during the third week that Mr James asked me to come and see him during my lunch hour. It had come to his attention, he said, that I was avoiding "the team" at lunchtimes and he wanted to know why. I was brutally honest with him. He listened dispassionately,

20. Celeste

then shrugged his shoulders. 'Fair enough,' was his only comment. So, I took it he had no objection to my enforced isolation.

Jayne's cooking was plain but wholesome and there was always enough. "Meat and two veg" was the typical evening meal followed by desserts usually served with ice cream. Jayne's enthusiasm for gardening included a passion for growing her own vegetables together with an array of fruits in season. After work I started helping Jayne in her extensive garden and under her guidance began to learn more about basic horticulture. Initially it was simple weeding or digging over a garden bed, but as I slowly became more proficient, Jayne showed me how to plant, use fertilisers and prune at the appropriate time of year. Now that I was earning a regular wage, I had no problem paying my weekly board. On the whole, Jayne and I continued to get along well.

Whilst working in Jayne's garden I spent time observing the birdlife that frequented the area. As a nature lover, it was a privilege to sit quietly and watch the antics of these feathery friends. There were the common bird varieties you see in everyone's garden: sparrows, starlings, galahs, parrots, willy wagtails. Pigeons, noisy miners and magpies, but some of the shyer, less common varieties could be seen in certain parts of the garden at particular times. A pair of tawny frogmouths frequented the old eucalyptus tree at the back of the garden where they sat together motionless all day, pretending to be pieces of timber. There was also a family of superb blue wrens that flitted in and out of the bushes catching insects. In another part of the garden was a nest of the colourful striated pardalote.

My relationship with Celeste was rather more problematic. It became apparent early on that she had developed a "crush" on me so that living in the same house together started to present some challenges. I didn't consciously encourage Celeste, it just happened. Neither of us wanted Jayne to know. In my case, I was worried Jayne might decide I would have to leave if she thought I was getting too close to her daughter. Celeste, on the other hand, was convinced her mother would never approve of her fifteen-year-old daughter having a romantic relationship with a boy and would be furious. These mutual fears led to a weird, secretive flirtation between us. We never spoke about it, it was just there.

It was at mealtimes that Celeste and I made eyes at each other whenever we felt it safe. I still longed to have Janice as my life partner, but I had to admit it was really positive for my ego to have the adoration of this beautiful fifteen-year-old girl. Janice had her own boyfriend, so I reasoned she couldn't possibly begrudge me having a bit of a flirt with Celeste. Janice would probably never find out about it anyway. After all, our flirting was nothing more than a bit of harmless fun.

Celeste was lovely to look at, but she had other fine attributes too. She never seemed to do much homework yet her school grades were consistently well above average. The lass never boasted about the high marks she was receiving. However, Jayne seldom missed an opportunity to make a complimentary comment about them at meal times. Celeste would remain silent whenever this happened, blushing prettily to an attractive shade of pink. She also had a remarkable talent for drawing. Sometimes, when waiting for Jayne to finish cooking tea, Celeste would grab a pencil and dash off a quick sketch. It might be something she could observe in the kitchen: a bowl of fruit, Jayne at the sink or a bunch of flowers. At other times, Celeste would sketch a picture completely from her vivid imagination, something in her mind's eye. One time it was a teacher at her school, another time a dancing couple and on one occasion, a magnificent galloping horse. As if by magic, she was able to capture the essence of her subject with a few well-chosen lines. A great natural talent.

Celeste also had a strong yearning for adventure. Whenever opportunities arose at school to do something out of the ordinary, she was the first to put her hand up and volunteer. She was doing the Duke of Edinburgh Award, had had a go at archery, slept out one night to raise money for the homeless and had even volunteered to go on a trip to Nigeria to help in a primary school. She liked nothing more than a challenge. There was so much to admire about Celeste.

20. Celeste

For weeks our relationship was restricted to making eyes at each other over the kitchen table. We seldom saw each other at other times. I used the bathroom first in the mornings and left for work before Celeste emerged. In the evenings I helped Jayne in the garden or went shopping. Celeste was kept busy in the evenings with homework, netball training and her Duke of Edinburgh activities. At weekends I had driving lessons and walked with the local bush walking club. I also volunteered at the Salvation Army depot most Sundays. Any spare time Celeste had at weekends was spent with girl friends or catching up on sleep.

One afternoon I was working as usual in the back garden. It had been raining earlier in the day, leaving the garden beds well soaked and the weeds amenable to being pulled out. After tuition from Jayne, I was now proficient at knowing the difference between a wanted plant and an undesirable weed. Mr Franchanji had landscaped the garden extensively when they had first moved into the house and the fruits of his labours were now easy to appreciate. Thankfully, Jayne was keen to continue his good work despite their recent break-up. Much to Celeste's disappointment, the back garden had never had a swimming pool installed although there was ample space. The Franchanji's' had stuck faithfully to their original landscaping concept and a swimming pool was not part of that design.

I was attacking a large clump of yellow flowering mustard weed when I heard a soft voice behind me.

'Hi Norman…'

I spun round to find Celeste standing there in her netball uniform and showing off her long-tanned legs to perfection.

'Oh, hi Celeste, I didn't hear you coming.'

'Netball was cancelled, so I came home early.'

'Why the cancellation?' I asked.

'The coach was sick and there wasn't time to let everyone know. Most of us turned up in our gear ready for training.'

'Sorry to hear that.'

'Where's mum?'

'Gone to the shops before they close. Had to get some more tomato sauce, I think.'

'Will she come back into the garden, do you think?'

I looked at my watch. It was already ten past five. Jayne usually started preparing tea about half past five. 'I very much doubt it,' I replied.

Celeste moved closer and was now standing only a yard from me. She looked stunning.

'So...Norman, we're here on our own then? Just you and me?'

'I think so.' I felt a strong urge to take Celeste in my arms, to hold her close, to kiss those beautiful lips.

'Do you mind if I draw you, Norman?' she asked, as she unexpectedly produced a drawing pad and pencil from behind her back.

'It'll cost you ten pounds.'

'That's a price worth paying,' she replied with a smile and moved a little closer.

'So...do you want me to pose or what?'

Celeste giggled mischievously, 'You can do whatever you want, Norman,' she said, seductively.

I decided to ham it up and adopted a pose standing like a Soviet peasant worker tensing up my mighty muscles. Celeste laughed, 'I think I prefer you as a gardener. I'll just sit on this bench and sketch you. I'll be done in ten minutes.'

I picked up my trowel and went back to work digging weeds out by hand while Celeste watched and scribbled, then watched and scribbled some more. I must have worked for ten minutes before Celeste called me over to take a look. I sat down next to her on the garden bench in the warm evening sunshine, tingling with excitement now that we were, at last, almost touching. The drawing was amazing. Celeste had skilfully captured me bending over the weeds digging away with my trowel. She had made it look more authentic by dressing me in gardener's clothes, complete with boots and an old straw hat. What I liked most was the way she had depicted me as being strong and virile, a well-built young man.

'Do you like it, Norman?'

I thought it was a terrific drawing and was about to tell her so when there was a strident shout from the house, 'Celeste, are you out there? Celeste, where are you?'

'Yes, I'm here mum. I've been doing some drawing.'

Another few seconds and I think I might have had my first kiss!

* * *

That evening, as Celeste and I stole our usual glances across the dining room table, we both knew how close we had come to kissing and how much we had wanted that close contact. For me, it felt as though we had ignited a fuse and I wondered where this was all heading. Janice, back home, was the only other girl I had ever felt powerful feelings for, but that liaison was not going anywhere while she was still dating Dean Hartcher. Janice and I had virtually grown up together and it seemed almost a natural progression for us to come together, although clearly, Janice was busily testing that assumption. My rapidly developing feelings for Celeste, on the other hand, were quite the opposite. We had only known each other for a few short weeks, yet seemed to be falling headlong into a relationship. Celeste was crazy about me and I knew I was falling for her.

Also, in the back of my mind, was the peer pressure I felt from a few of the young blokes I knew who were roundabout my age. I had met them at school, on the school bus and even in the hiking club I had recently joined. They bragged about kissing girls and one or two made out they had "gone all the way." I formed the impression I was not just a slow learner with my school education, but I was also being left for dead in my liaisons with the fairer sex. Next birthday I would turn seventeen, but I still hadn't even kissed a girl. Was there something wrong with me?

* * *

Like many successful new Australians, Mr Franchanji had poured his hard-earned money into building a grand double storied house for his family. It was a badge of office. To be acceptable the house had to be double red brick with a couple of ornamental columns at the entrance and be surrounded by a decent sized garden. It had to be palatial enough to send photographs proudly back to the relatives in Italy.

The Franchanji house must have been almost double the size of my family home. The spacious entry hall revealed a broad carpeted staircase leading up to four large bedrooms, two on either side of the staircase. The master bedroom included an ensuite, walk-in-robes and a marble spa bath. Jayne slept there with Celeste in the bedroom immediately next door. My bedroom was over on the other side of the staircase. Jayne used her well-appointed ensuite leaving Celeste and I to share the other bathroom on my side of the staircase. Early during my stay, Celeste and I had formed the sensible habit of always locking the door when we used the bathroom. As an extra precaution we always knocked on the bathroom door before entering. So far, we had not had any embarrassing situations.

I have to admit after that magic moment when Celeste and I sat together on the garden bench looking at her drawing of me, I felt a heightened interest in Celeste's movements. I found myself fantasising about what she was doing at various times of the day and wondering whether she was doing the same about me. It became a pleasant distraction to visualise Celeste's world during the many tedious hours I cleaned wards three and four or washed the floors. No doubt her life was far more exciting than mine, with her high school activities and friends both there and at netball. I longed to

20. Celeste

spend more time with Celeste, to get to know her better and develop our relationship. But how was I to do this? Jayne knew nothing about our blossoming relationship and Celeste and I wanted to keep it that way. However, I felt a growing unease about our shroud of secrecy; it just didn't seem right.

Matters came to a head, unexpectedly, a few evenings later. The three of us had enjoyed dinner together and were washing up afterwards when the phone rang. It was a call for Jayne. When she came back into the kitchen she looked stressed. She explained a close work colleague had just been driven home from the emergency department at the hospital after having x-rays for a suspected broken wrist. This friend lived on her own and was struggling to prepare her evening meal with one arm stuck in a sling and still feeling groggy. Jayne had agreed to drive over immediately to help her friend and told us she expected to be out for a couple of hours. Celeste and I immediately exchanged knowing looks.

As soon as we heard Jayne's car drive out of the garage, Celeste approached me. She took hold of my hands, 'Norman, let's put on some music and dance, mum's going to be out for at least a couple of hours.' Holding hands we hurried into the lounge and over to the record-player. Celeste began thumbing through their collection of LPs. 'What music do you like, Norman?'

'Anything that's recently been on top of the Australian charts. What about a bit of Elvis? "It's Now or Never" or "Are You Lonesome Tonight?"'

Celeste continued looking through the collection. Presumably, she was not a big Elvis fan. 'Do you like musicals? We've got Lionel Bart's, "Oliver." I'd love to see that one day. Oh, here's "The Drifters." Do you remember "Save the Last Dance for Me?"' She looked up with the sweetest of smiles.

'That'll do nicely.'

I watched as she placed the LP on the turntable and the music started.

For several minutes we moved together to the music. Celeste was a lovely, graceful mover and must have had dancing lessons, but after a couple of tracks she pulled me over to the couch. We were both hungry for something more.

'Can I sit on your lap, Norman?'

'I don't think that's a good idea.'

'Why ever not?'

I leaned over and took Celeste in my arms. Clumsily, we sought each other's mouths and began to kiss. It was a very amateurish first effort for us both. Our hands began to roam and I remember wondering how far this was going to go; Celeste's thirst for adventure might not be easily quelled. Gradually, she slipped herself down beneath me until I found I was virtually lying on top of her, feeling intensely embarrassed about my solid erection. She made no objection though and began kissing me even more passionately.

'What the hell are you two up to?' Jayne had forgotten something and come home early.

PART TWO

21. TWO YEARS LATER...

Looking back, I guess Jayne was quite decent about finding Celeste and myself in such a compromising situation on her couch. Furious at the time, she ordered me to leave her house first thing next morning. I had nowhere to go at such short notice, but to my surprise Jayne arranged with the friend she had gone to help for me to stay there. Jayne convinced her friend it would be a big help if she sent her boarder, Norman McDade, to stay with her for a few days until she was better able to manage. Amazingly, this worked! Miss Trillon welcomed me into her home, provided I promised to help with domestic duties about the house including the cooking. Jayne sang my praises, saying I was decent, reliable and trustworthy as long as there were no teenage daughters about the place. I helped Miss Trillon for a fortnight by which time she was coping reasonably well. Then I moved into digs with three other guys who wanted an extra person to share the rental expenses. Two years after my abrupt departure from the Franchanji household, I was still living in the same digs.

I continued as a cleaner at the hospital for another six months, by which time I felt I needed a change. With mum's help, I secured a new cleaning job at the Cessna Aircraft factory on the edge of town, the largest employer in the district. I was far happier at the Cessna factory. No more abusive colleagues and a greater variety of work made life more enjoyable. They were an interesting bunch of people at the factory too: engineers, electricians, carpenters, designers, pilots, secretarial and administrative staff, as well as other highly specialised trades people.

Being a non-smoker and a non-drinker, I had saved a bit of money which I deposited in my bank account. I used this money to pay a driving instructor for six lessons after mum had first given me some basic lessons. Mum was marvellous. She spent hours reading to me from "The Highway Code" until I had memorised virtually the whole book. Shortly after my seventeenth birthday I qualified for my driver's licence and started looking around to purchase a decent second-hand vehicle.

The news about dad was positive. He eventually shook off the depression that had prevented him making progress at the rehabilitation hospital and cooperated fully with the staff. He never regained the use of his legs but adjusted well to a wheelchair. Almost eight months after that horrendous car accident, he finally returned home. Mum took off the first week of his homecoming to help get him settled. He did well. He now enjoys an invalid's pension and has become active in the local community as an advocate for those with disabilities. Dad's also been elected onto the Shire Council and is the non-playing president of the Bowling Club. He's often seen there egging on his mates or sharing a beer with the bowlers. I've heard he's doing a good job as president and is well liked.

My love life has been disappointing, though. Occasionally I see Celeste in town. I think we both recognise our lusty encounter on the couch was no more than a fascination with exploring our sexual desires and we've moved on. Celeste is currently finishing her matriculation and hopes to be accepted into a university. Janice is at the Sydney Teachers' College finishing her second year of a Teachers Certificate. We haven't met up again since I left town and its mum who keeps me abreast of her doings. Apparently, she and Dean Hartcher split up and she's going out with another student from university. I still harbour strong feelings for Janice. I've dated two or three other girls over the last couple of years but these relationships soon fizzled out. I guess it's not surprising; going out with an illiterate cleaner with modest prospects is hardly a good catch for a woman.

* * *

Sometimes the cleaners at the Cessna factory were asked to work strange hours. If there was a big order and the assembly line was working overtime, cleaners fussing around with their mops and brooms were unwelcome and potentially a dangerous hazard. So, when this happened, we cleaners had to switch to night shifts. Being single, it often fell to me to do these night shifts since the married guys had families to look after. I quite enjoyed working on my own at night when the factory was quiet. The wages were better too! One night when I was on cleaning duty, I was witness to a suspicious event.

The Cessna factory employed a number of night security staff. They were mostly rough sorts of characters who spent much of their time wandering about, half asleep. This particular night, I was on cleaning duty with a security officer by the name of "Narky." I'm sure that wasn't his real name but he had been known by this name for many years and it had stuck. He never raised any objections. Narky was verging on being obese and was obliged to spend most of his time sitting about on his backside. I'm sure Narky knew every possible place in the factory where he could park his substantial posterior for a much-needed rest.

The security staff had a small office just inside the entrance to the administration building. Narky was there when I arrived, dozing peacefully with his head resting comfortably against the back of the large leather chair. I was required to sign in at the security office on arrival and Narky would have the necessary sheet of paper ready for me. I waited for a pause between snores.

'Narky, wake up. It's the CEO here.'

Narky shook like a jelly. His eyes flashed open as wide as saucers before he realised it was only me, the night cleaner, standing in front of him.

'Don't you bloody do that again, Norman. You scared the shit out of me!'

I laughed heartily while Narky glared unforgivingly and fumbled with the security badge on his chest.

'You could've given me a bloody heart attack waking me up like that.'

'Sorry Narky but I need the sign-in sheet, please.'

Narky propelled his groaning chair slowly towards the filing cabinet where he located the sign-in sheet and shoved the form in front of me, together with a pen. I signed.

'All quiet tonight?' I asked.

'Until you came barging in like a bloody bull,' protested Narky. 'Nobody has indicated they'll be working back late tonight so the place should be dead quiet, except for the rats.'

'Rats! Are they still about? I thought we'd killed them all off?'

Narky sniffed disapprovingly, 'They're still about lad. Nearly tripped over one of the little buggers last week.'

I grimaced. Rats gave me the creeps.

'See you about Narky. I'm being paid for four hours tonight and I'll be back here to sign out at eleven o'clock sharp. If you're out on one of your rounds, please leave the sign-out sheet for me.'

'Righto, Norman.' Narky yawned widely. It looked as though he would need a bit more shut-eye before rousing himself to do his rounds.

I headed off to the cleaners' store to collect my gear. This particular night, I was responsible for cleaning the three storeys of the admin building, a workload that was doable in four hours. In addition, I would have the luxury of a short smoko in the staff room with a cuppa. I wheeled out the cleaning trolley and collected the heavy bunch of keys that gave me access to any rooms that were locked. For a brief moment I allowed myself time to marvel at the sexy photograph of this month's naked pin-up girl discreetly posted on the inside of the door. When, I wondered, would I ever see a "real" naked woman?

I was a methodical cleaner and never cut corners. In fact, I took considerable pride in my work. Sadly, cleaners are rarely appreciated, we go about our work quietly and largely unnoticed. But we are the first to cop it if something is amiss. If an office item is lost or damaged some people are quick to blame the cleaners in their absence. An occasional word of thanks for enduring the drudgery of cleaning the same areas month after tedious month would be welcome.

Nobody ever complained to me that their work space wasn't properly cleaned but I have been falsely accused of moving things or breaking objects. Frequently valuables were left on a person's desk or in a workshop which were tempting for cleaners and then our honesty would come under scrutiny. For example, one of the middle managers, a woman, always left a tin of lollies or chocolates on her desk usually wide open and inviting. Often heaps of tools, scraps of useable timber, half used pots of paint or glue were left lying around in the workshops. These might come in useful on home projects. I'm proud to say I never gave in to such temptations, but I knew others who did. In fact, two cleaners were caught and sacked!

When cleaning the administration building, I always started on the top storey, it was by far the most interesting. I wheeled my cumbersome trolley into the lift and travelled up silently to the third floor. This was where the "top brass" worked. The CEO had a suite of rooms which included a ginormous office, a small private meeting annexe, the personal assistant's office and an ensuite bathroom, complete with a bath and shower. Next door was the spacious board room with its long mahogany table and twelve stylish leather chairs. One board room wall was covered with portraits of past CEOs and the other wall displayed photographs of famous Cessna models manufactured over the years.

I learnt at my induction that the company had been founded in 1927 by Clyde Cessna. He built himself an airplane in 1911 and by 1927 had established a factory in Wichita, Kansas, where he began production of a single engine, high winged aircraft that has since become famous around the world. There was a photograph on the wall of the Cessna headquarters in Wichita, another photograph of Clyde Cessna himself and all the Cessna models from the very first Cessna DG-6 (1929) through to the Cessna 172 Skyhawk (1956). It was the Skyhawk that our factory was currently manufacturing.

The board room always fascinated me. Cleaning it was simple enough although the size of the room meant I needed half an hour there. I would look at the row of distinguished CEOs and wonder what these men were like in real life. How had they risen to the top? Were they good family people? What challenges had they faced during their tenureship? Without exception, the CEOs were smartly clad and smiled down on us sagely. It was intriguing also to see how the photographs of the seven Cessna models showed how the Cessnas had become more streamlined and sophisticated over the years.

I stood back to admire my handiwork with the mahogany table that shone from my polishing so well that it reflected the outline of my body. Pleased with my efforts, I collected my trolley and moved towards the door. The next area for cleaning was the CEO's office and its annexe. As I opened the door, I was startled to find a man standing at the CEO's filing cabinet thumbing through papers. I froze for a second, satisfying myself this person was not the CEO himself. The stranger was so absorbed in what he was doing he didn't know I was watching. Whoever it was looked out of place, since he was wearing ordinary every-day clothes and thin rubber gloves. I hesitated, uncertain what to do.

At this point, something must have alerted the stranger for he turned around furtively as if worried there was someone else present. Seeing me, he flew into a panic and stupidly ran into the annexe hoping to escape that way since I was standing with my trolley blocking his exit. The annexe, however, led nowhere. It's an inside room with no way out. He was trapped. There were windows but to jump out from three floors up would mean certain death.

Clearly, the man was an intruder, illegally looking through confidential papers in the CEO's office. How had he acquired the keys to the filing cabinet? Had the intruder attacked Narky, or forced him to hand over the keys? Was Narky lying injured somewhere in the building? Perhaps this man was dangerous and likely to attack me if I got in his way. I thought back to my induction. The instructions about what to do if an intruder was discovered whilst on night duty were crystal clear. On no account try to stop an intruder. Call security and then, if necessary, the police. I moved forward into the room to use the CEO's telephone to call Narky. I reached the CEO's desk at the same time as the intruder emerged from the annexe holding a pistol.

'Don't you dare touch that phone. Turn round and raise your arms.' I obeyed, there was no point resisting. 'Now, you and me are going back down to the main entrance, nice and slow. This pistol is loaded and I'm not afraid to use it. Leave your cleaning stuff here. If you cause me any trouble, I'll kill you. Now start walking.'

I felt the pistol pushed hard up against the small of my back and moved slowly and reluctantly towards the door.

'Who are you?' I blurted out.

'Never you mind. Keep your mouth shut.'

'Yes.'

'We're going down the stairs. Keep moving...'

In silence we moved out of the CEO's office into the passageway and along to the top of the staircase. As we walked, I wondered where Narky was. Was he hurt or perhaps somewhere on his rounds? What was likely to happen if we came across Narky on our way to the main entrance? Then I started to worry what this stranger was going to do with me. Would he simply let me go or decide to kill me? It was rumoured a new Cessna model had been designed in Kansas and our factory would shortly be licensed to start production of this exciting new plane. The detailed plans of this major initiative would be highly valued by our commercial competitors both here and overseas. This must have been what the stranger was after.

Slowly but surely, we made our way down the three flights of stairs. Still no sign of Narky. Every few paces the pistol was jabbed hard into my back as a reminder to stay quiet and obey orders. As we approached the security office I looked about in vain for Narky. The stranger pushed me roughly towards the main entrance and out into the cool night air.

'Keep your gob shut. Walk over to those trees.'

We moved on, more quickly now. In a moment I would know what he had planned for me. Once we were out of sight, behind several tall pine trees, the man ordered me to lie down on my stomach. From somewhere he produced binder twine to tie up my wrists. Next, he forced my mouth open and roughly shoved in some kind of foul-tasting cloth material so I couldn't speak. Finally, he roped my ankles up tightly to prevent me trying to run for help. I lay on my stomach trussed up like a bacon roll.

'I'm going back to get what I was after before you so rudely disturbed me,' the man declared, 'no harm will come to you if you stay there.' He bent down, checked my hands and ankles were securely tied and with a satisfied grunt disappeared into the dark night.

I don't know how long I lay there becoming more and more uncomfortable. I rolled over onto my back to gaze up at the stars. Lying on my roped arms, however, was even more unpleasant so I rolled back onto my stomach. The stranger had done a good job lashing me up so tightly. The more I tried to loosen the bindings the more they dug into my skin. I thought of trying to get myself upright and then kangaroo hopping down the road to get away and raise the alarm. The nearest house was probably about four hundred yards away but such a journey would be slow and torturous.

What, I wondered, had happened to Narky? Was he even aware this man was inside the building stealing the company's secrets? Where was he? Perhaps he was in the staffroom having some refreshments or sleeping peacefully in some private retreat. Wherever he was, it made a mockery of having security personnel on night duty.

My thoughts returned to my own unpleasant predicament. Was the intruder going to leave me here all night until some early riser discovered me lying here cold, cramped and miserable? The man had a gun. Did he intend to use it? Stealing Cessna's trade secrets was a serious enough crime but adding murder would surely be a crazy thing to do. Unless, murder had already been committed in silencing Narky.

If I got out of this alive, the police would want to know everything about the intruder. As I lay there, I tried to recall what he looked like and how I would describe him. I rehearsed. The man was average height, perhaps in his thirties, slim build and spoke with an accent. He sounded Canadian or American. I rarely could distinguish between the two. I hadn't had time to see much more. If the man returned to release me, then I would do my utmost to observe him more carefully, noting what he was wearing, whether he was clean shaven or not, any distinguishing features.

The moon moved painstakingly slowly across the sky. As I lay there, I was amazed at the sounds of nature all about me. Somewhere nearby two owls communicated for quite some time whilst the leaves and grasses rustled and crackled with the frenetic movements of the creatures of the night. Nothing actually ran over the top of me but I'm sure curious animals checked me out from time to time annoyed I had been dumped in the middle of their hunting grounds. I imagined rats and mice and perhaps the odd echidna sniffing me out, maybe a potaroo or a feral cat.

Eventually, I concluded the intruder had decided not to bother to come back and release me and I wouldn't see him again. I guessed it was around two in the morning. The night security shift finished at six when the first of the day shifts came on duty. I was not prepared to lie on the damp ground for another four hours and then risk not being found by security at the six o'clock changeover so I made up my mind to get myself back to the road. The only way I could move was to roll sideways like a log. This was a painfully slow process. I would manage a couple of rolls and then come up against a tree trunk or have to negotiate loose rocks or clumps of phalaris grass. Nevertheless, in about half an hour I finally flopped over a gutter and rolled triumphantly onto the bitumen road that led to the main entrance of the Cessna factory. Here, near a street light, I was clearly visible to whoever turned up first. The energy needed to roll this far had warmed me up although I had suffered scratches and bruising as I made my unconventional journey through the scrub and trees.

Father Time can be a cruel master. When you're desperate for the hours to pass, he drags them on and on, interminably. I think I managed to sleep for a couple of short spells despite lying on such a hard unforgiving surface. At least it didn't rain! It was a joy to see the gradual glow of dawn begin in the east to the accompaniment of a cheerful chorus of birds waking for another day's activities. Best of all was the beam of light coming from an approaching car that suddenly encircled me. At last, I was about to escape my horrific night's bondage.

The Ute slowed, passed me and then pulled in to the curb a few metres away. I recognised the voice of the announcer from the local radio station conducting his "Wake Up with Walter" early morning program as the vehicle passed with its windows down. I heard a door slam and then a face I didn't recognise stared down at me.

'Blimey mate, what you been doing to yourself?'

I glared and grunted and wriggled in reply.

21. Two Years Later...

'Okay, let's get all this stuff off you,' and the stranger set to work, removing the mouth gag first and then the ties.

'Am I glad to see you,' I spluttered, 'I've been strung up like this for bloody hours.'

To the astonishment of my rescuer, I recounted what had happened overnight and stressed my concern for Narky and the likely theft of valuable files from the CEO's office.

22. HITTING THE HEADLINES!

My rescuer turned out to be Fred Tussack, the security officer reporting for the start of his six o'clock stint. With the aid of his Swiss army knife he had me free in a matter of minutes and together we entered the administration building to discover Narky fast asleep in the office blissfully unaware of the previous night's shenanigans. Somehow, I managed to refrain from stating the bleeding obvious about ineffectual security procedures and useless officers.

At first, Narky refused to believe what had happened to me, though he was more inclined to do so when I showed him my abrasions and lacerated wrists. Together, the three of us visited the CEO's office but it appeared to be safely locked up, clean and untouched. I remembered exactly where the stranger was standing at the filing system so I knew which files needed to be checked. My cleaning trolley was still parked in the corridor outside the CEO's suite of rooms.

'Narky, you're going to have to report this incident to the boss and write it up in the log book.'

'How can I bloody write up an incident I didn't know happened?' snorted Narky.

'Well, Norman here can help you. He was the one tied up all night and hidden away under the trees.'

22. Hitting the Headlines!

'I'll do whatever I can to help you, Narky,' I assured him, 'I can tell you everything I saw and experienced.'

'How about you write the bloody report then?' growled Narky.

'Sorry Narky, I can't read or write.'

'Bullshit! You went to school, didn't ya?'

'Yes.'

'Well then…what did you go to bloody school for, if you didn't learn to read?'

Fred stepped in with an excellent solution, 'Come on guys, you dictate Norman and I'll type the bloody report up for ya.'

And this is what happened. Over the next hour we three put together a two-page report ready for the Day Manager when he turned up around eight o'clock. Narky lived up to his name throughout the exercise, complaining bitterly he would be late for his breakfast. Narky's stomach was considerably more important than any concerns he had that under his watch vital trade secrets of the company had been stolen. With a final shrug of his shoulders, Narky stomped off home shortly after seven o'clock. I remained at work, anticipating the Day Manager would want to speak with me.

The Day Manager proved to be a man of action. He believed my story and after checking the CEO's office again, contacted the CEO and then the police. He was very concerned about my wellbeing since I had been through a frightening and sleepless night and sent me down to the canteen for breakfast "on the house." Bacon and eggs never tasted better followed by several rounds of toast with lashings of butter and marmalade. Half an hour later, two police arrived to interview me in the CEO's office with the CEO and the Day Manager present. Again, I recounted the details of the previous night. My story was vindicated when the CEO confirmed three highly confidential folders were missing from the files.

It was after nine when I was finally free to go home. I had never met the CEO face to face before. I think I made quite an impression on him. Before I left his office, he made a point of thanking me for the way I had conducted myself and expressed his concern that I get cleaned up and catch up on some sleep. In addition, he said he would have a letter of commendation placed in my file and that he would arrange for me to have two days off work without loss of wages to compensate for the hardship I had endured.

I remember the sense of relief when I pushed my bike out of the shed to ride home; relief because I had done everything I could in the best interests of the Cessna factory. Now I could go home and collapse into bed for a well-deserved mega sleep. There was one last hurdle, however, that I did not anticipate. As I rode my bike around to the front of the building, I was met by several excited young men armed with writing pads and cameras. Journalists! There was no escape. I faced a barrage of questions whilst their cameras flashed around me. I even had to roll up my sleeves to reveal the red sores on my wrists. Then the journalists insisted on photographing the precise place where I had spent much of my ghastly night. They wanted a blow-by-blow description of how I had rolled out to the road and details of my attacker. Eventually they let me go and I continued on my fifteen-minute ride home, only to be confronted by the same crew again when I arrived at our humble shared rental property. Yet another round of photos with me standing outside our place holding my bike.

I showered and climbed into bed where I slept deeply until woken by my flatmates returning home from work that evening. My nocturnal adventures were the main topic of conversation as we shared takeaway fish and chips followed by a few card games. Thankfully, there were no more journalists bashing down the door demanding additional information. We went to bed looking forward to seeing how the local paper would report matters next morning. My flatmates reckoned it would be a page two job with a picture of me and a half page story. As it turned out, the local rag must have been short of news because my little adventure became front-page headlines!

* * *

COURAGEOUS CLEANER'S SHOCKING ORDEAL

Nineteen-year-old cleaner, Norman McDade, endured a terrifying Wednesday night tied up, gagged and dumped under a tree in the grounds of the Cessna factory. Norman's harrowing story began when he reported to the administration building to carry out his late-night cleaning duties. But this was no ordinary night! It wasn't long before he disturbed an intruder searching through secret and confidential files in the CEO's office.

The news item went on for most of the front page covering everything the journalists had gleaned from me the day before, together with a few extra juicy bits they had made up to make the story sexier. My flat mates took great pleasure in reading me extracts from the paper and at the same time laughing and joking. Overall, however, I knew they were impressed with my exploits.

The story was continued on pages two and three and included no less than four photographs. On the front page was a picture of me with my sturdy bike standing outside our rental apartment. The caption read: "Norman McDade pleased to be home after his frightening ordeal." Also on the front page was a close up of the welts on my wrists where the rope had cut into my skin. Page two had a picture of the worn patch of vegetation where I had spent several painful hours. A piece of rope had been included for added effect. The fourth photograph showed the main entrance to the Cessna factory.

I soon discovered appearing as headline news in a newspaper brought instant, but short-lived, fame. The two days off work I had been granted were soon filled with requests for radio interviews on the local commercial station and the ABC's regional station. There was a flurry of "letters to the editor" about my exploits. Not surprisingly, the police were keen to speak to me again to double check facts and pick up on any details I may have overlooked. The editorial in the local newspaper tried to come to grips with the seriousness of what had happened at the Cessna factory. It was, the editorial claimed, a sad situation when highly confidential trade secrets could be so easily accessed and stolen. The security system at the Cessna factory was roundly condemned and the unfortunate Narky attacked ruthlessly.

The whole sorry saga hung about like a bad smell for weeks after the event. There was anger that the mysterious intruder had been allowed to escape without trace despite the best efforts of the police. Considerable attention was given to the possibility the intruder had been assisted by an insider. Suspicion fell on Narky who's grumpy, uncooperative responses to any questioning did not help his cause. In the end, it all became too much for Narky and he resigned. Cessna spent a considerable amount of money updating their security systems, retraining staff and improving their monitoring procedures.

There was one unexpected but most welcome outcome. My old flame, Janice, saw the headlines a few days later and called me one evening. I was at home on my own when the call came.

'Hello Norman, this is a blast from the past. It's Janice.'

'Oh wow, Janice, great to hear from you. How are you?'

'I'm good thanks. I wanted to commiserate with you about that awful night you had at the Cessna factory. It must have been horrible. Were you terrified?'

'Well…yes…I guess I was. I honestly didn't know whether the intruder was going to come back and finish me off.'

'I think you were really brave, Norman.'

'Thanks.'

'Guess what? I've graduated from Teachers' College and I'm now a fully qualified primary/infants' teacher.'

'That's wonderful Janice, many congratulations. What happens now?'

'Well, I'm home for the holidays and after Christmas I'll get a telegram telling me where I'm going to teach.'

'Exciting!'

22. Hitting the Headlines!

'It really is. Norman, I was wondering if you'd like to meet up for a coffee in the next week or so?'

'I'd love that. Where and when?'

'How about ten o'clock Saturday at the new place in the main street. It's called "The Red Roo". Do you know it?'

'I sure do. See you there....'

* * *

"The Red Roo" was all the rage amongst the young folk in town. It had opened a few weeks earlier and boasted a modern cuisine, an attractive airy interior and al fresco dining. Gone were the heavy wooden pew-like eating compartments common with Greek and Italian milk bars of yore. An attractive mural ran along the long wall depicting a mob of canny kangaroos seemingly headed towards the kitchen at the back of the establishment. The leader of the pack was a red kangaroo, larger and more handsome than his mates. The remaining décor was cleverly kangaroo-related. There were several pelts on display together with an assortment of objects made from kangaroo fur: small purses, handbags, hats and even moccasin-like kangaroo boots. In the centre of every table sat a cute toy kangaroo. Naturally, the menu included kangaroo tail soup!

I arrived first. Since it was a warm day, I procured a table for two outside under a shady awning. I hadn't seen Janice for over two years. I had moved into town seeking work when she started at Sydney Teachers' College. As I waited for her to appear, I wondered whether we still had that little bit of chemistry we had shared since our first time together in the infants' school almost fifteen years ago. The waitress appeared and left two menus on my table which I pretended to look through, thoughtfully. There were a few words I recognised but most of it was gobbledygook. I would have to wait for Janice to do the translating.

I must have been lost in my thoughts because I never saw Janice approach. Suddenly I felt two smooth, soft hands come from behind and cover my eyes. At the same time, a pleasant perfume washed over me.

'Guess who?'

Instinctively, my hands went to my face as I rose to my feet. Wow... Janice looked amazing! The two years absence had matured her into a lovely woman. It was still unmistakeably Janice but a slimmer more confident person stood before me with that same delightful smile and dancing blue eyes. For a fleeting moment I thought she was going to throw her arms around my neck and kiss me. I too, had matured over the last two years and my body had broadened out as a result of continuous physical work and frequent bush walks. I was now head and shoulders taller than Janice.

'You're looking great, Janice.'

'You don't look so bad yourself. Have you ordered?'

'No, I was waiting for you.'

'They do a lime soda to die for here. Can't beat it. What about you, Norman?'

'Well, I'm an earning man so this is my shout. How about you get something to snack on as well?'

'Oh, goodie...let's see the menu then.'

Ten minutes later we were deep in conversation enjoying lime sodas and warm doughnuts. I couldn't help noticing there were no rings on Janice's fingers so perhaps she was still available? She apologised for not inviting me to her graduation and we reminisced about the shocking events that followed my own humble graduation years earlier. We caught up on family news, the recent heroics at the Cessna factory, my continuing interest in bushwalking and the natural world. Janice spoke of her developing interest in classical music and her hopes for a teaching position somewhere in the bush. Taking a deep breath, I popped the question that was haunting me.

'Janice, forgive me for being nosey, but are you going out with anyone?'

To my surprise, she started to tear up and dived into her handbag for a handkerchief. After a few sniffles and the careful wiping away of tear-drops, Janice looked at me through watery eyes.

'I'm sorry Norman, I've just broken up from a long-term relationship and it's all quite raw still.' She forced a smile and looked away, shyly.

Instinctively I reached out for her hand, but couldn't think of something sensible to say. I waited a moment for Janice to recover her composure.

'I'm so sorry, Janice.'

She toyed with the last of her doughnut before replying.

'We were engaged to be married. He was at Teachers' College with me. We'd been going out together for twelve months and now it's all over.'

'Are you sure? Isn't there anyway the two of you can get back together?'

Janice shook her head vigorously.

'I left him and there's no going back. He cheated on me. He really wanted us to get back together again but I can't forget what he did and certainly can't forgive him. The only good thing about the whole sordid affair is that I got to find out what he's *really* like before we married.'

'Had you exchanged engagement rings and planned your wedding and everything?'

Janice nodded. 'I'm sorry to blabber on like this. To be honest, it's good to be able to tell somebody about it. I've only told my parents.'

I sat quietly, unsure how best to react. Perhaps Janice needed to spell out more details? I certainly didn't want her to feel I was prying into her past disastrous relationship. If she wanted to unload though, I hoped she felt I could be a good listener. We remained silent for a couple of minutes until the waitress suddenly re-appeared.

'Would you like anything else?' she asked cheerfully as she picked up our glasses and plates.

'Yes, please. Can we have two cappuccinos?'

'Of course,' and with a quick flick at a couple of offending doughnut crumbs, she left us.

'Thanks Norman, that's nice.'

'No problem.'

'I really loved this man. In a way I still do, but there's no way I can trust him anymore and that's certainly no basis for a marriage. I discovered he'd been sleeping with another woman. Can you believe it? One day he's asking me to marry him and I happily accepted then a month later I discover, quite by accident, what he's been up to.'

'Are you absolutely sure, Janice? It's hard to believe.'

'I know it's hard to believe, but it's true all right. The woman, who was also a close friend of mine, admitted they'd been sleeping together not once but on several occasions. All the time we were making our wedding arrangements; he was sleeping with Sonia! How shocking is that!'

23. UNIONISED?

Meeting up with Janice again after two years was a thrill for me, although I was saddened to hear of the awful experience she had recently suffered from the man she planned to spend the rest of her life with. I found it difficult to believe her ex-boyfriend could have behaved so despicably. As Janice sadly admitted, it was fortunate she found out about his shenanigans when she did, rather than later, when they had tied the knot. Janice deserved better.

Despite the obvious grieving process Janice was going through, our meeting had reignited my feelings for the girl I had known for most of my life. I didn't think it appropriate to ask her out again so soon after such a traumatic break-up, yet I was anxious to be around should she want my support. She told me she was going home to stay with her parents over the long Christmas holidays to await a telegram from the NSW Department of Education advising where she had been appointed for her first placement as a qualified teacher. So, I knew where to contact her.

I had become a bit of a hero at the Cessna factory after my unexpected run-in with the thieving intruder. I didn't think I had done anything particularly heroic but the local paper, the local radio station and my work colleagues did. I didn't mind basking in their glory for the short time it lasted. I had recently turned twenty and had already been at the Cessna factory for twelve months. I guess I liked it there. Unfortunately, wherever you work as a cleaner it always becomes boring and repetitive after a few weeks. The one thing that can keep a cleaner's life bearable is the folk you work alongside. The hospital had been a disaster in this regard but at the Cessna factory my fellow workers were a pretty decent bunch of people. The cleaners, as a group, got along well. There were precious few fringe benefits for the cleaners but like the other employees we were always invited to the Cessna Bumper Christmas Barbeque along with our immediate families (spouse and children).

A new cleaner unexpectedly joined the team during December and he came with a mission; he was determined to "unionise" the cleaning staff at the factory and make us sign up as paid-up members of the Miscellaneous Workers Union (MWU). Now, I have to confess to being strongly influenced by my parents who were stridently anti-union. This new arrival on the cleaning staff was likely to create problems for me.

Three generations of the McDade family had successfully managed the garage in my home town for over eighty years. Nobody knew exactly how many men had been employed in the business over the many years but it must have been dozens. In all that time nobody had found it necessary to become a member of a union. The reason was simple; the McDade in charge at the time always made it a top priority to see that his workers were well looked after. The bosses were generous, generous with pay, generous with the working conditions and generous with sympathy and empathy whenever required. Working for the McDades was regarded as a privilege and the McDade's generosity was repaid with hard work, honesty and loyalty. Being a financial member of a union at McDades was, quite simply, unnecessary.

During my short life I had absorbed much of the McDade's healthy attitudes to work and their employees. Treat the workers with the respect, care and consideration they deserve and it will pay dividends in the long run. Create a fair, sound work ethic and unions become irrelevant.

There were a dozen cleaners at the Cessna factory when I started there. We got along well and were quite satisfied with our pay and working conditions. There was generous sick leave and the boss was always prepared to listen if something was amiss. The cleaning rosters were carefully considered and we rotated through different jobs to give us more variety. Occasionally someone would have a bit of a whinge about something or other but overall everyone was perfectly happy with their employment. It was a good place to work. Things changed rapidly, however, with the arrival of the new cleaner, Brian McTavish.

Brian hailed from Scotland but turned out to be yet another angry young man exported from that beautiful land of whiskey, heather and bagpipes. Small in stature and wiry, Brian rarely smiled and gave the impression he was about to engage you in fisticuffs at any moment. McTavish had arrived in Australia a few months earlier and informed us he was determined to drag us into the nineteen-sixties. I think he saw us as a bunch of backward colonials. The Scottish accent is difficult to understand at the best of times; but someone brought up in the Gorbals of Glasgow is almost impossible! So, we cleaners had communication problems from the outset.

Brian McTavish was single and crazy about soccer. He was already playing "A" grade in town and every week would regale us with stories about his heroics on the soccer field as well as his beloved Celtic, undeniably the best club in the whole wide world. Nobody was game to disagree and we resorted to nodding enthusiastically as soon as Brian mentioned his beloved soccer team.

Within a few days of starting work at the Cessna factory, Brian began breaking up the contented dynamic amongst our cleaning staff. After a few weeks, things began to go seriously awry.

The troubles started because Brian was never satisfied. He constantly found fault or made unfavourable comparisons with "back 'ome". We felt like saying, if things were so great "back 'ome" why didn't he return there? He complained about the gear we were issued for cleaning, the brooms that didn't sweep properly, the polish which was "rat shit." Even the garbage bins were, in Brian's view, smelly and unhealthy. Cleaners, Brian attested, should never have to put up with sub-standard equipment. Why weren't we doing something about it? As for annual leave, he declared we were years behind the times. Twenty days leave a year was simply not good enough. These days every worker should receive at least twenty-five days leave per annum. Again, why weren't we fighting for our rights?

Perhaps we were a pretty docile group. A couple of the old hands had been faithfully cleaning at the Cessna factory for almost twenty years, ever since the company had opened its doors. Until Brian joined the staff, they had been perfectly happy and prepared to stay with the company until retirement. It wasn't long, however, before Brian had sown seeds of doubt in our collective minds. Nothing, it seemed, was good enough anymore.

'Forty minutes for lunch is bullshit. Every worker is entitled to a full hour and not a minute less.'

'But Brian, we are allowed to knock off twenty minutes early at the end of the day if we only take forty minutes for lunch.'

'You're abusing your body if you're taking only forty minutes mate. Your health is paramount. You're being exploited!'

'But Brian, we asked management for the forty-minute arrangement because most of us are married and we can get back to our families quicker this way. It's what we want.'

'Well, it's not right. Management should never have agreed. You need the time to digest your food properly and digestive systems need a full hour,' Brian strongly asserted, 'and while we're talking about lunch, you guys should be provided with a decent staff room. This room is lousy. Half the chairs are broken, there's no air conditioning and even the cord on the bloody kettle's frayed. That's a safety hazard. Somebody's going to be electrocuted one day and could even be killed.

23. Unionised?

If you were in a union, you'd at least get decent compensation for any injuries.'

This made sense, Brian certainly had a point. Next, Brian McTavish turned and confronted me head-on.

'Norman, I bet you got no compensation for what you bloody well went through a few weeks ago? What did management do for you when you were attacked that night and left to die out on the street? Eh? Did they pay you any compensation? Eh? Did they get you a counsellor to help you deal with the trauma? I bet they did fuck-all!'

I hastily recalled what had happened at the time. Perhaps Brian was right? Possibly, more could have been done for me? When it happened, though, I felt I had been fairly treated. I was given two days special leave on full pay; my boss was most concerned and sympathetic and the CEO even called me into his office to specially compliment me on the way I had conducted myself. Now, however, Brian McTavish was sowing seeds of doubt in my mind and in the minds of my colleagues. Before I even tried to answer Brian's challenge, he was off again…

'Norman, if you were a paid-up member of my union, the MWU, management would have been forced to pay you generous compensation. Being left out in the cold all bleeding night, tied up and in fear of your life should have been worth bloody thousands of smackers, mate.'

'Well… I hadn't thought of it like that,' I mumbled, unconvincingly.

Round one to Brian, the ardent unionist.

* * *

Brian relentlessly pursued his campaign to sign us up as members of the MWU over the ensuing weeks. The more he persisted, the more we came around to his way of thinking. Steadily but surely, like a successful fisherman, he hauled us in. The MWU, according to McTavish, was there to give us workers a fair deal and prevent

Cessna management shamelessly exploiting us. Matters finally came to a head early in February.

Several of us were sitting in the staffroom smoking and chatting before work one morning, when Brian sailed in and dropped a bundle of papers on the table.

'MWU membership forms,' he announced proudly, 'take one each, have a read and we can chat about them tomorrow. Some of you might already be happy to fill 'em in straightaway.'

I picked up a form, keeping up the pretence I could read and dutifully took the form home after work. That evening I passed the form around my three flat mates and sought their views. A lively discussion followed for we held differing opinions about the advantages and disadvantages of joining unions. I had, of course, heard most of the arguments before. One of my flat-mates was totally opposed to the concept of workers uniting; for him it smacked of communism, an ideology espoused by the Union of Soviet Socialist Republics and, in his opinion, doomed to failure. He believed people were inherently decent and that most workers were well looked after without reverting to the militant tactics often espoused by trade unions. He was also at pains to point out that when you paid your annual union dues you had no say as to how that money was going to be spent. He asserted it went into the union's bank account to pay for the salaries of the union staff and their benefits and any remaining money went to the Labour Party as a political donation.

A second flat-mate was a reluctant member of a union. His gripe was that in the building and construction industry, where he was employed, you *had* to join the union before you could get a job. Compulsory unionism was demanded and he resented the fact that if you wanted to work, you had no choice in the matter. What's more, if the union decided strike action was necessary you had to go out, whether you wanted to or not. Often, the dispute was not even at your own workplace but you were called upon to "go out in sympathy."

Over the next few days my cleaner colleagues made up their minds about whether or not to join the Miscellaneous Workers Union. Brian did everything to convince us to sign-up. In the end, nine of the twelve did. The two older guys, who had been with the Cessna company for over twenty years and were close to retirement declined and so did I. Brian immediately became antagonistic towards me. He accepted the resistance of the two old timers, who would be gone within a couple of years anyway, but I was a thorny, irritating problem. Intent on achieving one hundred percent union membership amongst the cleaning staff, with himself as the self-appointed union delegate, he set out to make my life thoroughly unpleasant unless I changed my mind.

A few days later I resigned. Compulsory unionism was against my principles.

* * *

Sometimes, taking strong decisive action can end up paying dividends. Shortly after I left the Cessna factory, a series of fortuitous events worked in my favour.

Out of a job and feeling dejected, I contacted Janice and told her of my resignation. When she answered the phone, it was as if she'd been longing for me to ring all along and couldn't hide her pleasure at hearing my voice. She urged me to come over and visit. I rang my parents, arranged to stay with them for a couple of nights and set off that same afternoon. Three hours later, I was sitting down enjoying one of mum's roasts and catching up on old times. My parents strongly supported my decision to resign rather than be dragooned into joining the MWU. After dinner I rang Janice again and we agreed I would come over to her place at ten next morning.

It was cool for the time of year and the car remained at a pleasant temperature as I drove across town to Janice's place. For once, Mrs Fenton didn't welcome me at the door with her usual barrage of subjects to talk about. Instead, it was the adorable smiling Janice who ushered me indoors.

'Oh Norman, I'm so pleased to see you. Thanks so much for coming over.'

'The pleasure's all mine.'

'Mum and Dad are both out. It's lovely and cool in the back garden. Let's go out there. I have a cooled bottle of chardonnay and cheese and biscuits ready. Come on.'

I followed Janice to find she had arranged everything beautifully under a shady tree. The picnic table had a clean tablecloth and an ice bucket keeping the chardonnay cool. There was even a small plate of sandwiches and the last of the Christmas cake.

'Is this some kind of a special celebration?' I asked.

'Sure is,' Janice replied, 'one door closes and another one opens.'

'What do you mean?'

'I've stopped grieving over my ex and I'm looking forward to my new relationship.'

I wasn't sure what to make of this comment. I didn't dare think *I* could be Janice's new relationship, so I said nothing. Janice gave me a sweet smile.

'Chardonnay?'

'Yes please.'

Janice poured expertly and handed me my glass. 'Now Norman, tell me all about this business with the Cessna factory and the union.'

We discussed my situation for a few minutes. Janice was most understanding. 'What are you going to do now?' she asked.

'Well, as you know, I've always wanted to start up my own cleaning business. I can be my own boss and anyone who works for me will not be obliged to join a union.

Janice laughed and passed me the sandwiches.

'I have some exciting news, Norman. Yesterday I received my telegram from the Education Department. I've been appointed the infants' teacher at a small three teacher school about thirty miles from here. It's called Peppercorn Gully and I'm leaving for the school the day after tomorrow. There's a two-bedroom house available for the Infants teacher to rent at a very reasonable price. It would be really great if I could find a second person to share the house with me and pay half the rent.'

'That is fabulous news Janice. I'm so pleased for you. You'll be a marvellous teacher.'

'Here, let me top up your glass Norman and prepare yourself for a surprise question.'

I held out my glass and watched as Janice expertly filled it again. I caught the faintest waft of perfume and marvelled at how attractive Janice was, dressed in a light lemon-yellow summer frock.

She giggled mischievously, 'Are you ready for my surprise question?'

I nodded.

'Will you come and live with me in my new house?'

'What?' I exclaimed, 'are you serious?'

'Never been more so Norman. Think of all the advantages. The main one for me is that I have at last come to my senses and know who I want to have my new relationship with. It's you! Over the last few years, I've had half a dozen boyfriends and all the time I've been ignoring you. What do you think?'

'I can't think of anything I would like more, Janice. I've been crazy about you for years, ever since we first met under that peppercorn tree sixteen years ago.'

Janice jumped up, ran around the table and sat on my lap, planting a generous kiss on my mouth.

'Think of all the other advantages Norman. I can help you with the paper work as you set up your own business. Peppercorn Gully's only thirty miles from Shelford, a town you already know and where you should be able to drum up enough customers to make your business a goer.'

24. PEPPERCORN GULLY

I found it hard to contain my excitement. Over a glass or two of chardonnay the two most important things in my life suddenly and unexpectedly were coming to fruition; teaming up with my childhood sweetheart and kick starting my very own cleaning business. My parents were equally pleased to hear the good news and quite understood when I explained I must leave early to get packed up and move my gear out to the house in Peppercorn Gully.

Before I left Janice's place, she laid down the ground rules for the two of us sharing her house in Peppercorn Gully. We agreed to share the domestic duties and expenses, the rent, the electricity, food and any other costs. I had no problem with these rules, they seemed entirely fair. Then Janice went on to stipulate there was one thing we would not be sharing: her bed! I think the wine was beginning to talk for Janice when she blushingly confessed that she was no longer a virgin. Apparently, she had slept with two of boyfriends whilst at Teachers' College but now regretted her promiscuity. Janice was pleasantly surprised to hear I had not yet lost my virginity. I accepted this final condition. Living in the same space with Janice, although not intimately, would still be fantastic.

The house in Peppercorn Gully turned out to be modestly but adequately furnished. Our landlords were a Mr and Mrs Cruickshank, who together ran a sheep station a few miles out of Peppercorn Gully. There was another house on their property occupied by old grandma Cruickshank, now in her nineties. Mrs Cruickshank senior stubbornly refused to even think of moving out. The house in town, which had been purchased expressly for her use had become a liability. The partial solution was to make the town house permanently available to the infants' teacher at Peppercorn Gully Public School. This arrangement had worked particularly well for the last eight years since the infants' teachers were young single women delighted to be accommodated only a hundred yards from the school.

The house could use a lick of paint. However, everything was neat and tidy when we arrived. Mrs Cruickshank had placed a vase of scented roses and a welcome card on the dining room table. The curtains were a touch faded but still did the job. Like many semi-rural houses, it was set in the middle of a large block of land that included a few ageing eucalypts, some she-oaks and a couple of fruit trees seriously in need of a drastic pruning. There was a carport, a shed for storing wood and even a dilapidated brick barbeque. I had no idea how long Janice and I would live in Peppercorn Gully but could see several projects I could immerse myself in to smarten the property up.

Janice was more interested in the interior. She gave the kitchen the tick of approval and was delighted to find her bedroom included an ensuite. The second bedroom was smaller with a single bed and another bathroom. The laundry was small and cramped and led out through a back door to a newly installed Hills hoist. The washing machine was an old model and looked as though it might be on its last legs.

'Well, what do you think Norman. Will this do?'

'Certainly. Much better than any accommodation offer I've had so far.'

'You're not upset because I won't sleep with you?'

'No, I respect your wishes.'

'Are you angry with me because I'm not a virgin?'
'Disappointed more like. There is something beautiful and special, I guess, if two people remain virgins before they marry.'
'Are you thinking of marrying me, Norman?'
'I've often thought about it, Janice.'
'But you've never asked me!'
'That's because we've never really been boyfriend and girlfriend. You've always been with someone else.'
'Perhaps that can change now?'
'I hope so.'
Janice came over and gave me an adoring kiss.

* * *

School started next week. I had absolutely no idea how much work was involved in being an infants' teacher. Janice was out of bed at six in the morning and left for work shortly after seven. She always took a small picnic lunch with her. She would arrive home exhausted around five o'clock and then start marking and preparing lessons for the following day. This became the routine from Mondays to Fridays and it was only at weekends that the pressure eased off somewhat. This meant I took on the cooking duties in the evenings to give Janice more time.

Each day I drove into Shelford looking for work. In the first week I only managed to pick up three small cleaning jobs working for elderly folk for two or three hours a week in their private homes. This meant I was seriously under-employed and not bringing in nearly enough money to pay my part of the rent and expenses. Over the last couple of years, I had been regularly putting money in the bank, which I estimated would allow me to stay with Janice for maybe three months. Unless I found a much more substantial cleaning job, the future looked bleak. Each evening, I would bring home the local paper and Janice would flick through the advertisements to see if there were any jobs I could apply for.

After four weeks a position came up for a cleaner at a new store called Woolworths. I applied and landed the job; however, the hours were horrendous. Start at six in the evening and work through until midnight six nights a week. It was one in the morning before I usually collapsed into bed. Disappointingly, I was not always able to get tea for Janice each night. Thankfully, together with my three small day jobs, I was now earning just enough money to pay my way at Peppercorn Gully.

Despite Janice's long hours and my crazy night-time shifts our relationship steadily blossomed. By mid-year we were seriously in love. On Janice's twenty-second birthday, a Saturday night, I took her into Shelford to the best restaurant in town. It was a cold, clear night and after the meal we drove up to the Shelford Lookout. I had everything planned. Below us the lights of Shelford twinkled magically, while a full moon lit up the volcanic rocks surrounding us. It was quiet and peaceful, nobody else about. We sat together in the warmth of the car holding hands. Fumbling in my pocket, I clumsily extracted an engagement ring and popped the question. Janice had been hoping something special was going to happen for her birthday.

We were married twelve weeks later. Now we share everything…

25. A CAREER CHANGE

Marriage to Janice was everything I ever wanted. For the first time in my life, I was truly happy. We stayed on in our house in Peppercorn Gully and did as much as we could, in the limited time available, to develop the garden and grow our own vegetables. Janice took more pride in the interior and added her own touches to the décor. It felt like home. Janice loved her work at Peppercorn Gully Public School and adored the children in her care. Clearly, she was most successful in her work. The parents were supportive and never a bad word was spoken of Janice. Her confidence grew and as she became more skilled and knowledgeable, she streamlined her work-load so that not so many hours were needed for report writing, marking and lesson preparation.

Working night shifts at Woolworths was not conducive to the life of a newly married young couple. I resigned the week before our marriage.

Sadly, I struggled with launching my own cleaning business. It soon became obvious cleaners were at the bottom of the employment pecking order and nobody was prepared to pay above the basic wage. When Janice and I summed up the situation at the end of the financial year I was only bringing in the equivalent of 50% of Janice's teacher's salary. This began to haunt me. I was not contributing sufficiently to the family's coffers. Janice was good about it and never made any disparaging comments. Furthermore, she did everything she could to help me with reading the newspaper advertisements and completing written work on my behalf. It was decided I must try again to launch my own cleaning business.

I sold my second-hand car and bought a mini-van which was cheap to run, yet large enough to carry my cleaning gear. On both sides of the van and on the back, I promoted my business…

NORM'S CLEANING SERVICES
NO JOB TOO BIG OR SMALL
RING 684 395 FOR A FREE QUOTE

I had virtually no overheads since the van was my office, my storage shed and my mode of transport.

* * *

Early in 1965, after we had been married about eighteen months, two significant events occurred. Janice announced one morning that she was pregnant and that our first born was due in early September. You can imagine the excitement this news created! Planning started immediately. Both sets of parents were roped in and the thrilling news passed on to everyone we knew and even some we didn't know!

The second event appeared mundane at the time but proved to be hugely significant in the long run. Shelford boasted an army recruitment centre, which doubled as a base for the army reservists living in the district. One evening, Janice spotted a promising advertisement in the local paper. The army recruiting centre wanted a cleaner for six hours a week. I applied and was successful. Little did I know where this cleaning job was going to lead.

There were roughly twenty Shelford army reservists who trained twice a week on Mondays and Thursdays after work. My job as the cleaner was to come in the following morning and fix everything. This meant cleaning the showers, the change rooms, the toilets, the captain's office and the recruitment offices. There was also a room referred to as "the mess" where the reservists had "smoko" as well as a kitchen area that they always managed to leave in an untidy state. The cleaning work was easily handled in the three hours allotted and for once the pay was fractionally above the basic wage.

Six hours work per week wasn't much but it was enough time for me to get to know the three regular army blokes who ran the recruitment centre. The "dogsbody" about the place was Private Frank Morcom, an uncouth character, who readily admitted he'd only signed up because the army did everything for him and he didn't have to do any planning or thinking for himself. The army paid him, fed him, housed him and even told him what to do every day. Frank was perfectly content to do whatever he was ordered to do during duty hours as long as the army didn't try to organise his life when off duty. Without fail Frank could be found every night at his local watering hole, "The Shelford Arms." The only time Frank was absent from the pub was when he managed to persuade one of the local sheilas to pleasure him. This didn't happen often because it was too expensive a distraction. Somehow, despite his drinking and occasional womanising, Frank always reported for duty on time next day looking smart and remained tolerably sociable all day.

Responsible for the day-to-day basic training of the reservists was Sergeant Jimmy Snares, a surprisingly versatile fellow and expert at solving the frequent problems the reservists threw at him. Married with three young nippers, he and his family occupied the only married quarters available at the base. Hard working and dedicated, Sergeant Snares had earned his three stripes having seen active service in the Malayan campaign. Athletically built and in his mid-thirties, the reservists had considerable respect for him. Since Shelford was also a recruiting base, Sergeant Snares was passionate about attracting new recruits to the armed services and usually met the quota for Shelford, a minimum of six new recruits per annum.

The officer in charge of the Shelford Recruitment Office was Captain Ralph Guinness. Running a small recruitment centre like

Shelford was seen by his colleagues to be a cushy job with minimal stress, stable hours and safe. Captain Guinness was well aware, however, that if he was to ever earn another promotion he needed to excel in Shelford. After completing two or three years he could then hot foot it back into mainstream army activities. Tucked away in Shelford, it was easy to be "out of sight and out of mind" and hence ignored or forgotten by his superiors. Guinness enjoyed the job especially speaking to high schools, service clubs, sporting clubs and anywhere else he might be able to enthuse a young man to seriously consider the army as a career. Captain Guiness was fortunate to have Sergeant Snares, an excellent man, as his number two.

One morning, when my cleaning was finished, I was chatting with Sergeant Snares who was bemoaning the fact that two promising young men he had lined up to be new army recruits had, at the very last minute, pulled out.

'These bloody young blokes! They were as keen as mustard last week. Told me they were definite starters. If they'd both signed up we'd have recruited seven for the year, one more than our quota. God knows what changed their minds.'

'Sorry to hear they let you down, Sarge.'

'Four weeks remain until the end of this recruiting period and we're sitting on only five starters for the year. The colonel will be really snarly if we can't find at least one more.'

'What's the pay like for privates when they join up?' I asked.

'Overall, the conditions are pretty bloody good Norman. Take home pay isn't as much as the basic wage but remember you get free training, free accommodation, free tucker and an interesting lifestyle thrown in, along with a great bunch of mates for company. I don't know why more young blokes don't jump at the chance. Suits married fellas too. Rent free housing, even some help with the kids' education if you're sent overseas.'

'It sounds really tempting. You know we are expecting our first child in a few months and finding regular work as a cleaner is not easy. If you're in the army, you're sure of a regular pay packet and somewhere to live.'

'Ever thought of joining up yourself, Norman? You're the right age, fit and healthy. I reckon you'd do well in the army.'

I laughed, 'There's one big problem, Sarge. I'm illiterate.'

'Oh shit, I didn't know that.'

The sergeant went quiet. 'That's a great pity,' he added, 'can't you do a crash course, or something?'

Briefly, I filled Sergeant Jimmy Snares in on my various learning problems and explained that despite specially trained teachers, nobody had ever been able to help me.

'Sorry to hear that mate,' was the only comment the sergeant made.

* * *

Janice and I threw ourselves into planning for the new arrival. I had no idea how many things had to be prepared, borrowed or purchased. First up was considering the suitability of the house we were currently renting. There was a spare bedroom but it needed a paint job for starters, new carpet, better curtains, more appropriate furniture and finally to be decorated in a way that would make the baby positively gurgle with delight (Janice's words, not mine). We headed off to talk to our landlords, Mr and Mrs Cruickshank, to see if they would be receptive to our needs.

Janice and I had never missed a monthly rental payment and had looked after the house well. The garden had been brought back to life and the Cruickshanks had remarked on how beautifully clean and neat everything was. On a couple of occasions, we had visited the Cruickshanks and given them boxes of fresh produce grown in the garden. We were sure we were in their good books and hoped they'd be receptive to the improvements and adaptations we wanted to make.

Mrs Cruickshank welcomed us at the door and invited us to stay

25. A Career Change

for afternoon tea. Mr Cruickshank was unusually subdued, seated in his comfortable armchair but not looking well. They were full of congratulations for the good news of the expected new arrival. As we started to explain what we would like permission to do in their house, Janice and I quickly sensed something wasn't right. The Cruickshanks were becoming increasingly agitated. After a few minutes, Mr Cruickshank raised his hand.

'Ahum...sorry to interrupt you folks, but there's a bit of a problem.'

We stopped and looked at Mr Cruickshank, nonplussed.

'I'm afraid there's a very real difficulty,' he repeated, 'we're going to sell your house.'

'Really?'

'Yes, I'm afraid so,' continued Mr Cruickshank, 'I've been diagnosed with terminal cancer. The doctors think I have less than six months left.'

Janice and I tried to find appropriate words for such shocking news. It was Mrs Cruickshank, who kindly added more details.

'As I'm sure you can understand, we have had to make some major and rather sudden decisions. News like this is quite devastating and we've had to make drastic changes to the plans we have for our future. We are selling the farm, your house and even the place old Mrs Cruickshank still lives in.'

'We are so sorry to hear this,' Janice managed at last, 'of course, we quite understand your decision.'

'The house you are living in goes on the market next week and we must give you the required one month notice to leave. Believe me, we are awfully sorry to do this to you. You have been superb tenants.' Mr Cruickshank had to stop at this point to catch his breath. Mrs Cruickshank continued for him.

'We feel very bad about this because there doesn't seem to be anywhere else in Peppercorn Gully where you can live. It's such a small place and there's nothing else here for sale, nor are there any vacant houses around that you could move into.'

We left the Cruickshank's house a little time later feeling desperately sad for them and wondering what we should do for our baby due in six months.

* * *

The necessity to leave our rented house in Peppercorn Gully within the month presented a host of challenges, the most immediate being where were we going to live. If there was no rental accommodation available in Peppercorn Gully, then we would be forced to move back into Shelford and Janice would have to drive to work every day. We only owned the one vehicle, my work van, so it would mean purchasing another car, something we could ill afford. Janice would only be able to work another four or five months anyway before going on maternity leave. Without Janice's salary coming in for the next three or four years, we would be seriously struggling financially and my employment prospects as a cleaner had not improved. One thing was clear; I must find work that paid better than a cleaner's wage. My chances of procuring better paid employment were grim.

Next morning, with these concerns eating away at me, I turned up for work at the Shelford recruitment centre. When my cleaning jobs were done, as was my custom, I visited Sergeant Jimmy Snares' office for a chat before leaving. Jimmy was expecting me and had a cup of coffee ready.

'Morning Norman, got your jobs done?'

'Sure have.'

'Here, I've made you a coffee.'

"Thanks.'

'Norman, do you remember me telling you I've only enlisted five new recruits this year?'

'Yup, and you're expected to recruit at least six.'

I stirred a spoonful of sugar into my coffee and wondered where the sergeant was going with this.

'I don't think any young blokes are going to sign up this late in the year and I'll be in deep shit with the captain. This will be the first time I've failed to make, or exceed, the quota of six new recruits.'

'I'm sorry to hear that, Sarge.'

'I have a serious proposal to put to you Norman. Please go home and discuss the proposal with your lovely wife.'

I took a sip of my coffee and helped myself to a biscuit.

'I'd like to offer you the chance to sign up and join the army.'

'Jimmy, I've told you before. I can't read so the army won't take me.'

'Well, that's where you might be wrong young fella. If you're interested in serving in the army, I'm prepared to help you fill up the forms and officially recruit you. Apart from your one problem with reading, I think you have what it takes. It'll be a win-win situation. I'll get my quota; you'll get a job for as long as you like which pays much better than what you're getting at the moment as a cleaner.'

'Are you serious, Jimmy?'

'I sure am. For both our sakes though, don't go around telling everyone you got into the army when you can't read.'

'But surely I'll need to read and write to cope in the army?'

'Probably not, as long as you've got good mates around you who can give you a hand.'

'That's amazing. This might just get Janice and me out of a tricky situation. When would I start?'

'Three weeks.'

'Three weeks! Where would I have to go for training?'

'Kapooka near Wagga Wagga or Puckapunyal in Victoria.'

'When would I get paid?'

'Fortnightly from the time you commence training.'

'What about accommodation?'

'Well, obviously the army provides accommodation for you when you are training but not for your wife. When your training is finished you can apply for married quarters. The houses are nothing special, nevertheless, heaps of couples find them satisfactory. Families with kids always get a three-bedroom place.'

'Are married quarters expensive?'

'No. A small part of your pay is taken out to help cover maintenance.'

'How long is the training?'

'Six months.'

'The accommodation for Janice while I'm training is going to be the problem, especially if she's pregnant.'

'Well, go home tonight and think about it.'

* * *

As I drove home that evening to our rented house in Peppercorn Gully, I considered Sergeant Jimmy Snares' amazing offer. If it materialised it would be a win-win for us both; Jimmy would get his quota and I would begin a new career that would be permanent and pay better. The security of an army job could be a blessing with our first child due and Janice unable to work for a few years. Furthermore, Jimmy was prepared to bend the rules to get me enlisted, an extraordinarily generous opportunity. Life in the army appealed to me, although I had to admit, I didn't really know what to expect. My vague impressions of army life were solely based on a couple of war movies I'd seen in which the allies were portrayed as the gutsy heroes during the second world war.

Whereas the prospect of joining the Australian army excited me, this decision had to be one that Janice was also happy about. How would she take to being the wife of a serving soldier? It could mean long periods of time when I would be away on manoeuvres and she would have to cope on her own. How would she manage when I was posted to different places and we had to up sticks at short notice and move? What about her career prospects? Quite likely we would have to move to other states and territories and this might present problems for Janice when seeking teaching posts. Janice has always had an adventurous streak, perhaps tonight would test how strong that streak really was.

It was after six o'clock when I parked in our car port. One of our resident possums watched wearily from above as I made my way indoors. Janice was busily preparing dinner using some of our home-grown potatoes, zucchini and carrots. I told her I had an exciting matter to discuss with her and promptly disappeared into the shower to remove the day's sweat, dirt and grime, leaving Janice intrigued but none the wiser.

During dinner I outlined everything that had transpired with Sergeant Snares and went on to say I was keen to sign up but only if she was happy about it. Janice was immediately excited by the possibilities.

'When do you have to give Sergeant Snares our decision?'

'The day after tomorrow. That's the day he has to submit his final annual quota to his boss.'

Janice chased an errant raspberry around her plate, another product of our gardening expertise. Then she sat back and looked at me with a serious expression on her face.

'Have you heard of the domino theory?'

'No, what the heck is that?'

'It's the reason you might be sent overseas to fight for your country.'

'What?'

'It could happen, Norman. I learnt about the domino theory at Teachers' College. The theory was originally pushed by President Dwight Eisenhower back in 1954 and it's the justification for why the United States sends its troops to overseas countries to resist communism. Eisenhower believed communism spreads quickly through countries. One by one nations surrender to communism, just like a row of dominoes.'

'That's interesting Janice, but how does that affect me?'

'If the United States gets involved in any wars in South East Asia Australia is likely to have to go to help, because of the treaty that Australia and New Zealand have signed with the USA. It's called the ANZUS Treaty. The USA is already in South Vietnam defending democracy against the communist Viet Cong. What's more, Australia has already sent thirty military advisers there. The Australian Army Training Team (AATTV) was first sent to Vietnam in July last year.'

'I still don't see how this affects me?'

'Well, if the war in Vietnam escalates and it looks like doing so, then many more Australian troops will be sent there to fight the communists and you might be one of them!'

'I see.'

'I just thought you should realise you could be volunteering to kill or, God forbid, be killed.'

'I hadn't thought of it that way.'

'I didn't think you had, that's why I'm mentioning it now. Being a soldier can be a dangerous occupation!'

'Thanks, it's a sobering thought. Anyway, how do you feel about the idea of my joining up?'

'You know me Norman, I love a bit of adventure. After all, variety *is* the spice of life. I think it would be really exciting. Moving about might be a pain but if it means we can be together as a family, then I can put up with it.'

'There's one big problem I haven't mentioned though.'

'Oh yes, what's that?'

'During my six months of training there's no accommodation provided for wives and families.'

'What? With me pregnant and preparing to give birth? What am I supposed to do? I can't stay here in Peppercorn Gully. Where am I expected to live? Go back to my parents? Mum would drive me crazy fussing about my pregnancy.'

'Well, if I can arrange to do my training in Wagga at Kapooka Army Camp, I thought perhaps you could stay with that friend

25. A Career Change

of yours from Teachers' College you've told me about a few times. Doreen somebody…She lives in Wagga, doesn't she?'

'You didn't tell me Wagga Wagga was one of the training camps. Doreen Ostromoff was my best friend at college and she's teaching at a school somewhere in Wagga. I could certainly try. I could offer to contribute towards my board. That's a brilliant idea, Norman. I'll give her a ring right now. You can do the washing up!'

Half an hour later a smiling Janice returned. 'Doreen was thrilled and said I can stay as long as I need. We even arranged how much board I should pay.'

Next day I sat down with Sergeant Jimmy Snares and together we completed the necessary forms. He was thrilled to get his quota of six new recruits and sent me off immediately for my medical check-up with Doctor Redness. I passed my medical with flying colours.

I was to commence training at Kapooka Army Training Camp, Wagga Wagga in less than three weeks!

26. TRAINING

During my final three weeks before setting off for Kapooka, I spent extra time with Sergeant Jimmy Snares. He was a fatherly figure and felt it his duty to bring me up to date with what was happening in Australia and overseas militarily. Being unable to read severely limited my ability to know what was going on in the world and I relied on the occasional news broadcasts on the radio or what Janice and others told me. According to Jimmy, the situation in Vietnam in March 1965 was alarming and Australia's response equally so. Australia was determined to do more to support its American ally by substantially increasing its forces in South Vietnam.

The good sergeant told me that controversially, and for the first time ever, the Australian Government had approved the conscription of young men into the armed services. The first "National Service birthday ballot" had already been held in Melbourne on March 10th 1965 only a few days before I signed up. In typically Australian style they used a Tattersall's lottery barrel. Inside the barrel were 181 wooden marbles marked with a number from 1 to 181. Each number represented a date falling between 1st January and 30th June 1945. A total of 96 marbles were then extracted each number corresponding to the specific birthdates of 4,200 twenty-year-old men from around the country. These men were sent letters informing them they were required for National Service to serve for a minimum of two years,

26. Training

subject to passing their health checks. Medically fit conscripts were to commence their ten weeks "boot camp" on 1st July. My own "boot camp" started earlier on April 1st, April fools' day!

Although Sergeant Snares had tried to warn me that "boot camp" was no bed of roses, I was totally ill-prepared for what happened as soon as the bus loads of new recruits entered Kapooka Army Recruit Training Centre on April 1st.

'Right, get off this fucking bus or you'll do push-ups until this place is below sea level,' yelled a red-faced sergeant as mad as a cut snake. 'Form up in three ranks, girlies. Get over there you dickhead. Not there you stupid arsehole. What are you, a fuckwit or something? Answer me you penis with ears…or I'll come down on you so fucking hard you won't get up for a month. What's your name dopey prick?'

'Norman McDade sir and I'm a cleaner from Shelford.'

'A bloody scrubber, eh? Well, *that* life's dead and buried. You're in the fucking army now and believe it or not, we're going to make a fucking soldier out of you!'

From that moment on, my army nick-name was "Scrubber."

First up, we were issued with a regimental number, our uniform, ill-fitting boots and had a short back and sides haircut. Already our individuality was disappearing as we became increasingly look-alikes. Then we were assigned, in groups of twelve, to World War II Nissen huts, our accommodation for the next ten weeks. Looking like giant rusty tins cut in half and slapped on the ground with doors at each end, the Nissen huts did little to keep out the cold winds at night. We soon found out why the aboriginal folk called this place Kapooka, "the place of winds."

Mornings started at 0530 hours. We had an hour to shower, dress, make our bunks, polish our boots and clean our rifles before going on mess parade at 0630 hours. For the next hour we were put through marching drill, whatever the weather, before being allowed half an hour for breakfast. The rest of the day was designed to push us physically and mentally to reach a high level of fitness and strength.

To achieve this, we suffered never-ending rounds of drill parades, route marches in full army fatigues carrying our rifles, running increasingly long distances, completing challenging obstacle courses and climbing activities. At times my muscles screamed with pain forced as they were to do things they had never done before. At the end of most days, I staggered back to my Nissen hut and collapsed exhausted on my bunk.

It was a great relief to know Janice was happy staying with her close college friend and had even managed to pick up some short-term casual teaching work around Wagga Wagga ("the place of many crows"). Her pregnancy was proceeding normally. After four weeks we were given two days leave over the weekend and, thankfully, I was able to spend mine with Janice. There was no way we could plan for the baby's arrival yet, since where I would be stationed after graduating from Kapooka remained a total mystery. Apparently, we would be informed at the start of the tenth week which regiment we would be joining and where we would be based.

Janice was impressed when she saw me after the completion of my first four weeks of boot camp. She was not overly keen about my cropped hair but physically I had slimmed down and muscled up so that I cut quite an athletic figure. She also reckoned army life was doing heaps for my confidence. Sex that weekend was fantastic.

Leave over, we returned to Kapooka for more medicine but more demanding than before. Half a dozen of the boys did not report back for duty and so joined the small number of "wimps" who hadn't adapted to army discipline and had already dropped out. The training steadily became more and more challenging as we started to learn new skills. A few of our number were called out at mess parade one morning and informed they had been handpicked for officer training. These guys had three hours to be ready before being whisked off for six months officer training at Scheyville Officer Training Unit, a camp outside Sydney. For the rest of us it didn't take long to adjust to the routines of army life and some actually began to enjoy the

26. Training

experience. Certain army dictums were soon being bandied about, 'if it moves salute it, if it doesn't move, pick it up and if you can't pick it up, paint it' and 'tell them what you're going to tell them, tell them, then tell them what you told them.'

With a couple of hundred recruits being thrown into the deep end at Kapooka, it didn't take long for close friendships to form. A kind of mateship developed as collectively we endured pain, discomfort, the constant abuse of the sergeants, staying out on exercises all night without sleep and suffering a host of minor injuries. Soon we were assigned to sections, groups of ten men, the basic building block of the army. Sections consisted of four riflemen, two scouts, who took the forward positions when out on patrol, a machine gunner and his "number two." These eight men were commanded by a corporal and his second in command, a lance-corporal. Three sections when combined made up a platoon of thirty-four men. In charge of a platoon was a lieutenant and his second in command was an experienced sergeant. These two were joined in the platoon's headquarters by a medic and a radio operator. Three platoons together made up a company of around 108 men and four companies formed a battalion.

As the training continued our introduction to other basic skills broadened. Soon we were learning ceremonial parade work, weapons handling, accurate shooting, field craft, map reading, navigating across-country, how to live off the land, combat first aid and the vital silent hand signals used by all sections. We were permitted two more days leave at the eight-week mark and then three more days at graduation (after ten weeks). It was an absolute joy to be back with Janice for these short leave periods.

During week ten we were handed a form on which we had to indicate which speciality training we wished to pursue for the next three months. The choices were wide-ranging: infantryman, signaller, engineer, medical corps, artillery, bomb disposal, transport, catering, dental and a few more. We were required to list our first, second and third choices. Of course, I couldn't read the wretched form or complete it, so I had to rely on my best mate, Sparksie, for help. His first preference was infantryman, followed by engineer and thirdly, signaller. The least I could do was to follow his lead, so we could perhaps stay together. It worked and we were both posted to the newly formed 6th Battalion of the Royal Australian Regiment.

Normally, Sparksie and I would have been sent to complete our three months of speciality infantry training to the Infantry Centre at Ingleburn Army Camp, south-west of Sydney. However, such was the urgency to get more troops into Vietnam, normal procedures were abandoned. The Australian Army was rapidly increasing its fighting force from three to nine battalions and it was decided the three months at Ingleburn would be scrapped. Instead, new infantrymen would join their battalions immediately and "learn on the job" like apprentices. The 6th Battalion was based at the Enoggera Barracks in Brisbane. When I joined Janice after graduation, I was able to tell her we were off to the capital of Queensland for the foreseeable future. Neither of us had been to Queensland before so this was a new adventure. At least Brisbane was a large city with excellent maternity wards!

Sparksie and I met up again at Enoggera and were thrilled to discover we had both been assigned to 10 Platoon, Delta Company, under the command of a bloke called Major Harry Smith. Sparksie was single but in a serious relationship with a lass from Sydney which was his home town. Janice and I were allotted married quarters which were basic but passably clean. There were three bedrooms, standard army issue furniture and the essential ceiling fans for making the hot clammy weather of summer more bearable. Janice was now seven months pregnant and immediately set about arranging which hospital the baby would be born at and began purchasing the essentials: a cot, nappies, a decent washing machine, a change table, toys and a pram. It was a relief to know we were to be based here for at least three more months and if I was posted to Vietnam, Janice and the baby could remain here. She said she felt reasonably settled. After the rigours of living in a Nissen hut for ten weeks, having a house and wife to come home to every night was a luxury.

Mid-June, 1965 and the forty new members of Delta Company were turned out smartly, standing at attention on the parade ground at Enoggera Barracks. We were keen to impress our commanding officer, Major Harry Smith. The major inspected his new batch, casting a critical eye over each man. We thought we had presented surprisingly well but the major knew he had a horrendous task ahead of him. We had been sent directly to him from Kapooka or Puckapunyal after only ten weeks of "boot camp." None of us had completed the three months additional training that infantrymen normally had received in the past. Somehow Major Smith had to bring us up to standard so we were tough enough and battle ready. In the major's opinion "boot camp" did little more than get rid of the wimps. The real training started now.

Important for us new comers would be learning how to work as part of a ten-man section. Then, in a few weeks' time, sections learnt how to interact as part of a thirty-four-man platoon. Thereafter, the platoons learnt how to participate as part of a company and finally, these companies learnt to work together cohesively as a battalion.

Without further delay, we were organised into ten-men sections. As the result of clever manoeuvring, Sparksie and I made sure we ended up in the same section: Section Two, 10 Platoon, Delta Company. Being with a close mate from the outset was affirming for us both. In our sections we practised patrolling and tracking using the full range of silent hand signals. We refined our skills of navigation and map reading. Map reading presented problems for me but once I learnt what the many symbols represented and Sparksie helped as well, I managed to scrape a pass. There were detailed instructions on firing and stripping down machine guns, operating radios and dressing wounds. Every man in the section had to be multi-skilled so we could immediately take over other roles if there were casualties.

Six weeks later, our intensive section training moved on to learning how to function within a platoon and the three sections of 10 Platoon paraded before our newly appointed commanding officer, Lieutenant Geoff Kendall for the first time. The whole parade was closely watched over by Major Harry Smith, the hardened veteran of the Malayan Emergency during which Australian troops fought the communists in the jungles of Malaysia. At 32, Major Smith was considered a veteran and one of the most experienced serving officers. He was more than ably supported by Company Sergeant Major Jack Kirby, a veteran of both the Korean War and the Malayan Emergency. Together they made a formidable pair. Kirby was the disciplinarian and Major Smith the brains of the show.

The first intake of "Nashos" began their ten-week "boot-camp" training on July 1st. A few of their number eventually ended up joining Delta Company. Mid-1965, most Australians were generally supportive of conscription and Australia's participation in the war in Vietnam. The Prime Minister, Sir Robert Menzies, strongly believed Australia must honour the ANZUS Treaty and support the United States. New Zealand agreed too and also committed troops. Not all Australians, however, were in favour of our participation in Vietnam. Chief critic was Arthur Caldwell, elderly leader of the Labor opposition party. As Australia's commitment to Vietnam increased, his remarks, made in May 1965 became prophetic. 'To exhaust our resources in the bottomless pit of jungle warfare, in a war in which we have not even defined our purpose, or explained what we would accept as victory, is the very height of folly.'

Early in September 1965 we were told the newly formed fifth and sixth battalions would be heading to Vietnam sometime during May 1966. This news inspired our company commander, Harry Smith, to drive us even harder. He knew from personal battle experience the skills and level of fitness that would stand us in good stead in the jungles fighting the Viet Cong and was determined to see every man in Delta Company reached the highest of professional standards.

Each week that passed, we grew stronger, fitter, tougher and more capable.

I will never forget Major Smith's advice to us about the Viet Cong.

'The Viet Cong are fair dinkum fighters and make no mistake, very good soldiers. They are well trained, seriously experienced and don't know how to back off. Soon you are going to meet them and fight against them. We are going to have to train harder than ever to make sure we are ready. The Viet Cong are masters of camouflage, able to strike from close up when you least expect it before instantly disappearing. Generally, they shoot and scoot, avoiding pitched battles unless they outnumber you. They're better equipped than you and know how to live off the land. And… there are hundreds of thousands of them!'

On September 14th I was ordered to report to my platoon commander, Lieutenant Geoff Kendall.

'McDade, your wife has just contacted us to advise that she has been admitted to the maternity ward at your local hospital. Starting from today, you have seven days compassionate leave to be by her side. Good luck!'

I saluted smartly. 'Thank you, sir,' and excitedly caught the first bus to the hospital.

27. PETER FREDERICK MCDADE

Half an hour later still dressed in my battle fatigues; I arrived at the hospital. I was intrigued at how often people stared at me, a soldier in town was still something unusual. Most people seemed to admire me, a few of the younger women were quite flirty but I also received a nasty comment from one man, 'Get lost trooper, don't go to bloody Vietnam.'

I was directed along low-ceilinged corridors smelling of hospital disinfectant. Rows of donated pictures graced the walls and nurses and members of the public bustled around like ants. Finally, I arrived at some double doors proclaiming, "Maternity Ward." As I ventured through these doors, the realisation hit me hard that Janice and I were about to become parents, responsible for a tiny, helpless little human. God forbid; I might already be a dad!

A formidable woman sat at a desk immediately in front of me, clearly the on-duty sentry. I half expected her to challenge me with, 'Who goes there?' Instead, she eyed me suspiciously and asked, 'who are you, young man?'

I almost saluted. 'Private Norman McDade,' I snapped back in far too loud a voice.

The sentry figure seemed amused, 'You can stand easy in here, Private McDade. Your wife's waters have broken and she's in room 14 on the left. Make sure you speak to the duty nurse in the centre of the ward before entering.'

I hurried through the ward, accompanied by the sounds of crying babies and found two smartly dressed nurses discussing a report. I waited politely until they had finished.

'Ah,' said the pretty younger one, 'you must be Norman? Your wife has been asking for you. The contractions have started. Please come with me and we'll see if it's convenient for you to be with her.'

I felt very much the male intruder in this female domain, exacerbated by my army battle fatigues. I was still wearing heavy army boots and carrying my slouch hat. The two nurses, however, had eyed me over appreciatively. Now I clumped my way behind the neat little figure of the younger nurse along to room 14. She popped her head in and spoke quietly to whoever was there, then turned to me and flashed a smile before inviting me in. I think entering room 14 was more terrifying than conducting a left flanking platoon attack when under heavy enemy fire.

Janice was lying in the bed and gave me a lovely smile as I entered. Her left hand was resting on the bed covers so I went straight over, gave her a kiss and sat on the chair provided, holding her hand.

'So glad the army could spare you, darling.'

'No problem…I've been scaring all the old ladies walking around in my battle fatigues. How are things going?'

'They are going exactly as they should be,' replied a voice from the corner of the room. 'Hello, I'm the mid-wife looking after your wife. I'm Sister Glenis.'

I looked across to see a middle-aged portly woman with her hair done up in a bun, 'Hello Sister, glad to meet you.'

'Your wife's contractions started about ten minutes ago. You may stay for a short time only. We don't like husbands to stay too long. This is women's business and it's best if you go home and stay there until we ring you. Your wife has given us your phone number.'

'I don't see why he can't stay if I want him to,' said Janice.

'I'm sorry dear, it's hospital policy,' Sister Glenis responded, firmly.

Sister Glenis had missed her vocation, I mused. She was definitely Company Sergeant Major or even Regimental Sergeant Major material.

I was allowed to remain for another ten minutes before being unceremoniously chuffed off. Janice had driven herself to the hospital so I was able to drive the car home. I stopped to pick up fish and chips on the way back to Enoggera Barracks, then rang Janice's mum. Excitedly, she promised to book her Sydney to Brisbane flight next morning and assured me she would be arriving before the week was up. No need to worry, she assured me, all mums and their babies stayed in the maternity ward for a week anyway. Next, I opened a beer and rang my parents to alert them to the coming event. Now it was a waiting game, waiting for the all-important phone call from the hospital.

At eleven o'clock there was still no phone call so I retired to bed but sleep escaped me. Janice must have been in labour for several hours by now and I knew the shorter the time in labour the better. I debated whether or not to ring the hospital. In the end I resolved to ring at mid-night. I was just putting on my dressing gown to do so, when the phone rang. Fabulous news… Peter Frederick McDade was born at 11.45pm and mother and child were doing well. Sister Glenis told me I could visit at eight o'clock in the morning. That was 0800 hours, I translated. I rang both sets of parents again.

* * *

Most of my leave was spent with Janice and Peter at the hospital that week. It was wonderful to see how naturally mother and child bonded; it seemed so right, so beautiful. When I was first presented with my son, I confess to feeling less than impressed. He was not particularly attractive to look at, although I could only see his face and hands. By the end of the week Peter was looking more normal, more like a chubby, soft baby. Janice recovered quickly and was pleased to have the opportunity for almost complete rest for seven days.

The day before they were due to be discharged, I brought Janice's mother to see them both. Of course, she drooled over Peter and soon embarked on a weird sort of identification exercise.

'Oh, Janice dear, he's got your lovely snub nose and his mouth looks just like yours did when you were born. Isn't nature remarkable. Peter definitely has your big ears Norman and his eyes look like yours too. Does he have a lot of wind, Janice? That was the main problem I had with you, dear. So much wind and it was hard to burp you. Unless I could burp you properly you wouldn't let me put you down. I remember we would yell for joy when you finally expelled the last of that excess wind and we might then get some peace and quiet. Have the nurses shown you the best way to burp him?'

Mrs Fenton was her usual excitable, talkative self and was likely to continue babbling on for at least another half hour without drawing breath. It was an ideal opportunity for me to take in some fresh air and enjoy a cigarette, a nasty new habit I had acquired since joining the army.

Janice and Peter came home the day before my leave expired. My mother-in-law, Belinda Fenton, had swung into action as if she had done this sort of thing a hundred times before. Everything was set up in Peter's room, the cot made, the change-table ready for action with an impressive pile of nappies on hand. Belinda even had a roast cooking in the oven and the table laid ready for dinner. There was a small bottle of champagne in the fridge for Belinda and I to enjoy. Janice, quite rightly, had resolved to avoid alcohol whilst Peter was on the breast. It was a lovely home-coming, although Peter insisted on the occasional yell when he felt the need for some sustenance. It was a joy to see Janice looking so well, so happy and proud.

I was back on the Enoggera parade ground at 0630 hours next morning and endured good-natured ribbing throughout the rest of the day's training. Each night, whilst Janice and Peter were in hospital, I had enjoyed celebratory drinks with my mates. Soon my recent fatherhood became stale news. There were plenty of other events to toast with my army colleagues in the weeks ahead: birthdays, anniversaries, engagements and in a couple of cases, loss of virginity.

28. GETTING UP TO SPEED

It was another eight months before the newly formed fifth and sixth battalions were expected to sail for Vietnam. This seemed a long way ahead. The senior ranks were becoming more and more proficient at motivating us to achieve ever higher standards. Scare tactics were a common ploy. I particularly remember one talk from CSM Chinn that did much to renew our focus.

'The Viet Cong are masters of the booby trap. They have punji sticks, sharp bamboo stakes covered with piss and excrement. They put these at the bottom of pits, pointing up. They cover the pit with bamboo and a light covering of earth. If you happen to fall through, you'll be impaled. You may not die immediately but the toxins are likely to finish you off a few days later. Then there are the snake pits. They tie snakes to the grates that are at the entrances to their tunnels. Move a grate and you're likely to find a batch of cranky vipers. They also leave snakes in backpacks. If you find an abandoned backpack, watch out! And of course, there are trip wires. Trip over one of these and a couple of hand grenades will explode in your face. A variation is the bamboo whip. Tread on this trip wire and a long bamboo with evil spikes will spring into your face or chest leaving you in a bloody mess. The message is, when out on patrol in Vietnam, never relax. Now, learn how to be attentive every step you take when out on patrol. We will be using harmless booby traps during training to keep reminding you.'

Message received! The forward scout in every section was now far more aware.

As if this wasn't enough, there were training sessions when we were ambushed and had to respond instantly. A mock Vietnamese village had been set up and as our section walked through, the image of a VC soldier would suddenly pop out from behind a building. We had about a second to fire two rounds at the figure. Aim for the legs we were told. This way we will probably hit the VC in the torso, because when firing instantaneously a soldier tends to instinctively lift the rifle a little. A single VC figure jumping out we could usually despatch, but then they started making it more difficult with two or three VC popping out from both sides. Towards the end of our training there were as many as five or six VC in the mock ambushes. It was amazing to see how our skill levels improved.

Other major hazards were the networks of underground tunnels the Viet Cong had established over many years. These tunnels, sometimes over a kilometre long, often connected villages so that when you thought you had dispensed of the enemy in one village, you found them suddenly popping up again behind you in another village. The tunnels were cleverly utilised to hide the VC fighters, to store ammunition, food supplies and even provided underground medical facilities. The lesson was, watch your back at all times! Apparently, a few selected volunteers were currently being trained as "tunnel rats." The task for these courageous guys would be to blow up the tunnels and in some cases, enter them to kill the occupants and destroy everything stored therein.

The great thing about training in and around the Enoggera barracks was being able to come home to Janice and Peter every night. Belinda stayed for five weeks until she was confident Janice was completely recovered and managing well. Peter was so cute, so cuddly and playful. Mother and baby had bonded beautifully. Psychologically, Janice and I had blocked out any thoughts about my going to Vietnam in May. We didn't want to face up to the fact I would be on a twelve-month posting and would not return until May 1967. The possibility I might never return or come back seriously maimed or in a body bag, was never discussed. We just got on with our domestic life as best we could and left the dark cloud of Vietnam to float around unheeded.

January 1966 marked another major shift in our training regime. Vietnam was covered in thick tropical jungle and was hot and humid and it was time for us to start training in similar conditions in the northern parts of Queensland. For me, this necessitated long spells in the bush far away from Janice and Peter. Endlessly, we practised moving silently through the vegetation, using offensive and defensive formations and following the hand signals of our leaders. In addition, we learnt to camp out at night with limited rations and how to stay awake when on sentry duty. After a night of camping, we moved on leaving no trace of where we had spent the previous night. We became experts in the art of camouflage and comfortable with using live ammunition in the wild.

Time and again we went through drills for jungle fighting, constantly striving to perform faster and better under the critical eyes of senior staff who pushed and pushed us until it became second nature. Our days began before sunrise, completing fifteen-kilometre hikes in battle fatigues and carrying full kit. Often training continued for up to eighteen hours. The officers who trained with us, wanted us to be exhausted, lacking sleep, frazzled but *still* performing. Sometimes we slept without a tent and simply used our "hoochies" (a stretch of cloth we were all issued with) to provide some limited protection from the rain. We learnt to live with the native animals and to tolerate innumerable mosquitoes, leeches, scorpions and other nasties. Life was tough. Nevertheless, camaraderie and respect for our colleagues grew.

Sparksie and I remained firm mates in Section two, Platoon 10, Delta Company. I was still known by everyone as "Scrubber McDade" in recognition of my previous life as a cleaner. Sometimes, Sparksie came round to our house for a meal and a quiet beer. At these times he would often talk about his girlfriend down in Sydney who he missed terribly. He had high hopes we would be allowed a few days leave before our departure for Vietnam in May and hinted he was going to use this leave time to pop the question.

Section two moulded into a tight-knit unit led by the indefatigable Corporal Ordo, a regular soldier with six years' experience but frustrated he had served this long and not yet seen any real action. A fine rugby league player, Ordo took his responsibilities seriously and conscientiously looked after his nine charges. Second-in-command was Lance Corporal Charlie Anders, the comedian in the section. Also, a regular army man, it had taken him twelve years to finally earn his first stripe. Charlie was guaranteed to ease the tension when the going got tough with a wise crack, a crude joke or just a silly face. Our machine-gunner was the hefty Lance Gourmet, selected for the job because of his physicality. A one-time weight-lifter, Lance could handle the heavy machine gun as if it weighed no more than a couple of balloons. Lance's off-sider was a quiet Tongan guy with an impossibly long and convoluted name so he was simply called "Tonga." Like Lance, Tonga was a substantially large unit. The four riflemen in the section were wiry teenagers from the outback who knocked about together, fought occasionally and drank too much but mostly managed to stay reasonably sober. Last, but not least, were Sparksie and myself specially trained to be the section's forward scouts.

Forward scouts needed to be alert to every minute detail as we led our section through the jungle. Failure to pick up signs of the enemy lurking in the dense vegetation could mean leading our ten-man team into an ambush. Using silent hand signals became second nature to Sparksie and myself as we learnt to hunt for booby traps, trip wires or traces of recent Viet Cong activity. After a bit of experimenting, we agreed I would take the front left and Sparksie the front right and be positioned three or four metres in front of the two machine gunners. Next in line came the four riflemen, then the signaller and finally "Tail End Charlie," more affectionately known as "Arse End Arnold." More often than not, the corporal or his second-in-command functioned as one of the riflemen or the signaller, or even "Tail End Charlie."

Major Harry Smith, officer commanding Delta Company, was convinced the most effective fighting force for Vietnam was the small mobile section that moved stealthily through the jungle environment, undetected and able to switch from defence to attack in a split second. To this end, he redoubled his efforts to improve the performance of the twelve sections under his command. We went on exercises as sections, we trained in our sections, marched in our sections, travelled in sections and fought in our sections. Each section was like a squad of commandos, fit and highly trained, a band of brothers capable of operating independently or as part of a larger cohesive force.

Enoggera Barracks closed down for three weeks over Christmas and New Year with only a small and disgruntled skeleton crew remaining to look after the base. Everyone else went on three weeks' leave. It was enough time for the soldiers to get home, wherever in this vast country home happened to be. Janice, Peter and I drove back to Rinsdorf where both sets of our parents still lived. Baby Peter was a little over three months old and guaranteed to attract people's attention like a magnet. That year we observed all the Christmas traditions with a fine Christmas tree, decorations everywhere, even carol singing around the village. Santa appeared and baby Peter received his first ever Christmas gifts. I don't think he was overly impressed with the Christmas dinner, preferring mum's breast. It was a wonderful festive time together as a full family.

It was tough going back to Enoggera after three weeks of relaxation, over-eating and over-imbibing. Our officers and NCOs gave us hell for the first few weeks to get us up to speed again. As always happens after an extended leave, a few blokes never returned and the military police were called in. Sparksie told me, confidentially, he had been sorely tempted to stay in Sydney with Rosie, his girlfriend. Thankfully, all ten members of Section two reported back for duty and we remained intact as a fighting unit.

By early March, 1966 we had reached a plateau. We knew our stuff, were superbly fit and ready for action in Vietnam but still had to wait another two months before departure. This was a difficult time. 6RAR was battle ready and champing at the bit. The officers and NCOs were stretched to the limit finding different ways to challenge us and some bizarre activities were devised. It was as if, like elite professional athletes, we had peaked too early and now had to try to sustain our motivation and enthusiasm until deployed.

The final major training activity for 6RAR began on 15 April, 1966. The entire regiment was flown in RAAF troop carriers to Shoalwater Bay, half-way between Brisbane and Cairns for "Operation Foxhole." "Operation Foxhole" was the nearest thing to a real battle with the Viet Cong the army could simulate. For three weeks we lived in the bush and did our best to eliminate the enemy, known as the "Queensland Cong." The "Queensland Cong" was, in fact, a company of men from 2RAR. Heat, humidity, tropical rain, rough country, leeches and innumerable other creepy crawlies provided the backdrop for these taxing exercises. For the first time the troops experienced travel in APCs (Armoured Personnel Carriers) more aptly referred to as "heat boxes." In addition, we lived off army rations for the whole time and discovered what it was like to have heavy artillery firing over our heads continuously for hours on end. "Operation Foxhole" was a realistic, sobering introduction to what we might expect in Vietnam.

During the first week of May we returned to Enoggera Barracks and were informed our date for departure to Vietnam was May 23rd. There was now a mad flurry of activity to get everything packed and stowed away in time. Heavy machinery from the Quartermaster's stores had to be broken down, cleaned, stowed and audited. Because of my previous experience as a cleaner, I was especially assigned to

28. Getting up to Speed

assist the Quartermaster Sergeant with his cleaning duties. The contents of our personal kit-bags were inspected and then packed ready for boarding. During this massive packing process, we fronted up for our vaccinations against cholera, typhus and yellow fever.

On 13 May, ten days before departure, we went on leave one more time to say our farewells to family and friends. With little Peter just nine months old, Janice and I decided not to drive the long way back home to see our parents. Instead, we hired a holiday flat for a week down by the beach and introduced Peter to the wonders of the seaside.

29. DEPARTURE

On Saturday morning 21st May 1966, the men of 6RAR marched along Queen Street in the centre of Brisbane for our farewell parade. Kitted out in jungle greens, slouch hats and rifles with fixed bayonets, we felt invincible. The crowds were five deep on both sides of the street clapping, whistling, cheering and yelling for the regiment that had become known as "Brisbane's Own." From the windows, balconies and rooftops people tossed confetti, rose petals and torn up paper over their heroes. We marched past the official podium offering our smartest salutes to His Excellency the Governor of Queensland Sir Allan Mansfield, the Minister for the Army the Honourable Malcolm Fraser, the Queensland Premier Frank Nicklin together with some of the top brass from the Australian Army. It was the proudest moment of my life and sure beat a cleaning career.

Somewhere in the crowd were Janice with a few of her friends as well as Sparksie's girlfriend, Rosie, up from Sydney. Sleeping blissfully in his pram was little Peter totally oblivious to the significance of the event unfolding before him. Janice told me later that evening she and Rosie were moved to tears by the parade. It was really special for Rosie because she and Sparksie had just announced their engagement. They planned to marry as soon as possible after Sparksie's return in twelve months' time.

29. Departure

The official march past over, I was left with two final nights at home with the family before I had to report for duty early on 23rd May, the day of our departure. It was a lovely time. Peter was at a cute stage clapping his hands and starting to crawl. He was "talking" incessantly, although there were no recognisable words being uttered so far. Every night we read stories to him, although often they were snatched away and ended up in his mouth. You might say he was an active reader!

My imminent departure to one of the most dangerous places on earth was never openly discussed. It was sensed, however, through the tenderness we showed towards each other and the loving way we did everything together during our last hours. The army had urged the men serving in Vietnam to write a will before they left. This I had done, with Janice's help. My meagre earthly belongings had all been left to Janice, should I fail to return. I rang my parents on my last night and was surprised to hear them have a cry at the other end. The dawn start next morning required an early night and Janice and I made it a very special one.

The shrill of the alarm clock woke us at 0500 hours. A quick shower, some cereal and a piece of toast and I was ready to leave. Peter was wide awake by now and he and Janice were hovering at the front door for a last farewell. I hate farewells; afraid of letting go and becoming too emotional, I suppose. Little Peter reached out for a last cuddle and as he did so, I could have sworn he said "ad-ad." A final touch of magic to remember him by.

* * *

The USA, Australia and New Zealand may have been allies under the auspices of the ANZUS Treaty, but they had different ideas about how best to conduct a war in a foreign country. To be candid, the senior Australian officers were appalled at the antics of the Americans and decided from the outset that the ANZACS would establish their own base well apart from the Americans. In March 1966 senior Australian officers flew over the south Vietnamese countryside searching for a suitable tract of land to be cleared and established as the base for the 1st Australian Task Force. They found what they were looking for as their helicopter hovered above part of the Phuoc Tuy province. Below them was a prominent hill called Nui Dat (Dirt Hill in the Vietnamese language) surrounded by extensive rubber plantations. The plantations were on flat land, easy to clear and Nui Dat itself could provide an excellent vantage point to observe enemy movements. 5RAR had left for Nui Dat in April 1966, a month before 6RAR and had the initial task of clearing this land and establishing the boundaries.

On the edge of the area designated to become the Australian base was the long-established traditional village of Long Tan. Families had prospered here peacefully for hundreds of years. Without warning on April 4th a host of helicopters descended from the sky at the same time as a troop of armoured personnel carriers trundled into the village from the south. The unwelcome visitors were from the ARVN, the South Vietnamese Army. Their mission, to give the outraged villagers thirty minutes to collect their belongings and leave for other nearby villages. As they did so, American soldiers approached from the north and conducted a ruthless "search and destroy" exercise looking for any VC soldiers who may have been living there or down in the tunnels.

The Australian base was to be built to house up to 5,000 personnel with an exclusion zone of four miles around the base to be known as the "Alpha Line." No Vietnamese would be allowed to reside or work inside the Alpha Line which explains the need for the sudden and tragic demise of the village of Long Tan. Anyone found inside the Alpha Line would be assumed to be enemy and shot or arrested.

The preparatory work of 5RAR in establishing the base continued apace. Patrols combed the entire area within the Alpha

29. Departure

Line ensuring it was free of unwelcome locals. The headquarters building was erected and they started building a wire fence around the entire base. Weapons pits were dug and bunkers built to hold machine guns. The climate was stinking hot and humid and the men sweated so much it became a very real challenge to stay hydrated. Every afternoon the heavens opened and torrential rain tumbled down out of an ashen sky for an hour or so. Welcome to Vietnam!

* * *

Scores of buses and army trucks were lined up along the edge of the Enoggera parade ground on our day of departure. By mid-day the men of 6RAR and their equipment were on the move headed for Brisbane's International Airport where several Qantas Boeing 707s waited patiently. Embarking was an endless process of checking, re-checking and then checking again. We didn't have liftoff until after midnight, squashed as we were into seats that were far too small for hulking great soldiers carrying kit-bags and trying to find spaces to put their rifles. As we watched the lights of Brisbane twinkling happily below, many of us wondered if and when we would return. First stop was Manilla where we transferred onto US Airforce troop planes and flew on to Saigon, Vietnam.

Tan Son Nhut International Airport, Saigon, was extraordinary. We had landed in a war zone! Domestic flights, war planes, private aircraft and helicopters were taking off and landing in all directions. How they weren't colliding was a miracle. We stumbled out onto the tarmac blinking in the blazing heat and debilitating humidity to be ushered straight onto Australian Caribous from the RAAF's No 35 Squadron. Known as "Wallaby Airlines" we walked up the ramps at the back of these massive planes already feeling somewhat shell shocked. An hour later we landed at the far smaller relatively quiet airport of Vung Tau.

Our first few nights were spent camped near a mangrove swamp on the outskirts of the city of Vung Tau, a place unpretentiously named Back Beach. Here we were supposed to be acclimatising to the intense heat, monstrous mosquitoes and humidity. Even the boys from North Queensland couldn't believe this climate. There was not a great deal of training we could do for the first few days and visits into the town of Vung Tau and the neighbourhood were encouraged so we could become better acquainted with Vietnam and the Vietnamese. The countryside was not dissimilar to parts of Northern Queensland where we had trained: swamps, open fields, plantations, bamboo thickets and steep hills covered in scrub. Scores of women, wearing conical hats, were digging with wooden hoes in rice paddies while men on buffalo carts moved ponderously along the dirt roads.

Like everyone else, Sparksie and I headed off into town; a cultural shock if ever there was one! The narrow streets were crawling with people, animals, rickshaws, trundling old buses and the occasional motor car all fighting for a space. Pedlars hawked their wares while bare-footed children ran about everywhere, some totally naked. Stunningly beautiful young women, dressed in long colourful garments moved gracefully around earning high praise from the eager young men of 6RAR. With staggering casualness, butchers slaughtered animals and then carved up the meat on the side of the streets before hanging up the cuts on hooks, the meat still dripping with blood. Through this teeming melee of people came men and women on ancient bicycles wending their way and balancing impossibly heavy loads of goods and shackles. There was an excited buzz of conversation everywhere we went in a strange sounding language. Exotic aromas swept over us as we made our way painfully slowly through this mass of humanity, every step a fresh revelation.

Vung Tau was colonised and then partially developed by the French as a resort town. They erected a number of grand European style mansions and government offices. These faded old gems had become the hotels, bars, cafes and brothels now frequented by thousands of American soldiers on R & R (Rest and Recreation

29. Departure

leave). Despite the war to the north, Vung Tau was a booming city. The never-ending arrival of cashed up Americans was superb for business. However, it only took a couple of days before some of our Australian boys started turning up at the medical officer's tent requesting treatment for various types of venereal disease.

Young Australians had never seen or experienced anything remotely like Vung Tau. Every other building was either a bar or a brothel. The most notable watering holes, according to the Yanks, were the Blue Angel, the Rose Bar and the glittering, Lily Bar. At these bars you could be reasonably certain the drinks were clean, genuine and not watered down. The same could not be said for the many other dark dives that claimed to be proper bars. The boom-boom girls were everywhere. The going rate $2.50 US for three hours. The pox was free…

Sparksie and I were not interested in the boom-boom girls so we spent much of our time wandering the streets, seeing the sights or sitting in one of the more reputable bars yarning to American GIs who were only too keen to boast about their exploits in the war fighting "Charlie" as they called the Viet Cong. They claimed there were up to 300,000 Americans currently in Vietnam and regarded the Australians as totally crazy setting up a base camp in the middle of the VC's heartland. Nui Dat, they reckoned, was crawling with "Charlie."

After a few days "acclimatising" at Back Beach we were once again involved in intensive training. As usual, Delta Company set the pace. Now that we were so close to the real action, our training became deadly serious. We practised firing smoke grenades used to guide a chopper in to pick up a wounded colleague or to drop supplies. We learnt how to enter and exit Huey choppers at breakneck speed, ten seconds to board and five to get off. Patrol work intensified and sentries were posted around the camp now equipped with live ammunition. Fitness runs escalated and night patrols increased. On night patrols, we found ourselves wading through swamps holding our rifles above our heads as we tried to get accustomed to the conditions: mud, vines, stinging plants, leeches, snakes, spiders, monkeys, mosquitoes, wasps and a host of other nasties.

After two weeks at Back Beach, the order came through for us to move immediately to the newly established base at Nui Dat. Enemy activity in the vicinity had been increasing so our arrival had been brought forward. This was it, at last. We had mixed feelings. Finally, we were to be tested in the theatre of war. Were we up to the task? Had we trained hard enough? Did we have the jungle craft, the guts and resilience to overcome "Charlie" on his home ground?

30. NUI DAT

5RAR had been digging in at Nui Dat for a few weeks establishing the Australian base but there was still much to do. Reports were coming in from patrols that a full regiment of Viet Cong (around 1000 men) was positioned only a half-day's march away to the North-west. Reinforcements were needed urgently. Within hours, a number of Armoured Personnel Carriers (APCs) set off for Nui Dat each carrying eleven men. The remainder of 6RAR were to be transported next day in "Chinooks." As always, Sparksie and I planned to travel together.

Already the two of us had written home a couple of times but were yet to receive replies. Mail, we were advised, was sporadic. The best guess was two weeks for a letter to reach a letter box in Australia and probably rather longer for mail coming the other way. We'd been in Vietnam for two weeks already so hoped to receive our first letters from our loved ones shortly after arriving in Nui Dat.

Chinooks are huge, heavily armed American choppers with dual rotors. Eight of these monsters were lined up at Vung Tau airport ready to transport the remainder of the regiment. 'Ten seconds to board' barked the sergeant as we raced, heads down, across the tarmac. With a roar we took off and in an impressive convoy flew north for six minutes before descending one by one into the heart of our new base, Nui Dat. 'Five seconds to exit' and we ran to the edge of the landing pad fittingly christened "The Kangaroo Pad."

Nui Dat was under the overall command of Brigadier Oliver Jackson, reputedly a man not to be trifled with. Jackson was responsible for close to 2,000 men made up of the 5RAR, the 6RAR, the 1st Armoured Personnel Carrier Unit, artillery units, engineers, signallers, medics, intelligence and sundry others. The brigadier was tall and gaunt and exuded total confidence. He could be described as "having presence."

The base was being established in a rubber plantation which afforded some relief from the relentless sun. The men of 5RAR, after several weeks of building, were exhausted and badly needed a break. The arrival of the relatively fresh 6RAR was more than welcome. Those that needed to climbed to the top of Nui Dat Hill which provided a 360-degree vista of the surrounding area including villages, roads, plantations and any Viet Cong movements. Little wonder the Viet Cong were not impressed with the sudden arrival of close to 2,000 additional enemy. Located less than 50 kilometres north of Vung Tau the climate at Nui Dat was no different, stinking hot and humid with heavy rains arriving every day around 16.00 hours. In fact, the rain was so predictable that "see you after the rain" was synonymous with "see you at 17.00 hundred hours."

Initially things were pretty grim for the men of 6RAR. Our tents had not arrived and we were forced to sleep under our 'hoochies' that gave little protection from sudden tropical downpours meaning we stayed permanently wet for days. Failure to keep dry frequently led to tinea and other nasty fungal infections. Adding to our misery was the absence of proper field kitchens wherein to cook our meals, instead we were reliant on uninspiring ration packs. At least we had ablution pits!

Our first task was to complete the erection of the defensible perimeter fence extending for a total of twelve kilometres around the entire base. This meant driving in fence posts then stringing up several strands of wire between them. This was the easy part.

30. Nui Dat

Near the fencing we dug trenches deep enough for soldiers to take cover and fire at attackers. Other members of 6RAR were employed digging out the bunkers for the HQ, various storage areas and, most importantly, dry pits for the safe storage of ammunition. It was gruelling, backbreaking work and half the time there was not enough equipment to get the job done properly. We were short of fencing, short of fence posts and even short of machine guns. But we persevered hoping like hell the VC wouldn't attack while we were still establishing some semblance of a secure base.

Mail distribution times were interesting. Choppers travelled regularly between Vung Tau and Nui Dat and every second day they usually brought in mail. The mail was sorted into platoons and the platoon sergeants had the job of calling out the names of the lucky ones when each platoon was dismissed at the end of the working day. All thirty-four members of the 10th platoon would hang around Sergeant Bob Buick in a melee while he yelled out names…

'Harris'

'Here, Sergeant.'

'Corporal Creighton'

'Here, Serg.'

'McDade'

'Over here, Sergeant.'

And so, it went on. We, the fortunate ones, hurried away excitedly, desperate to spend quiet time with our loved ones. Others, less fortunate, mooched off despondently. I felt particularly sorry for those who seldom heard from home. Getting a letter from someone special meant so much and lifted our spirits. It was good to be reminded a better, happier place still existed across the seas, a place where one day we would re-unite with our loved ones. Sparksie and I both received our first letters from home with the second postal delivery and together we raced back to our freshly erected tent to devour their contents. It was too much for Sparksie and he couldn't avoid a cry when he read a beautiful loving letter from his fiancée.

Being a married man I was made of sterner stuff, but was still deeply moved to hear Sparksie read out my letter from Janice. Everything was fine at home, although little Peter often asked for his 'Da-da.'

The hard work at Nui Dat continued for several more weeks. It was generally believed there were fewer than 500 enemy in the vicinity and this was considered too small a force to seriously threaten the base. Nevertheless, enemy patrols were active around the perimeter and minor skirmishes were frequent. Our intelligence unit thought the enemy patrols were trying to assess our overall strength and map the positions of our facilities in preparation for a major attack once their reinforcements arrived. The best form of defence was for night patrols to venture outside the perimeter of our base into enemy territory. Consequently, each company was assigned an arc along part of the perimeter and held responsible for patrolling this area. So, we worked our guts out during the daytime and then often, at night, would be out again on patrol or sentry duty. Sleep became a precious commodity.

Sparksie and I had trained hard to be the forward scouts for our section. It was generally recognised that the forward scouts had the most dangerous position in the section. Should the section encounter the foe, it was the forward scouts who were most likely to be the first targets. Not only did Sparksie and I have to focus our desperately tired, sleep-deprived eyes, on everything that moved or seemed to move, but we had to also be searching for a range of cleverly hidden booby-traps. Gradually, despite our exhaustion, we became more expert at finding our way through the thick jungle vegetation and knowing how to proceed almost noiselessly. We began to appreciate the varying sounds and smells of the jungle; when to be cautious, when to be confident. Section two was steadily developing into a highly skilled unit, a team in which the members almost instinctively understood each other. Confident as we were, we knew to guard against complacency. Patrols from other companies had been ambushed and casualties experienced. Next time it could be us!

30. Nui Dat

There were few creature comforts in Nui Dat. Our tents turned out to be 20 feet by 20 feet white canvas and in a shocking state of disrepair. There were holes in the roofs that allowed the rain in. Apparently, these tents had been in use during World War II, more than twenty years ago. It was a process of trial-and-error finding positions for our beds-between the rain leaks. Trying to keep clothing and the inside of the tents clean and dry was a nightmare since we were surrounded by red oozing mud that somehow managed to penetrate everywhere.

On the few occasions we had time to relax, we wrote letters home, played cards, or caught up on sleep. Occasionally the Yanks of 2/35th Artillery invited some of us "Ossies" to come over to watch "R" rated movies and drink Budweiser beer in an enormous tent set up especially for this purpose. The Americans had an ill-disciplined, sloppy approach to war. They were often observed going out on patrol, smoking cigarettes, talking and even listening to music. Not surprisingly, they attracted the attention of the VC and suffered horrific casualties. Whenever this happened, they called in their heavy fire power and bombed the hell out of the place where the attack had occurred. Of course, the VC had already well and truly disappeared by the time their aircraft arrived. Saddest of all, the Yanks never seemed to learn.

Every four weeks each company at the Australian base was given two days and two nights leave in Vung Tau. Most of the single blokes took the chance to let their hair down and spend time drinking cheap liquor to excess, gambling and enjoying the delights offered by the plentiful supply of prostitutes. Absconding was rare. The men returned to base with heavy hangovers and many with nasty venereal diseases. Nevertheless, the next leave in Vung Tau was something eagerly anticipated and leave undoubtedly helped maintain morale.

Sparksie and I always looked after each other during our Vung Tau leave. We stayed away from the gambling halls and spent most of our time wandering around the markets before retiring to a reasonably decent pub for a few quiet drinks. We were fortunate to find a small one room flat to sleep in, run by an elderly lady and her senile husband. It was located along an out of the way side street a couple of kilometres from all the action in the centre of town. It was basic but the place was reasonably clean and there were no bed bugs. The dear old lady with only a smattering of teeth, took a liking to us. The couple badly needed the money and didn't want to attract servicemen who would return late at night drunk and disorderly with a couple of prostitutes for company.

Over the next couple of months, the personnel at the first Australian Task Force swelled to almost 3,000. We were joined by the 161st Field Battery from New Zealand in an echo of the time the two nations fought side by side at ANZAC. More crews of Armoured Personnel Carriers (APCs) arrived and were quickly dubbed the "turret heads." The artillery and engineers also moved in and set up camp. The artillery guys were soon referred to as the "drop-shorts." Finally, there were the "Brylcream Boys," the fellows involved with the RAAF. Sadly, there was little time for socialising with all these new arrivals although we sometimes met up with them when on leave in Vung Tau. Piece by piece the base was completed until finally it included extensive medical facilities, canteens, streets, tented villages, a chapel, a post office, a rubbish dump and even a dentist. It was more like a small town.

The greatest thrills at the base were the three concerts given by the seventeen-year-old sensation from Sydney, Little Pattie, together with pop stars, Col Joye and the Joye Boys. What an incredible day that was! Everything was geared to having as many as possible of the 3,000 men at the base present. There were minimal patrols out that day, no training exercises, no routine duties to be done, no briefings. Even the staff and patients at the medical centre limped and staggered out for the concerts. Had the Viet Cong known, this would have been the ideal time to launch a full-scale assault

30. Nui Dat

on the base. The performers didn't disappoint and overall morale immediately shot up a couple of notches.

Wonderful letters from home arrived every few days. Around week nine of our time in Nui Dat one particular letter from Janice floored me. At first, I thought Sparksie was making it up as he read Janice's letter out loud to me.

My Darling Norman,

It was wonderful to receive another lovely letter from you today. As always, Sparksie is doing a wonderful job writing your letters for you. Please tell him once again how much I appreciate his generous help.

It must be awful trying to live in that ghastly heat and rain and all that horrible red mud. Peter and I are so proud of you! I'm glad the perimeter fence is nearly finished at last. Perhaps when it is finally completed you will have less to do during the daytime and can catch up on sleep? It sounds like you and Sparksie are the best forward scouts in the world…

Now, I have some very very exciting news for you, dearest. I hope you will be pleased? I'm pregnant again! I think it must have happened on the very last night you were here with me. What a wonderful present you left me that night. I missed a period and then a second one and have been feeling a bit crook in the mornings. Yesterday the doctor confirmed it. I'm due mid-February, only three months before you'll be home. So, when you arrive home, you'll be the father of TWO littlies. What do you think of that?!?

I've rung both sets of parents and they are thrilled to hear they will be grandparents again. Mum has promised to come and stay as soon as I give her the word. She's going to knit some yellow booties that can be worn by either a baby girl or boy. It's going to be a bit crowded with four of us in the house. If we have a third one, we will be eligible for a larger place!?!

I'm already counting down the weeks until you are home. I keep telling Peter that 'da-da' will be coming home in May next year but he doesn't understand. He loves to look at the photo of you in your uniform by our bed and it sends him into a chorus of 'da-da, da-da' for several minutes. So cute!

It's really cold. Lots of snow in the Snowy Mountains.

Got to go and do the nappies...

All my love, darling and keep writing with Sparksie's help.

Janice XXX OOO XXX

That evening Sparksie and I celebrated my happy news at the canteen. News from his fiancée was good too but I knew Sparksie fretted whether she would stay faithful for another nine months.

31. ENEMY BUILD-UP?

Sparksie and I and others from our platoon frequented the same canteen when we had a bit of spare time. Usually, we knocked over a couple of beers and indulged in some packets of crisps. We were modest drinkers in comparison to most of our mates. Over the weeks we gradually befriended an eccentric guy who was often in the canteen in the evenings by the name of Captain Trent Cunliffe. The fact he preferred to drink in *our* canteen rather than in the officers' mess, marked him out straightaway as being a strange bloke. Everything about Trent was unusual. He usually drank on his own and then only whiskey which he had purchased in the officers' mess and smuggled into our canteen in a knapsack (only beer was available in our canteen).

I don't remember how it was that Sparksie and I first got chatting to Trent. Anyway, our antennae were soon twitching when we discovered, much to our surprise, he was head of intelligence and had direct access to none other than Brigadier Jackson the commander of the entire base. If anyone knew what was going on in the province of Phuoc Tuy, it was likely to be Captain Cunliffe. The captain had no qualms about talking to a couple of lowly privates like us, seemingly unmoved by the huge differential in our rank.

Captain Trent Cunliffe was clearly an eccentric, a total mis-fit in the Australian Army. He told us he had been approached by the army one day whilst lecturing about Babylonian history at the University of Sydney. He had received virtually no basic army training and was measured up and handed two military uniforms almost immediately. To entice him to stay, the army gave him the rank of a captain, three pips on his shoulder lapels and a salary to match. Within a week he was rushed to Phuoc Tuy to head up the small intelligence unit based there. Now it had become Trent's responsibility to inform Brigadier Jackson of any significant enemy movements or troop build-ups in the province.

Tall and gangly with heavy framed spectacles, Trent sat at the same table every night surreptitiously swigging the occasional mouthful of whiskey from a bottle well concealed in his knapsack. Invariably, he was surrounded by maps and papers and could be seen scribbling down his observations onto a thick pad of paper with a red Parker fountain pen. It transpired that Trent had been singled out as a man with an exceptional brain sharpened by becoming a world authority on the deciphering of Egyptian hieroglyphs. Trent's outstanding powers of analysis were now required in the province of Phuoc Tuy to fathom out what the Viet Cong were doing and where and when they might attack. Later, we discovered, as if we didn't already know he was brilliant, that Captain Cunliffe had two PhDs to his name and had been awarded an honorary doctorate from the University of Cairo. For someone like me who cannot read or write, making sense of those weird Egyptian squiggles was truly miraculous.

Trent was quite happy to chat to us about his work and how he pieced together the intelligences he received. Essentially, he had three main sources of information; reports from the American 173rd Airborne boys, observations of the South Vietnamese operatives in the province and encounters and reports from the constant patrols that ventured outside the perimeter of the Nui Dat camp both day and night. Trent was an excitable, restless fellow. It was as though his brain was constantly in overdrive. At times he became quite agitated as he relentlessly analysed and re-analysed the mass of information coming to him and tried to make overall sense of this plethora of detail.

Sparksie and I will never forget one particular evening when we were sitting with the enigmatic captain and he suddenly stared at us through his heavily framed spectacles and announced, 'The Viet Cong have assembled a large enough force to attack and virtually wipe out this entire camp! Unless we take urgent steps to prepare for this attack, few of us will be around to tell the story in the future.'

'Hey, that's a bloody alarming thing to say,' responded a startled Sparksie, 'how do you know?'

Trent took another nip of his beloved whiskey before he replied.

'I've been keeping meticulously careful records of all the data coming in ever since I first came here with 5RAR nearly four months ago. For a long time, there was virtually no change. Sporadic reports came in of small groups of Viet Cong moving about within the province but it appeared to be quite random. Sections of VC were occasionally encountered and their movements indicated they were primarily interested in finding out what *we* were doing, but that was all. Throughout the whole province, the VC didn't number more than perhaps 500 men, in toto. A few times they ambushed us. What we now call "strike then scatter." They certainly didn't want to stand and fight. However, in the last week or so, things have drastically changed.'

'Crikey!' I said, 'what have you done about it?'

'I've been jumping up and down in front of the brigadier, trying to convince him and the other top brass that a major attack is imminent.'

'Do they believe you?' asked Sparksie.

'I don't think so. Some of them regard me as a nutcase and simply laugh at my advice. If you don't have the gravitas, it's difficult to be taken seriously.'

Sparksie and I exchanged looks. Neither of us had heard the word "gravitas" before but we still understood what the good captain meant.

'How can you be sure you're right?' I asked.

Trent waved an arm loosely across the papers and graphs scattered about in front of him. 'Because I'm the only person in this whole bloody camp who has access to every tiny bit of information coming in from the scores of patrols, from the Yanks aerial reconnaissance, from the South Vietnamese observers and our own patrols and can put the whole bloody lot together into something meaningful.'

'So, what can you do to convince the brigadier you are right, captain? This is really bloody serious! We could all end up being slaughtered by the VC!' Sparksie demanded.

'Read this...' Trent pushed a statement he had written towards me, not knowing I was illiterate. I gently pushed it over to Sparksie who started reading it out loud.

OFFICIAL STATEMENT

ENEMY FORCES SITUATION (Captain Cunliffe, Head of Intelligence)

The main force controlling operations in the province of Phuoc Tuy is the VC's 5th Division. This division has two sub-units, namely the 274th Regiment and the 275th Regiment, totalling approximately 3,850 men. The 274th Regiment comprises 2,000 well trained men and is currently moving slowly towards us from the North-east with the intention of launching a major attack. These troops have the normal complement of weapons but it is strongly suspected they now also possess 120mm mortars. The 275th Regiment is also on the move a few miles behind the 274th and will be used as reinforcements, should this be necessary, or to surround us and cut off our retreat.

Evidence of this military build-up has been mounting over the last ten days. I am convinced a full-scale attack with the intent of destroying this camp is imminent. Steps need to be taken immediately to prepare for this major assault.

There was a moment of silence as Sparksie and I contemplated the full impact such a bold statement should have had on the top brass.

'How can they ignore a statement like that?' I inquired.

Trent shrugged his shoulders, 'They're a conceited lot and I'm the only one alerting them to the impending situation. The Kiwis have no intelligence officers here and the Yanks are hopeless at intelligence gathering. The VC could be drinking American Budweisers in one of their canteens before the Yanks would twig something was amiss.'

We laughed nervously, although it was no laughing matter.

* * *

Sparksie was an incredible mate. It was over a year since we had teamed up at Kapooka and I have lost count of the number of times he has helped me when something had to be read, a form needed to be filled in or a letter written. He never complained and always found time to read my letters from Janice a second time or even a third time if I felt homesick. Every second or third night, if we were not out on patrol, he would write my letters to Janice as I dictated. Then he would compose his own letter for Rosie, his fiancée. Infrequently, I also wrote to my parents but didn't like to do this too often in case Sparksie objected to doing so much letter writing.

I did what I could to repay Sparksie for his generosity. There were a few simple ways of doing this that Sparksie accepted as my attempts to thank him. For example, I provided the postage stamps, pens, envelopes and writing paper and I was the one who always took our letters along to the camp post office for posting after the sergeant had read them through to check we were not offending the powers that be or giving away military secrets. There were other ways to repay Sparksie too. An extra beer or I might clean his rifle or, on a couple of occasions, I even polished his dress boots for him. When on leave in Vung Tau I would pay for one of his meals sometimes. Sparksie accepted my small tokens of thanks without saying a word. It was a tacit understanding between mates.

The news from Janice was always uplifting; her letters upbeat, optimistic and full of amusing little anecdotes about what Peter had been up to. Sometimes there would be a couple of black and white photographs of Peter or the pair of them together. They had recently acquired a puppy spaniel that got along famously with Peter. The puppy's name was Rusty and there was a photo of him playing with Peter as well. Janice reported her bump was starting to show, very exciting!

Sparksie was receiving heaps of letters from Rosie but he only told me snippets. They were very much in love and some of what Rosie was writing might have been a bit risqué. The fact that all outgoing letters had to be vetted by the sergeant seriously curtailed what Sparksie felt he could say in reply. This really annoyed him but it was a censorship cross we all had to endure.

* * *

The next time Sparksie and I met up with Captain Trent Cunliffe he was sitting in his usual place in the canteen feeling a little more positive. Apparently, Brigadier Jackson had at last taken *some* notice of the many intelligences Trent had been feeding him. The brigadier was still not convinced a force of 3,500 Viet Cong was nearby and planning a major attack, but as a compromise he agreed to take the initiative with regard to a village called Long Phuoc and ordered 6RAR with 13 Armoured Personnel Carriers to move the villagers out and then totally destroy the village. Trent had been telling the brigadier for weeks that Long Phuoc, situated two miles outside the perimeter fence, was strongly pro-Viet Cong and quietly harbouring the VC and storing their supplies of ammunition and food. When the main VC force attacked, Trent believed it was sure to use Long Phuoc as a staging post. Its elimination would, therefore, make the defence of the Australian base easier.

The very next day 6RAR was given its orders with regard to the village of Long Phuoc. "Operation Enoggera" involved the safe removal of the villagers and the destruction of every building together with the network of underground tunnels. Any suspected VC were to be killed or captured. Our troops were to be transported using a shuttle service of Armoured Personnel Carriers. We were told Long Phuoc offered an enemy fortress only a few kilometres out of Nui Dat. It was suspected the village was riddled with trapdoors leading down to a sophisticated system of tunnels and that one tunnel went three kilometres underground before surfacing in the village of Long Tan. We were under no illusions; this was going to be dangerous work. At any moment trapped VC were likely to open fire or toss hand grenades amongst us. We also needed to be wary of booby traps, trip wires and the ghastly punji stakes.

Like most of my mates I felt bad about kicking out these villagers. We gave them thirty minutes to collect their most valuable belongings and start walking. Understandably, the villagers were livid and didn't waste time telling us what they thought of us. Then, a steady trickle of elderly folk, together with mothers and mobs of children began moving slowly and grudgingly away using donkeys, carts and any other form of transport available as they headed for the nearest village. If these people weren't already ardent supporters of the Viet Cong, they definitely were now! The job had to be done. If we didn't move the villagers on and destroy the place, the VC would use the well-established village to kill Australians.

With Long Phuoc surrounded the four companies of 6RAR each took responsibility for roughly a quarter of the village. We conscientiously searched every building, one by one, collecting any religious artifacts we found, which we handed back to the villagers. It was a relatively prosperous village with houses made of stone or brick that had stood there for perhaps a couple of hundred years. We were also under strict instructions not to touch shrines or pagodas.

Once every house in the village had been cleared of people and the religious artefacts removed, the next step was to go through again looking for hidden trapdoors leading down to the tunnels that honey-combed the village. These trapdoors were cleverly hidden, under mats, behind cupboards, under beds, in the small vegetable gardens. Once a trapdoor was found, it was opened up and at least one hand grenade lobbed in. Finally, the whole village was torched to the ground (except the religious structures). An acrid smell filled the skies as a warning to other villages not to welcome the Viet Cong. Most of us feared we were already too late.

The job done, we returned to base having suffered no casualties.

* * *

That evening Captain Cunliffe was again in the canteen keen to find out how everything had transpired. He was much relieved to hear we had completed "Operation Enoggera" efficiently and without loss. He felt vindicated when we told him we had discovered dozens of trapdoors and interconnected tunnels as well as caches of ammunition and armaments. The Viet Cong had been happily using Long Phuoc for quite some time.

The captain took an extra-large gulp of his secret whiskey by way of celebration and announced he had some news of his own.

'I'm being moved on…'

Sparksie and I registered our surprise at this news. By now we had become quite friendly with this eccentric intelligence officer and more than pleased to hear what "intelligence" was thinking.

'I believe they've had enough of me. My reports are too alarming and top brass simply don't want to hear them, let alone believe them. Mind you, I've been shown to be one hundred percent on the money with Long Phuoc!'

We nodded our agreement.

'So, what happens now?' I asked.

'Tomorrow, I'm to be choppered out to Vung Tau for a few days leave while they decide what to do with me.'

'They're bloody bonkers!' exclaimed Sparksie with more than a trace of anger in his voice.

31. Enemy Build-up?

Trent shrugged his shoulders, 'Maybe they'll send me home?'

'You'd be a lucky devil,' I added.

'Hey, you can get among all those gorgeous bang-bang girls when you're on leave in Yung Tau,' joked Sparksie and then thought better of his crude suggestion for the captain wasn't really the type to be attracted by the local tarts.

'Who's going to take your place here then?' I asked.

'Probably my number two, Lieutenant Gibbs, unless they send someone else out from Australia.'

Sadly, that was the last evening we enjoyed with Trent. We heard later he had been "invalided" back to Australia as being "unfit for duty."

Trent's prediction the Viet Cong were amassing troops for a full-scale attack proved correct. Top brass's failure to properly heed and act on his intelligence reports cost us dearly.

32. "OPERATION HOBART"

With Captain Trent Cunliffe invalided back to Australia, the remaining Intelligence Unit struggled to bring further meaningful and credible advice to the brigadier. Cunliffe's claims of a force of some 3,500 well-armed, highly trained Viet Cong amassing only a few miles North-east of Nui Dat was largely ignored, even ridiculed. What little intelligence information trickled in suggested there was a maximum of 300 Viet Cong in and around Nui Dat 2, a hill to the north east smaller than Nui Dat.

On July 24th 1966 "Operation Hobart" was launched; a search and destroy mission to find and destroy this force of 300 Viet Cong. 5RAR was ordered to remain at Nui Dat to defend the base while 6RAR was given the job of carrying out "Operation Hobart." Finally, the men of 6RAR were being given the chance to prove their worth in battle. After twelve months intensive training we were to demonstrate our fighting skills in a real situation. We left the perimeter of Nui Dat feeling confident and strong as we anticipated the likely combat ahead.

The element of surprise is invaluable in battle strategy so we left at 0100 hours in total blackness. Pushing through dense jungle in daylight was tough work, pushing through jungle in total darkness was madness. Nevertheless, we pushed on. By 0400 hours we had traversed five exhausting kilometres and it was estimated we were only a kilometre away from our destination. Here we stopped and slept or rested for two hours until dawn. Sparksie and I found the trunk of an ancient rubber tree to lean up against and fell into a fitful sleep almost as soon as we sat down.

Shortly before dawn we were awoken by the deafening chorus of birds of the jungle, no doubt annoyed to find some 550 men occupying their territory. Breakfast rations were hurriedly consumed and we formed up separately into our four companies ready to advance slowly towards the suspected enemy position. Last night no signs of the Viet Cong had been detected, but the adrenalin was pumping now as we expected to make contact, or at least find signs of Viet Cong activity, very soon.

Delta Company (our company) was the first to discover clear traces of the enemy. Heavy tracks of troops moving south and estimated to be as much as company strength, that is, around a hundred men. Orders came through for Delta Company to break up immediately into its twelve sections and proceed with extreme caution. Sparksie and I took up our places as the right and left forward scouts respectively. Long ago we had lost track of how many hours we had led section two as its forward scouts. We still had the same ten men we had trained with in Queensland and we worked together like clockwork. After spending hundreds of hours functioning as a section, we knew each other's strengths and weaknesses. Instinctively, we made any necessary adjustments and quickly adapted to our surroundings.

Lieutenant Geoff Kendall, our platoon commander, indicated we would be departing in ten minutes. A last chance to have a pee, adjust equipment and check our rifles were loaded. The boys of our section gathered for a few quiet whispers. We were a nervous lot but none of us wanted to admit it or let our peers suspect we were feeling tense. We sensed we were at last about to see real action. This was it! We were so close to the VC. However, we had no way of telling whether the VC knew of our presence and were perhaps, at this very moment, organising an ambush or setting up their trip wires.

Sparksie and I shared a few final thoughts.

'This is looking a bit serious, Sparksie. Don't forget, if anything happens to me, please write to Janice and return her photos. Tell her what happened.'

'Come on Scrubber, don't even think about it. You'll be fine mate. We might not even have to fire a shot in anger. We are only one of twelve bloody sections moving towards the VC. Chances are we won't see any action.'

'All the same, Sparksie, it's good to know you'll do the right thing by me, if it's necessary.'

'And what happens Scrubber if *I'm* the one that gets hit?' asked Sparksie.

'I might not be able to actually write a letter for you mate, but I'll be sure to find someone in our section to do it for you. I'll dictate the letter and that's a promise.'

'Okay, sounds good. Be sure to tell Rosie she's the most beautiful person in the world.'

'I'll do more than that Sparksie. When we get out of this wretched hell-hole, I'll go and visit Rosie for you.'

'Likewise, I'll visit Janice and little Peter for you.'

Our solemn pledges made, we took up our places at the head of section two and waited for the order to advance. From here on there would be no more talking, only hand signals.

* * *

The signal to advance came as the first sizzling rays of the sun hit and sweat started to eke out of our pores. Sparksie and I separated so there were four or five metres between us and began picking our way carefully through the undergrowth. In thick jungle like this it was impossible to always keep the same distance apart because impenetrable plants sometimes blocked our way. Then there were stinging plants that reputedly could inject so much poison into your body that you would be writhing in agony and need to be hospitalised. It was rumoured that too much of this poison and you could die!

There were also many amazing plants to admire. Apart from the native rubber trees, there were strangler figs, walking palms, lupuna, tangarana and lofty ironwoods. Closer to the ground were varieties of colourful orchids, ginger plants, vines, mosses and slippery tree roots. Occasionally someone in our section tripped over roots, or slipped over in the mud and came crashing to the ground. Part of our training had involved learning how to fall and, most importantly, controlling any loud expletives that might give away our position. Appreciation of the plethora of flora and fauna of the tropical rain forest was far from our thoughts though as we picked our way carefully and silently forward. Amongst this dense foliage the enemy could be as close as five metres ahead and we might never see them.

We had only been advancing for a few minutes when there was a sudden exchange of fire to the north of us where another section was also slowly advancing. We learnt later they had stumbled on a couple of unsuspecting Viet Cong surveying the area. Both men were instantly mown down. If the VC didn't already know we were in the vicinity, they certainly did now. Unscathed, Sparksie and I continued on along our compass bearing, silently, in tight section formation, using hand signals only. Everything was eerily quiet. The sudden explosion of gun fire had frightened the wildlife too.

"Operation Hobart" was planned as a seek and destroy exercise. We were the aggressors, intent on eliminating any Viet Cong we came across. According to the limited intelligence available since Captain Cunliffe was so shamefully dismissed, there were less than 300 Viet Cong in the area. 6RAR numbered roughly 550 men so we believed we had the advantage numerically. However, as we were to discover very soon, our mate, Trent Cunliffe, was right. We were being sucked into a situation where, unbeknown to us, an entire Viet Cong Division (3,500 men) was now awaiting our arrival. If only Brigadier Jackson had heeded the advice provided by Captain Cunliffe we would not be walking into this ghastly encounter.

Stealthily we moved on. Sparksie and I frequently exchanged glances which helped keep up our spirits until the jungle abruptly thinned out in front of us. I signalled for the section to halt and drop to the ground while Sparksie and I crawled on to investigate further. We were right to do so because we had stumbled upon a forest clearing. As the vegetation thinned the intensity of the sun increased. On the other side of the clearing we heard voices, Vietnamese voices. Peering out from behind some kind of a palm, we saw a dozen Viet Cong soldiers sitting on a couple of logs eating and drinking, oblivious to our presence. They were no more than fifty metres away on the opposite side of the clearing, sitting ducks. We stayed and observed for a couple of minutes more, making sure there were no more VC soldiers nearby.

'What do you reckon, Sparksie? We can't miss at this range. If we bring the machine gunners up, they can polish these guys off quick time.'

'Sure can, Scrubber. How come these idiots never heard us killing off those other blokes fifteen minutes ago?'

'Too far away, I guess. With this dense jungle around us it stops much of the sound travelling.'

'I guess you're right. Do you think there are any others?'

'Well, I've counted eleven blokes. Section size, I'd say.'

'How about I crawl back and talk to Corporal Ordo? He'll want to come up and see for himself.'

'No need Sparksie, he's coming up behind you right now.'

The corporal crawled up between us, sweating profusely. As always, he was vigorously gnawing on an exhausted piece of chewing gum. On seeing the VC chatting unsuspectingly on the far side of the clearing, Ordo's eyes lit up and he gave the thumbs up sign. He whispered that he would instruct Lance, our machine gunner, to get himself set up and tell Dave, our signaller, to call the platoon commander. 'I'd better check in with the boss first just in case he has other plans. Watch for my signal in a few minutes.' With a broad grin our corporal crawled back until it was safe for him to stand up again.

A few minutes later all was in readiness. Lieutenant Kendall approved our planned action and the ten men in our section were in their positions spread out along the edge of the clearing. Lance was in the centre with his sights set firmly on the VC. The enemy were still blissfully unaware but showing signs of packing up, having more or less finished their meal. Each of us selected one of the VC as a target and had our rifles trained. We waited for the corporal's command to 'fire.'

When the order came all hell broke loose. The sound was deafening. We watched in awe as the VC screamed and dived for cover. We kept firing until the corporal ordered us to stop. At least eight of the VC had been hit and several lay on the ground, motionless. Two others began desperately crawling for cover. Another machine gun burst from Lance stopped that. From the trees on the other side of the clearing came wild and sporadic enemy fire. Clearly, they were in retreat and firing randomly. Corporal Ordo gave the order to charge and, as one, the ten of us rose up from our cover and ran steadily towards the decimated VC. It was exactly as we had trained a thousand times. Firing as we advanced, we maintained an impressive straight line and kept our proper spacing, a couple of metres apart. One of the VC was still alive and half rose to shoot at us but he never managed it.

We continued running until we were a few yards into the jungle on the other side of the clearing where the corporal called a halt. 'Take up defensive positions' he yelled and we formed the circle we had been trained to make with each man in the kneeling position facing outwards in case of a counter attack. The corporal went back and inspected the fallen VC. Seven dead and two badly wounded. Five minutes later Ordo was back having unloaded and discarded the weapons he had found. We reckoned only two had survived our attack and they'd fled into the thick jungle ahead of us. Blood on the ground indicated at least one of the two had been wounded.

Except for Corporal Ordo, we had just killed or wounded our first enemy soldier (the corporal had served in the Malaysian campaign and seen action there). There were mixed feelings amongst us. Horror at the devastation our weapons had inflicted, relief that we had been up to the task and a sense of excitement that we had actually seen action at last. During training we were constantly instructed to regard the enemy as someone who wanted to kill us. There was nothing humane about it. These were ruthless killers out to get us. We were never allowed to think of them as husbands, fathers, sons or brothers. 'Don't be bloody sentimental…it's quite simple, kill or be killed!'

Corporal Ordo briefly congratulated us, then radioed Lieutenant Kendall to report a successful engagement with enemy casualties as eight confirmed dead and three wounded. Section two had sustained no casualties and was now holding a defensive position and awaiting further orders. The message came back to pursue the two or three VC who had escaped, but for ten minutes only. Apparently, there had been a couple of skirmishes involving other sections and signs had been picked up indicating there may well be more than 300 VC ahead.

We resumed our single-file formation with Sparksie and I serving again as the two forward scouts. Corporal Ordo had received orders that we were to maintain the same compass bearing we were following earlier to avoid crossing the path of one of our other nearby sections. No hurry, proceed with utmost caution. The blood trail lasted for about fifty metres, then disappeared. We never found the wounded man.

So far "Operation Hobart" was going to plan. As 6RAR steadily advanced, a total of sixteen VC had definitely been dispatched with only one of our guys being injured (a broken leg, not a bullet). If the Intelligence Unit had it right, we still had around 285 VC to find and destroy. The northern end of 6RAR's advance was nearing Nui Dat 2 and the southern end was approaching the village of Long Tan. More action was keenly anticipated.

33. DAY TWO

As the heat and humidity of the day intensified there were more sporadic encounters with the enemy. They were short bloody affairs, over in a few minutes. Small VC patrols appeared to be out and about, assessing the strength of the advancing Australian force. Bravo Company was hit particularly hard with two men killed and fifteen wounded most of whom were quickly evacuated to Nui Dat. Choppers were called in to convey the three critically wounded men direct to the military hospital in Vung Tau.

Right on time, the heavens opened up at sixteen hundred hours and the rain belted down as if disapproving of what was happening on the ground. The advance was halted and the troops ordered to eat their evening rations and turn in for the night. Every platoon appointed sentries. Unfortunately, I picked the short straw and had to be on sentry duty from 18.00 hours through to 22.00 hours.

The men of 6RAR were exhausted. We had had only a few hours' sleep in the last 72 hours. This, combined with the stress and tension of trying to outwit and overcome the VC, had taken its toll. The opportunity to catch up on sleep was hugely appreciated despite the discomfort of lying on soggy ground and being constantly attacked by mosquitoes, biting flies and the occasional scorpion. Spare a thought for us poor buggers though, struggling to stay awake on sentry duty!

This was not the first time I had undertaken sentry duty. During training in Queensland, sentry duty had been strictly rotated so everybody completed at least one four-hour spell. It was a duty that was universally loathed because it was so demanding when you were desperately wanting to sleep and your mates were flaked out snoring their heads off. Yet, it was vital someone took on this responsibility to lessen the chance of an attack during the night. Falling asleep while on sentry duty was a cardinal sin and severe punishments were meted out to anyone that succumbed. It was rumoured the British Army shot sentries who fell asleep!

Like most of my mates, I had developed my own techniques for staying awake for the four seemingly never-ending hours of sentry duty. Every ten minutes I would move to another place, silently hum tunes I knew and spend time thinking about Janice and Peter and the baby yet to be born. I also watched and listened to the jungle around me for signs of life. It was a moon-lit night so there was some visibility. After a time, my eyes began to play tricks on me. Trees seemed to move or I sensed something was peering at me from the shadows. Soon the occasional weird sounds of the jungle at night started to spook me. Could I hear voices? Was that brushing sound a person coming towards me? And that strange tapping noise…was it an animal or a VC soldier sending a message to a mate nearby? The jungle at night was alive with mysterious sounds and smells.

After a couple of hours standing about and moving to another spot every ten minutes, I was totally spent. My legs were like lead and my rifle getting heavier by the minute. I needed to get off my feet for a short time, so I picked the trunk of a large rubber tree and sat down leaning back against the welcoming bark. It was such a relief to ease my fatigued leg muscles. I intended to stay seated for ten minutes only before getting up and moving to the next place along my arc of responsibility.

I don't know how it happened. Something kicked my ankle hard and I sat up with a jolt to find myself staring at a pair of army boots. I

33. Day Two

blinked and allowed my gaze to travel slowly up from the boots to the face of none other than Regimental Sergeant Major George Chinn, the most feared member of 6RAR. RSM Chinn was responsible for discipline across the entire regiment. He was regarded as tough but fair. The men, without exception, had great respect for RSM Chinn, undoubtedly the most experienced soldier in 6RAR.

I scrambled terrified to my feet and realised my rifle was still lying on the ground. I grabbed it hastily and stood up straight. 'I'm sorry Sergeant, I must have nearly dozed off for a moment.' The punishment for being found asleep on sentry duty was known to be 21 days without pay and 21 days of field punishments. I immediately thought of poor Janice discovering her bank account was missing three weeks of pay and how she would manage for the next month. But RSM Chinn surprised me.

'Keeping your eyes out, are you, digger?'

'Yes, sir,' I stammered.

RSM Chinn gave me a look that said it all…don't ever fall asleep on sentry duty again!

* * *

We were woken at 0400 hours by a rapid exchange of gunfire coming from Charlie platoon, a hundred yards to our north. It lasted a few minutes only and typical of the VC's strategy of attack and disappear, a technique they'd perfected over the many years they had been engaged in jungle warfare. I had not had enough sleep since coming off sentry duty. Shamefully, I confessed to Sparksie about my unplanned meeting with RSM Chinn. He reckoned the RSM knew I was a married man with kids and could ill-afford to miss three weeks of pay, which is why he let it pass this time. 'He'll have your guts for garters if it ever happens again,' he added.

Now we were all awake Major Harry Smith, Delta Company commander, ordered everyone to consume their breakfast rations and be ready to push on towards Nui Dat 2 by 0500 hours. Once again we were relying on darkness to advance. The VC were unlikely to be expecting us to be on the move so early. We formed up in our sections and proceeded to march strictly along our compass bearings. As always, Sparksie and I were the forward scouts. Expectations were high. Unless the VC had made a tactical retreat from Nui Dat 2 and Long Tan overnight, we were likely to clash full on sometime today.

After an hour stumbling along in the dark, making painfully slow progress, the first glimmers of the dawn arose in the east. It was easier now to spot booby-traps or pits left behind by the VC. Sparksie and I had been fortunate so far; had there been any booby traps as we scrambled along in the dark, we would never have had a chance. The corporal ordered a five-minute rest at 0600 hours. It was a chance for a pee, a drink and a couple of minutes breather to scratch the worst of last night's mossie bites. Radio contact was made with company HQ. The message from HQ was that it was eerily quiet and no platoons had made contact with the VC. Be extra vigilant!

I wandered off to find a suitable tree to relieve myself. As I stood there, a strong stench of manure or excreta enveloped me. It was powerful and disgusting. I immediately thought of the dreaded punji sticks the Viet Cong placed at the bottom of pits covered with a thin layer of bamboo to catch unsuspecting foe. It was *so* pungent, I knew I must be horribly close to a trap. Gingerly, I turned around on the spot, looking for signs the ground had been tampered with. Sure enough, a few feet in front of me were definite signs the jungle floor had been recently disturbed.

As I rejoined my colleagues, I realised just how close we had been to falling into this ghastly cess-pit with its contaminated punji sticks. Had the corporal not called a halt when he did, either Sparksie or I might easily have fallen through the thin layer of bamboo saplings onto the fearsomely sharp punji sticks. So far, no Australians had become victims of these beastly booby traps but our American allies certainly had. When on leave one evening in a Vung Tau pub,

33. Day Two

Sparksie and I had been yarning with a young Yank who described in gory detail how the forward scout in his section had fallen into one of these "punji pits.' He almost died of his wounds. First, he had to be prised off four impregnated punji stakes as he screamed in agony and soon after suffered life threatening septicaemia. It was a miracle he had pulled through.

I told Corporal Ordo how close I had come to falling into the punji pit and that it was only the stench that had alerted me. He summoned the section together and ordered me to show them where the pit was. Ordo seized the opportunity to warn us again of the dangers of booby traps and finished by saying, 'You lot are bloody lucky you have Scrubber and Sparksie out there in front looking out for these bloody awful things.'

* * *

According to our map, we were now close to the deserted village of Long Tan. We still hadn't had further contact with the enemy and were beginning to think we were being drawn into an ambush. We found clear signs the VC had been in the vicinity recently; the remains of a campsite suggesting as many as thirty had stayed there last night and ten minutes later we came across a substantial track hacked through the jungle. The VC were certainly about, but where? More importantly, how large a force were they? Messages coming from HQ were now suggesting that 350 Viet Cong may be an underestimation and we may be up against a full regiment similar in size to 6RAR. Not good news!

Morale amongst 6RAR was being sorely tested. It was only day two of a five-day operation but the heat and humidity were debilitating and the general mood was smouldering also. It was the first time the great majority of the men had experienced real warfare and it was ten times more stressful than training. There was agreement amongst the men that the training they had received back in Australia was top quality and had prepared them well. Nothing, however, could quite prepare someone for a real life and death situation. There was a certain amount of tension between some of the officers and the lower ranks as the officers tried to maintain control. There were blow-ups between some of the men over silly, piffling matters and tempers easily frayed even amongst the mildest of men. The calmest soldiers in the regiment were the sergeants; tough, mature guys who had experienced it all before and were the undisputed backbone to 6RAR.

Morale amongst Sparksie's and my section seemed to be holding up reasonably well, though. We were a compatible bunch of guys who usually enjoyed each other's company. Our corporal was a decent enough bloke who had won our respect. With our five-minute spell over, we once again coated our faces and the backs of our hands with camouflage creams: green, brown and black. Our uniforms were jungle green with splotches of red, the colour of the soil beneath our feet. A couple of the guys had been issued with steel inserts for the soles of their feet; an attempt to reduce injuries if you fell into a punji pit. The inserts were most uncomfortable so it was debateable whether they were worth the bother. The owners of the inserts had no intention of falling into a punji pit to find out.

We were still in deep jungle and maintained our single-file formation until we emerged into some open country that had previously been farmed. Automatically we adjusted our formation to an arrow-head and moved on looking out for a glint of steel, a twist of rope or cut bamboo lying about on the ground. We felt horribly exposed out here in the open and quickly headed for a dense bamboo forest over to our right. Here we found more signs of the Viet Cong. Bamboo forests were perfect for VC snipers who could position themselves high up on bamboo platforms. We changed formation again, this time into threes. One person searched for booby traps, the second looked ahead for signs of the VC and the third kept his eyes skinned for snipers up above us. We found nothing. The only sound, our own laboured breathing.

On the other side of the bamboo forest, we came into scrubby land with low fast-growing bushes, rushes and sages. It must have been cleared for farming a couple of years ago but now lay abandoned. Most alarming though was the discovery of a peculiar curved object lurking in the undergrowth. The corporal was the only one to have seen these objects before. 'It's a claymore mine. Tread on one of those and at best you will lose a leg. Most don't survive!' Yet another murderous object to look out for…

A few minutes later all hell broke loose. A small group of Viet Cong (three or four?) opened fire on us. We instantly responded. Somehow, none of our section were hit but one of theirs was. His mates started to drag him along the ground but had to abandon him as we charged, firing with everything we had. It was another typical VC action, 'shoot and scarper.' Cautiously, we approached the wounded man and made sure he was totally disarmed. He was terrified and then astounded us by speaking in English, 'Please, please, please don't shoot.' We assured him he was safe and Tom, who had some very basic knowledge of medical matters, checked him over. He had been badly hit in the stomach and was bleeding profusely. We had no way of staunching such a flow of blood and set about trying to get information from him about where the VC were and how many.

As the minutes ticked by and he groaned in awful pain, we administered a massive shot of morphine. It was a blessed relief but we could see he was steadily fading from loss of blood. The corporal persisted, asking time and time again for information but the man remained tight-lipped. Finally, as his breathing became raspy, he smiled and whispered, 'Go easy, uc dai loi, go easy.' He passed away without disclosing anything useful. We admired the young man, gutsy to the end and so committed to his cause that he would not betray his colleagues. We buried him in a shallow grave with his rifle stuffed into the red mud as a marker.

This whole episode had taken nearly half an hour. It was starting to rain again so we huddled under some palms and ate our lunch rations. Contact was made once more with HQ. Our orders were unchanged: keep going and expect action. Major Harry Smith was pleased we had come off best in another exchange with the VC.

As it turned out, our section had no further contact with the VC on day two of "Operation Hobart." Other platoons reported sporadic minor contacts but nothing major. The movements and strength of the Viet Cong remained a mystery. For now, we were the aggressors moving relentlessly forward in an attempt to remove the VC from Phuoc Tuy Province. Complete eradication from the province would never happen because VC sympathisers could always creep back and live amongst the villagers. So far, however, "Operation Hobart" seemed to be proceeding passably well.

34. DAY THREE

Our section was cautiously approaching the deserted village of Long Tan. We were in single file, as usual, with me as the forward scout on the left front and Sparksie on the right. The sun blazed down unremittingly and our shirts clung to our backs with whatever perspiration we still had left. No talking, hand signals only. The road steamed and the last of the puddles from the previous night's downpour glinted in the sun. Red soil clung to our boots. Everything was eerily quiet.

Long Tan had been cleared of villagers some time back but a few of the houses were still more or less intact. It was not surprising that occasionally the displaced villagers returned, perhaps to try and find something they needed or just for old times' sake. More concerning was the possible use of the ruined village by members of the Viet Cong. Their underground tunnels had been blown up by our guys, however, we knew the ever-resourceful enemy may have been back to dig replacements. It was our job today to check the village was not being used by anyone.

Being at the front, I was the first to hear it. The sound of a small child crying, most likely a baby. Surely, we wouldn't harm an innocent child? If there was a child crying, presumably there was a mother nearby too. I raised my right hand above my head to signal the section to halt. Now we were standing still, the sound of the unhappy child's whimpering was audible to the rest of the section. As far as I could tell, the crying was coming from the third house on the left on my side of the road. It was one of the houses that had been less severely damaged by our boys.

A moment later the corporal joined me. We discussed the situation and agreed the killing of an innocent mother and her child would not happen even though they were in the wrong to have returned to the village. We would get them out of the house and send them on their way, making sure the mother understood we were very angry. What worried us most was the possibility that the father was also in the house; young men from a village like this could well be serving Viet Cong, or at least VC sympathisers. We would have to proceed with great caution three metres behind each other.

Corporal Ordo spoke quietly to each one of us in turn. His instruction was to hold our fire until he gave the order. Having explained the situation to everyone, Ordo came back to join me. The plan was for him as our leader, to enter the front of the house first with the rest of us positioned around the house in case anyone tried to escape. Slowly, we advanced towards the dwelling where the crying was coming from. As we did so, I remember thinking the sound of a baby crying was much the same anywhere around the world. This baby could so easily be my own little Peter.

When we were twenty metres from the house an extraordinary thing happened. A pram emerged (prams were unknown in Vietnam) pushed by an attractive white woman wearing a light green blouse and a long black skirt just like my Janice liked to wear. The lady turned and began walking slowly towards us. We were so stunned to see this western woman we stopped in our tracks and gawped. She didn't seem to see us though and walked slowly past as if we weren't there. It was as though we didn't exist. The woman came so close to me I could have touched her. It *was* Janice and the baby in the pram was Peter. Furthermore, there was a tell-tale bump on Janice's tummy. I tried desperately to move towards her but I was frozen in place, incapable of moving or speaking. Janice walked slowly on, pushing the pram past the entire section and then disappeared, like a wraith, into the jungle. Stunningly beautiful, but untouchable.

I awoke suddenly to find both my legs cramping and barely able to move. It took me five minutes to ease the cramps and come to terms with what, I now realised, had been a cruel dream. I was not usually into the meaning of dreams but this one worried me. It was definitely Janice with little Peter and our child-to-be who had walked out of that house. What frightened me most was seeing them go past me as though I didn't matter. I was invisible to Janice, no longer in her world. Was this some kind of a bad omen? I wondered whether to confide in Sparksie but decided against it. After all, it was just a stupid dream…forget it!

* * *

There was too much to do to spend any more time dwelling on my dream. We had to have breakfast, check rifles and grenades, put on more camouflage and have a briefing with the corporal. Overnight our signaller had received reports from base camp that it had been under attack from mortar shells for over an hour during the night. The VC had been accurately targeting the nerve centres of the camp, the HQ, artillery and the depot for armoured personnel carriers. They knew what they were doing and a number of casualties had occurred. It was even more important now that "Operation Hobart" be a success and we locate and destroy the enemy's mortar positions.

Mortar shells were more terrifying than other shells because we never knew where they were going to land. First you heard the PUMPH as the mortar was fired, then a roar like an express train approaching followed by a moment of silence. This was the time you wondered whether this particular mortar shell had your name on it. Next, there was a WHOOSH as the shell hit the ground and then the massive THUD as it burst sending out shrapnel in all directions.

Mortar shells can do serious damage and it took our artillery some time to pinpoint exactly where they were being fired from and to return fire.

Mortars date back to the fifteenth century and became particularly important in the two world wars because of their high arcing trajectories that enabled the shells to actually land *in* the trenches. They were light weight weapons usually consisting of a barrel fixed to a base plate with a bipod mount and a sight. A big advantage was their mobility. One strong man could carry a mortar to another location, set it up and start firing shells within minutes. Other men would, of course, be required to carry the shells. Before firing a mortar you needed to know the exact location of your target or you were wasting your time. Apparently, Viet Cong patrols had been able to get close enough to our base to relay this information.

Following the mortar attack the personnel at the base assessed the full extent of the carnage. There were no less than 67 mortar craters. 21 tents had been destroyed and seven army vehicles severely damaged. Despite the closeness of the shelling, the four artillery batteries remained virtually unharmed and continued to fire on the Viet Cong positions for an hour after the mortars ceased. 24 soldiers were wounded, mostly by shrapnel. Once stabilised, the seriously injured were safely choppered out to the military hospital in Vung Tau.

At the start of day three of "Operation Hobart" our section was well hidden in thick jungle, approximately one hundred metres away from one of these mortar positions. As far as we knew, the Viet Cong were unaware of our presence. Section three, two hundred metres to the north of us, was also closing in on the same mortar position. We believed a mortar position would be guarded by a force about the size of a section, that is ten men. If we attacked, the element of surprise would be crucial. The plan was that section three and our section would advance simultaneously by crawling, undetected, through the scrub towards our quarry. Once we were within close enough range, we would break cover and give them hell. The attack

34. Day Three

would be coordinated. Our corporal, more senior than section three's, would give the final order to attack.

Shortly after 0730 hours we spread out into a long line each man two or three metres apart and began our torturous long crawling through the bush. We forgot about the heat and humidity, the clouds of mosquitoes and gnats, the snakes and scorpions, the sharp-edged plants as the adrenalin kicked in. Every man was totally focused on remaining hidden and making minimal noise. At the same time, we maintained visual contact with the man on our left and the man on our right.

As we neared the VC's position, we could hear voices and muffled laughter. There didn't appear to be anyone on sentry duty. About thirty metres from the enemy, we stopped our strenuous crawling. Long distance crawling was hard work, arms and shoulders ached painfully from this prolonged and unaccustomed activity and we needed time to catch our breath and ease our muscles. Corporal Ordo was positioned in the centre of the line of twenty men from where he could best pass messages along in both directions. Section one, some hundred yards to our right, had also been made aware of our intentions and placed on standby ready to come to our aid if required.

With a blood curdling yell our corporal jumped up and led the charge. The fastest of us would be physically amongst the VC in less than ten seconds which gave the enemy little time to ready themselves. As one, we rushed at the foe screaming abuse and yelling profanities exactly as we had been trained to do. But this time we meant it! In a flash we were upon them each of us having fired off several rounds as we approached. We had caught them napping and they were clearly panicked and terrified. As we fell amongst them, we resorted to using our rifle butts to slam down any men still scrambling to find their rifles or grenades. And there, in the middle of the small clearing was the offending mortar gun still bolted to its base and already abandoned.

The Viet Cong soldiers who could bolted into the jungle. Barely a shot was fired back at us as flight rather than fight was their first reaction. It was a triumph almost too good to believe. Six VC lay on the ground dead or badly wounded. Our section's injuries? One slightly sprained ankle. We estimated four or five VC had managed to escape. Section three was just as elated as us. One of their number had been pinged on the side of his leg and would need medical attention.

I have to admit a feeling of euphoria came over me. I think we all felt as if we had just won the NRL grand final and were in the mood to celebrate. We relaxed momentarily, shook hands and slapped one another in victory giving heartfelt congratulations all round. Corporal Ordo was having none of it, however.

'Take up defensive positions. Expect a counter attack any moment,' he yelled more than once.

We quickly came back down to earth and both sections took up positions around the VC camp we had taken. We re-loaded in time before sporadic firing started coming in from several positions in the jungle. The almost impossible task now was to spot the shooters and return fire. As soon as we detected where shots were coming from, however, the sniper responsible would quickly move to a new position. The enemy was firing just enough to keep us pinned down. It soon became apparent these snipers had been joined by reinforcements and we were now up against a force equal to, or larger than ours. The question now was, should we hold our ground, try to advance further or make a well executed retreat?

The corporal was soon in touch with our platoon commander, Lieutenant Geoff Kendall. It was a heated discussion. Our hard-headed and more experienced corporal believed we were now in a no-win situation. He argued strongly that the two sections had already totally wiped out a mortar position and accounted for a number of Viet Cong casualties. However, the intensity of the counter offensive was increasing suggesting the number of the enemy we were up against was mounting and our present position was

34. Day Three

untenable. Kendall, on the other hand, thrilled at the success we had achieved so far, was most reluctant to withdraw. He was keen to send section one round to the enemy's right flank to attack from a new direction. Another surprise attack, he argued, might be enough to send the VC packing again and then we could advance even further. He reminded Corporal Ordo the objective of "Operation Hobart" was to destroy the enemy and ensure the province of Phuoc Toy was rid of the Viet Cong.

In the end, the matter was passed up the line to Major Harry Smith for a decision. A wise move. Smith had a far better overview of what was happening across the whole battle area since he was responsible for four companies. He ordered us to stay put so he could come and see for himself how we were positioned. It took him another ten minutes to join Geoff Kendall and review the situation by also speaking with our corporal. A decisive man, Smith gave the order for sections two and three to withdraw and take up new positions about a hundred yards back where there was better cover and a slight rise which would give us a strategic advantage. Section one would provide heavy covering fire to enable us to make our retreat.

A moment later all hell broke loose. Section one opened up with everything it had which was our signal to retreat to the small rise behind us as fast as possible. Keeping low and zig-zagging as the ground permitted, the men of sections two and three belted back while section one kept up its heavy covering fire. We all made it, except the poor guy who had already sustained a grazing injury to his leg. His injury must have been more serious than he let on because running caused him acute pain. He fell behind the rest of us and collected another bullet to the back of his neck. He died instantly a couple of metres from the rise where we were taking up our new defensive position.

The decision to withdraw fifty metres to a more defensible position was the right one. In the next ten minutes the number of

VC facing us increased alarmingly. It was now estimated they were at about company strength (100 men). With section one dropping back to join us to help hold the line, we numbered a total of 29. This was a sudden and unexpected turn in our fortunes. A short time ago we had been advancing to put the mortar out of action believing the enemy numbers were small, perhaps a couple of sections at most. Now, heavily outnumbered, we were struggling to hold this new position.

Lieutenant Kendall quickly worked out the coordinates for the VC's position, checked them carefully, checked them again, and then called in the artillery. The four batteries back at base rallied fast and assumed their firing positions. Ten minutes later, using Kendall's coordinates, they opened fire. The only way we could hold out was if the artillery started dropping shells on the VC. The first round of shells landed some fifty metres behind the VC's position. Lieutenant Kendall radioed slightly adjusted coordinates which, hopefully, would result in greater accuracy. If Kendall got the coordinates wrong the shells might land on us!

Sections one, two and three kept up a steady rate of firing, cognisant of the fact we only had a limited supply of ammunition remaining. Additional ammunition needed to arrive within twenty minutes or we must retreat again. Kendall was in touch with Major Harry Smith again who promised a delivery of ammo from Company HQ within fifteen minutes.

Fire was coming in steadily from the VC now and we had to keep our heads down and stay behind substantial cover. In the next ten minutes two more of our number were hit, one being our section's machine gunner. A machine gunner can do so much more damage than a rifleman. Consequently, he becomes a prime target for the enemy. We had all been trained to operate a machine gun should the appointed man be unable to continue so I rolled him gently to the side and took over. As I did this, we were shocked to see a line of around fifty Viet Cong emerge from the cover of the trees and start

34. Day Three

charging towards us, yelling and screaming crazily. Clearly, they were intent on completely destroying us.

We commenced rapid firing and I had our machine gun operating fully again within seconds. The Viet Cong soldiers were still advancing but taking heavy casualties. What saved us was the second round of artillery. Four shells exploded amongst the advancing troops at precisely the right moment and in the right places. It couldn't have been better executed. Many of the attackers were killed or maimed by the shells. The few that remained on their feet staggered back to their lines. The attack had failed thanks to the timely help of the artillery.

A few minutes later we were joined by Alpha Company, sent to relieve us. We had successfully held out for nearly half an hour during which time three more of our men had been hit. We were exhausted and needed to get out of the front line and hand over to the more than welcome guys from Alpha Company who were coming in relatively fresh and unbloodied.

I heard a voice from someone lying on the ground just behind me. The guy told me to take a break. He had been ordered to take over my machine gun position. I felt a massive sense of relief. This was my chance to move safely away from the front line, have a well-earned rest and some refreshments. I looked up, sincerely thanked my replacement and started to crawl back. Encountering a large ant heap, I had to partially get to my feet to get around…

35. SPARKSIE

Scrubber McDade was killed in action near Long Tan on 18th August 1966. Death was instantaneous. As his best mate for the last year, the least I can do is try to finish off his story for him.

We dragged Scrubber's body back behind our lines where I dived into his top pocket to retrieve the photographs of Janice and little Peter that he always carried around with him. The photos were looking a bit worn and faded after our time in Vietnam but I knew they meant the world to Scrubber. Sometimes, when he thought nobody was looking, he would take the photographs out of his top pocket and give Janice a kiss. I had promised to return the photographs to Janice should anything happen to Scrubber.

Several Armoured Personnel Carriers had arrived behind our lines bringing additional supplies of ammunition, personnel and extra food rations. On their return trips the APCs carried the lightly wounded who could be patched up by the doctors at Nui Dat and returned to action. They also carried the corpses of the deceased. I helped load Scrubber into APC 2 and dearly wished I could travel back with him. I knew the driver and asked him to take special care of my best mate.

Until "Operation Hobart" started, we had only had a couple of diggers die. Already, we knew the proper routine for our departed mates. The body bags were choppered out to Vung Tau to be flown on to Australia for family burials. To give some respectability to the start of this process and to properly honour the lives of those who had died fighting for their country, the deceased were accorded a solemn military farewell. This meant a full parade of the regiment and the slow marching of the coffins, draped in Australian flags, to the helicopter. A horribly sombre business, even if you didn't know the diggers personally.

Scrubber had died bravely doing his duty in his own quiet way. A genuine bloke without airs and graces, just another decent man. His deep love for Janice and little Peter was both humbling and inspiring. Having written all his letters for him and read the incoming mail, I guess I knew him and his family unusually well.

Now, I had a couple of difficult promises to fulfill. First, I must write to Janice to express my deepest sympathy and assure her Scrubber fought courageously and had never stopped talking about her and little Peter. The children could grow up proud of their father, Private Norman McDade (Scrubber) of the Sixth Royal Australian Regiment. Later, if I safely returned to Australia, I must visit the Enoggera Barracks or wherever Janice had moved to, to commiserate with her. I also promised to march for Scrubber McDade every ANZAC Day until I could manage it no more.

R.I.P. Scrubber McDade.

EPILOGUE

Scrubber died early in what soon became known as the Battle of Long Tan. Delta Company fought heroically and, against the odds, went on to defeat the Viet Cong in this encounter. A third of the company were wounded or killed. The eighteen who gave their lives did not die in vain. The VC, after confronting the Australians for the first time at Long Tan, did whatever they could to avoid open conflict with the Australians in future. The Viet Cong learnt at the battle of Long Tan to respect the fighting capabilities of the diggers.

We may have won the battle but we didn't win the war. Ho Chi Minh had rightly predicted he could lose ten men for every one of the enemies and still win. On 30th January 1968, the "Tet Offensive" began. Thousands upon thousands of communist troops from North Vietnam simultaneously attacked over a hundred sites right across South Vietnam and the Americans and their allies were forced from offensive to defensive mode. Being forced into an overly defensive position eventually leads to defeat.

Soon the American people and their allies lost the stomach to fight on. Massive anti-Vietnam War marches and demonstrations helped change peoples' views. Nui Dat was handed over to the South Vietnamese Army in November 1971 and the last of the Australian infantry left the next month. At the time of their departure, the

Australian forces had suffered a total of 423 fatalities with 2,398 wounded. The Viet Cong soon ruled Vietnam unchallenged. Saigon fell on 30th April 1975. On that day there were shocking images on our television sets of the last American citizens in Saigon who wanted to escape, clinging desperately to helicopter skids on the roof of the American Embassy. North and South Vietnam were re-united to become The Socialist Republic of Vietnam.

Today, with the benefit of hindsight, it is hard to find anyone who believes the Americans and their allies should have ever gone to Vietnam. The "domino theory" remained just that. The dire predictions never eventuated.

18th August, the day Scrubber died, is now known as Long Tan Day. It has also become the official day of commemoration for the Vietnam War as well as Vietnam Veterans' Remembrance Day.

* * *

Twelve months after the start of our tour of duty in Vietnam, 6RAR returned home to Australia. At best we received a mixed reception, which made the tough times we had endured for a year in the tropics far more difficult to accept. We never received the unrestrained heroes' welcome accorded to those who had served their country in previous theatres of war. For some Vietnam veterans it was particularly hard when even some members of their own families remained antagonistic. It's no wonder the veterans of the Vietnam War have suffered more suicides, more mental illnesses and more problems than previous returned servicemen. This suffering is still rife today.

I was one of the more fortunate ones. Once I recovered from the cruel death of my best mate, Scrubber McDade, I came through the rest of my time in Vietnam more or less unscathed. The thought of coming home and marrying my sweetheart was a powerful motivator that helped me through the remaining months. Rosie and I were married exactly two weeks after I touched down in Sydney. We christened our first born, Norman.

One of the most difficult things I had to do was to visit Janice McDade, Peter and the newborn, Lynda Mc Dade.

A couple of weeks after we returned from our honeymoon, I arranged for Rosie and I to visit Mr and Mrs Fenton over the long weekend so I could spend a little time with Janice. Rosie had only met Janice a couple of times before Scrubber and I went off to Vietnam and felt it best to let me see Janice on my own. I had never met Janice's parents before. Scrubber had told me a little bit about them. They sounded like decent folk and were most understanding when I rang them and explained why I wanted to see Janice. Rosie and I had a little money left over after our honeymoon (amazingly!) so we booked into the better of the two pubs in Rinsdorf for a night.

Janice was as lovely and welcoming as ever. Despite her best efforts to hide it, I could feel the deep sense of loss she was experiencing. Her parents minded the two children while we shared a cup of coffee on the back porch. I handed back the photographs she had given Norman to take to Vietnam and we talked about Scrubber and cried together. I told her what good mates we had been and she thanked me for helping with their letters. It was a difficult conversation to have as we had both lost a person we had loved dearly.

Before I left, I offered to help Janice in any way I could. She thanked me for this but assured me she would get over it. As she said, 'Life goes on and I don't plan to spend the rest of my life moping. I have the kids to raise and when they're a few years older, I'll go back to teaching.' I also knew Legacy would generously provide assistance with the children's education and welfare.

I was heartened by Janice's determination and resilience and knew that if Scrubber was watching over her, this is what he would want to see.

ACKNOWLEDGEMENTS

Like all my books, the creation of *Scrubber McDade* has been a family effort. Editing and proofing were handled by my wife, Joy, and daughter, Wendy. Advice on technical matters was more than ably covered by my son-in-law, Simon. Thank you once again for your collective commitment, patience, advice and skill.

I particularly want to acknowledge the work of Peter Fitzsimons who in 2022 published his well researched book, The Battle of Long Tan. I have relied on this work to provide valuable background for the last part of this novel.

Special thanks go to Luke Harris from Working Type Studio who has done everything else including the cover design, type setting, printing and publishing. Luke's professional advice and great patience has been invaluable.

www.ingramcontent.com/pod-product-compliance
Lightning Source LLC
Chambersburg PA
CBHW031235290426
44109CB00012B/308